A Carrot is a Carrot
Memories and Reflections

A Carrot is a Carrot
Memories and Reflections

Zia Mohyeddin

2011

ISBN 978-969-9154-00-3

Printed in Pakistan 2011

Published by
Ushba Publishing International
74-C, 13 Commercial Street, Phase 2 Extension, DHA, Karachi,
Pakistan

To
Daud Rahbar

'So we rode and joked and smoked
With no miracles evoked...'

Louis MacNeice

'My inspiration has been genuine but worthless, like so much inspiration, and I have never sat down on a theme.'

E.M. Foster

CONTENTS

Introduction   *xi*

1. Kasur   1
2. Khadim Mohyeddin   15
3. Eat Your Heart Out   29
4. Ludhyana   35
5. Smudger   40
6. Music as I Knew it   45
7. Shadowplay   58
8. 'Oh that Dylan Thomas'   67
9. Must the King Submit? The King Shall Do It   77
10. The Hero Must Look Well-Fed   82
11. Tennessee Williams   85
12. Leela Lean   90
13. Talk is Cheap   110
14. Pino   115
15. Charms Fly at the Mere Touch of
    Cold Philosphy   121
16. The Peacock Dance   126
17. Dance: the Bugbear Word   131
18. A Doleful Song   136
19. An Unequal Music   141
20. Gajal   146
21. Your Deal Partner   151
22. Urdu Music   156

23. 'Why Ask For Happiness'   161
24. The Maverick   166
25. 'To Cynthia, From Her Cocker Spaniel'   176
26. Parsing and Kenning   181
27. Shiatsu   185
28. Sleepless Nights   189
29. Do Not Believe What You Read   194
30. Film Star is One Word   199
31. An 'Islamic' Robbery   204
32. Humour Doesn't Always Cross Borders Safely   210
33. Ignorance of Certainty   214
34. Language that Conceals Language   219
35. Let's Play Culture   224
36. New York, New York...   229
37. Oh For a Swizzle Stick   234
38. Punctual or Intellectual?   238
39. Punctuation—A matter of taste?   242
40. Culture Colonization and Forster   247
41. 'Sounds of the Heart'   252
42. Stirrings   257
43. Ten Men and a Horse   262
44. 'You Don't mind, is it?'   267
45. The Rattling of Bones   272
46. The Unprintable Poetry   278
47. Vain Faith and Courage Vain   284
48. Wattle and Woozle   290
49. 'What Else is On'   295
50. Santa   300
51. A Carrot Is A Carrot   305

Index   *311*

INTRODUCTION

Looking at some of my old photographs, I see that my face was plumper and less lined than it is now. My figure was good but somewhat slight. Of what was going on inside me, however, there is no indication. There seems an emptiness of expression, and there is a little brazenness in the arranged smiles and no trace of impatience; in this the cameras must have lied. I have always been impatient.

There is no earthly reason for me to look at these photographs, but every now and then I am asked to dig up some old photographs by people who, for reasons unknown to me, wish to burrow into my past. I have one photograph, taken over forty five years ago, showing me standing by a lamp post looking at a rubble in Harlem. (I have not shown this to anyone). God knows what I was doing there but I look exactly as I am today—partly morose, partly amused. It's uncanny but I managed to look like what I would become in four and a half decades. Child must be the father of man.

Before heading the National Academy of Performing Arts in Pakistan, I journeyed through the world of acting and directing in England and America, for some fifty years. I have had my share of triumphs and disasters, setbacks and jubilations. I have never been in any doubt that the compulsive irrational human instinct — the Need to Act — gives rise to more disappointments than anything else, but I'd rather live through these than own a chain of Wal Marts. The moment of elation as you step forward to take a bow and hear the surge of applause rise to a crescendo, compensates for all the frustrations that a theatrical career, necessarily, entails.

Many years ago I wrote a novel, which a year later, I thought was trash. The only thing good about it was the title, *Unreal City*, which I had borrowed from a poem by Eliot. I dumped the manuscript in a trunk, which also contained my discarded cricket gear, (boots, abdominal guards, gloves, fractured bats), old photographs and all my notices. The trunk was lost when I moved from one house to another in London. God knows what the removals people did with it.

I never collected another review. I didn't write for a long time, not until Peter Ustinov encouraged me — nay, coaxed me — to write. He had read a few pieces I had written in the vein of a colonial Blimp describing the 'native' rebellion of a frontier tribe, and he insisted that I should write more often.

All the pieces in this collection were written in the last ten years. Some of them have appeared, in an abridged form in the *The News on Sunday*. I am grateful to the Editor of *The News* for allowing me to include these.

KASUR*

It is uncanny: the swirl of dead leaves pulled along by the wind in the heat of the day reminds me of Kasur, a small provincial town that I have not visited since I was a school boy.

What can I tell you about Kasur? Very little except that it is my ancestral town. My father had a house there, which I never saw, but my two elder brothers were born and died in that house. This much I learnt from my mother, just as I learnt from others that he sold his house because he needed the money to provide dowries for his daughters. After he sold his house, his visits to Kasur became rarer. Once a year he would take his family to visit his sister, my aunt Ruqaiya — and his sister-in-law, whose small two-roomed house was not too far from my aunt's.

My aunt Ruqaiya's relatively spacious house was on the Circular Road overlooking a bare, bald field that stretched for miles and then merged into the sky.

* This is how the town is spelled these days. The actual word is *Qusoor*, the plural of *Qasr*, meaning palaces.

The rickety, creaky front door opened into a porch from which you stepped down to a large inner courtyard, which was not paved. The sweepress used to cover her mouth and nose with her veil before sweeping it with a heavy broom with sharp, spiky reeds. Clouds of dust rose from the earth and wafted in the air, leaving the earthen floor spotless, with serrated edges.

Cool air floated in when the front door was left open; even on the hottest day there was a lovely soft breeze. I used to sit on the uneven brick floor in the porch and watch long lines of ants moving purposefully in between the bricks, which were flaking at the edges. Outside, on the bald field, a cluster of dead leaves drifted in from nowhere, whispered among themselves and flew away in different directions. It was the most idyllic, somnolent setting.

The top of the house was approached through a step ladder that had been placed on the landing where people slept at night. Children were forbidden to go to the roof because their presence agitated the weird, mad woman who lived next door. I once climbed the ladder when no one was around. There was a boundary wall, almost my own height. From over the wall you looked into a backyard full of rubble and mounds of rubbish.

The yard was usually deserted, but sometimes, the mad woman, in tattered rags, could be seen there crouching and looking intently into the debris. She looked a witch incarnate. Everyone called her a *dain* (witch). Now, and then she would give off a scream followed by gibberish which sounded like '*enamardankuttay enabhobarbhor darodah*'.

I had been warned by the sweepress never to let her set her eyes on me. I decided to take a peak, fully prepared to back off, if I found her looking my way. I placed one foot on a bumpy lump on the wall and inched my way to the top. She was standing with her back to me looking in the opposite direction, rigid and mute. Suddenly, she turned and looked at me. Her mouth opened into a leer. I felt frozen, devoid of all energy. My legs shook and I sensed that any moment she would leap and gobble me up. She raised an arm and beckoned me to come to her.

Week-kneed and breaking into a cold sweat, I let go of the foot perched on the bumpy surface and somehow managed to slide down, bruising my thighs. The witch began to shriek '*enabharbhor darodah*'. I ran down as fast as I could and hid behind some cans on the landing. There was a strong odour of rancid butter coming from the cans; my heart was pounding so fast I thought I would collapse.

After some time, when I felt sure that the *dain* was not in pursuit, I ventured to creep out and, shaking the dirt off my clothes, allowed myself to be seen by the others. I thought I looked fairly normal, but my eldest sister, coming out of an inner room, took one look at me and stood, horrified. 'What have you been doing? Why are there filthy marks all over you?' 'Nothing,' I said, 'I was on the roof and that woman started shouting at me.' 'How many times have I told you not to go to the roof top on your own?' She

raised a hand and pursed her lips to make it clear
that if it was not for my aunt's house she would
have thwacked me. 'That woman is mad.' 'No *beta*,'
said my aunt coming towards my sister with her
slow, measured walk, 'She is an unfortunate woman,
a *bekas* (helpless).'

It was a relief to see my aunt. But for her
intervention, my sister would have led me to the
corner in the courtyard where there was a hand
pump with a bucket underneath, filled the bucket
with a few angry strokes and, making me take my
clothes off, disregarding my shame and horror,
begun to scrub me. She used to bathe me when I was
a baby and she felt that she had an inherent authority
over me. I remembered the harsh way in which she
cleaned my ears. I would squirm and wriggle, but
she would hold me firmly by one arm and scrape
the back of my neck as though it was a saucepan.
She was now married to my aunt's eldest son and,
therefore, had to be circumspect in her mother-in-
law's presence.

'You should be careful and not stare at that poor
wretch,' my aunt came closer to me, 'she lost her
mind when God took away her entire family. Ah!
His is the will,' she sighed.

My aunt Ruqaiya, spoke haltingly, in measured
tones, just like her walk. She had a kindly face and
sad eyes and she never raised her voice. Her teenage
daughter was a frightened little girl who could have
been salvaged from the morass if she had been
handled delicately, but she had been subjected to so

many mystical cures that she was now like a vegetable.

Aunt Ruqaiya had been suffering from all kinds of ailments, but she did not whine or groan like my other aunts who were, eternally, complaining of swollen abdomens and sharp pains in their backs or their necks. Her husband, a pink-cheeked man with an untrimmed grey beard, had never paid her the slightest attention; my aunt, in turn, had learnt to ignore his presence in the house. I never heard my uncle speak to my aunt just as I never saw him without a big white turban on his head.

Mianjee, my tall, turbaned uncle, rarely spoke to anyone else either. He looked like a patriarch but he was utterly devoid of any authority. Most of the time he was out of the house. We were told that he had work to attend to outside Kasur. In actual fact, he went to warehouses, picking up rejects; pencils, rubber balls, hair clips and an assortment of tinsel, arrange it in a *tokri* (a large wicker basket) which he then placed on his head — the heavy turban acted as a cushion — and walked from village to village, selling his wares. When night fell, he slept in a nearby mosque.

On the odd occasion when he was in the house, people called upon him. *Mianjee* never asked anyone in. He would open the front door, ever so suspiciously, and step out of the house, carefully closing the door behind him. He had a reedy, boy's voice and a peculiar speech impediment, which turned all his k's into t's, so that a 'cat' became a 'tat' and a 'queen', a 'tween'. I found it so comical that I once imitated his manner of speech in front of one of my timid cousins. My eldest sister overheard me and she boxed my ears and told me never to make fun of my elders.

When my father or one of my innumerable aunts enquired of *Mianjee*, my aunt, Ruqaiya, was prone to say '*kas nakushaid-o-nakushood*' or some such expression. She was fond of using Persian phrases in her everyday Punjabi. Aunt Ruqaiya was rare amongst women of her generation in that she was not only well versed in Urdu, but Persian classics as well. The peerless polymath, Daud Rahbar, (also her nephew), tells me that she had a sharp sense of drollery. Whether she made it up or heard from someone else, aunt Ruqaiya would, frequently, regale Rahbar and his brothers with doggerel like:

Bala khana nishasta boodam, it aiyee karkandi;
Gar sar-e-khud paran na kardam, sar noon par ke jandee

From somewhere came a missile, when I sat upon the terrace;
If I had not turned my head away, it would have been a menace.

The translation does not give you the flavour of how earthy Punjabi expressions have been woven into the fabric of refined Persian words.

She may have loved life once. I only saw aunt Ruqaiya as a morose, slightly droopy figure, walking hesitantly as though she was afraid she would fall down any moment. Perhaps she was weighed down not so much by her physical woes, but by an intellect that found no outlet from her surroundings.

If my aunt Raqaiya was lachrymose, my father's sister-in-law, *Taijee,* was a cheerful, silver-haired seraph. Her narrow, sculptured face was delicately wrinkled and her egg-white skin was as soft as a river bed. I don't remember her wearing anything other than white.

Taijee would welcome us with a radiant smile. Unlike other elderly ladies in my family she did not dole out benedictions to every child backed by scriptural sayings — as my other countless aunts were wont to do. She welcomed us with a beautiful smile and set down a large platter of white, sugar-coated nuts.

Taijee kept her small house as spotless as herself. The charpoys in her living/dining/storage room, which were used for seating guests, had crisp counterpanes with tambour work. The utensils displayed on high shelves gleamed when sunlight caught them. She was a petite bundle of energy. Her walk was so lithe, so self-possessed that it was hard to believe that her husband had died more than twenty years ago. Two of her married daughters had been widowed early and she was a grandmother of at least seven children. A neckless, mousy looking girl lurked behind her. She was the first born of one of her widowed daughters. The adopted daughter neither smiled nor frowned; she kept her eyes lowered to the ground and performed all the chores silently and obediently.

Taijee was deferential to my father, but she had a quaint, coquettish manner towards my portly uncle, my father's younger brother, a far more serious looking man than my father. My uncle responded to *Taijee's* playful inquiries with a mortified grin as though he was embarrassed that a woman could be so demonstrative towards him. Everyone knew that my uncle was quite small when our grandmother died and that *Taijee* had mothered him through his early childhood, but years of celibacy had made my uncle feel disconcerted in the presence of women. He may have looked uncomfortable about *Taijee's* open affection towards him in the presence of his children, but I think he rather enjoyed the special attention he received.

Which is probably why three times a year my uncle filled his Morris Oxford with four of his children and myself — if I happened to be around — and motor up to Kasur on a day trip. The journey, no more then 35 odd miles — and roads were deserted in those days — would take the best part of two hours because my uncle was a cautious driver who believed that a car should only run as fast as a man could run. He stopped first at *Taijee's* house and only after lunch and a siesta, called upon his sister, Ruqaiya, before motoring back.

Lunch at *Taijee's* was a big attraction for all of us. She was a legendary cook and her *Tinda Gosht*, considered to be an ordinary dish in our cuisine, was simply out of this world. The adopted daughter laid out the best china on a *dasterkhwan* placed over a square of rush matting which was spread on the floor. How she organised to send for fresh *andarsah* (sweet, buttery, rice pasties), a Kasur specialty, from the bazaar when there was no servant around, was a mystery to me.

Aunt Ruqaiya was never present at these lunches. There may have been no animosity between the two sisters-in-law, but they did not visit each other.

After lunch I would sneak out of the back door. Two steps from the door led to a back street, which had an open sewerage running in the middle of the street. Street is too grand a word for the narrow, slanting lane that zigzagged its way through featureless structures, which looked like mini warehouses. The lanes were so narrow that if two people came out from a house at the same time they had to walk single file. There were no windows in the walls, only heavy, traditional wooden doors with iron spikes. The joints of brickwork had corroded and yellow wasps flew in and out of the holes with abandon.

How can I ever forget the day when I dared to explore the mysteries of that narrow lane? It felt cool; the air, in spite of the sewerage stream running in the middle, was not fetid. The deserted, narrow lane didn't bend or curve, but turned, angularly, to the right or left. It was as thrilling as being in a maze. I kept following it until it ended abruptly, in front of a square.

I have a vivid recollection of reaching the end of the maze. It was as if the sound track of a movie that had gone dead, had suddenly come to life. There was an incoherent mixture of sounds, which only made sense once my mind became focused and I realized that what struck me as a chaotic uproar was, in fact, the urgings of the sherbet sellers, the cries of the hawkers, the pleas of beggars and the tingling bells of the bicycle riders.

The bazaar area had rough cobblestones. In between the shops, as well as in the open square, there were small stalls and barrows; men sat on low stools, behind big, round *tokris* laden with fruits or vegetables. The booming voice of the *ganderiwala* rose above every other cry. The man paused for a while as if to recharge himself and then began to shout the praises of his sugarcane cubes, which he announced were marzipans, laced with honey, and descended directly from heaven. Now, and then, he made a perfunctory gesture with his left hand to ward off the flies. No one paid him much attention.

Beggars groaned about their miseries but they did not pester anyone. They either lay prostrate underneath the platforms of makeshift kiosks, or squatted in doorways. From their respective positions they invoked the mercy of Allah, by rote. The shoppers, men mostly, hastened past them to bargain with ironmongers and haberdashers.

This was the bazaar that adjoined Kot Ruknuddin Khan and Kot Fateh Din Khan. Kasur was a town of Kots. Some of the Afghans who came to invade India in the 18th century settled down in Lahore. It is said that a few of those fell out of favour with the mighty Ahmed Shah Abdali, and moved to Kasur, where they established their Kots (forts or castles) in different areas. Later these Kots, were expanded into wards. My ancestors took domicile in Kot Ruknuddin—in Mianjee's jargon it was 'Kot Lukamdeen'—but I often heard my aunts tell me that some of my relations had taken up residence in Kot Murad Khan and Kot Hakim Khan.

There was an incredible commingling of smells in the bazaar. The acrid odour of tobacco and *gur* lying in open sacks, was soon overtaken by the aroma of freshly roasted grams. The cloth shops with their bolts of shiny silks and cottons gave off a whiff of vetiver; a few yards away was the soothing, breezy fragrance of sherbets which again dissolved into the tangy, spicy fumes of fried aubergines. The provision shops didn't smell of tumeric and coriander, but fenugreek, which was a great Kasur specialty. In fact, once you moved down the street away from the cloth shops, it was fenugreek, fenugreek all the way.

Pedlars coaxed me to buy their charms and amulets; the nougat-seller insisted I try a piece, even if I didn't want to buy any. I drifted from one stall to the other, stopping with no other motive than my uninhibited delight in the spirit of things. It was fascinating to watch the shaven-headed *Vataun-fryer* pick a mound of wet, flour-pasted triangularly sliced aubergines and drop them into a huge vat of oil, where they hissed and spluttered; their original saffron colour soon turning into a deep terracotta. The fryer knew exactly when to scoop them up. I was debating with myself whether to buy one or two pieces, when a hand on my shoulders turned me around. It was the woman who covered her mouth and nose before sweeping aunt Ruqaiya's courtyard. I had never realised that owing to the formation of her teeth she could never close her mouth. 'Oh son,' she shook her head in dismay. 'What a bother you have been. Everyone has been worried sick, but I told them I'd find the little blighter. Oh, praise the Lord.' She got hold of my arm and held it firmly as she led me back.

I did not think I had committed any wrong and yet a peculiar kind of uneasiness swelled inside me; my heart began to race as we approached aunt Ruqaiya's house. The backdoor was open. The sweepress still holding my arm, at last, released her grip. 'Here,' she said loudly, in a self-important tone, 'Take care of your precious one.'

It was late in the afternoon, well past the time my uncle had set for our departure. Fez in place, his *achkan* buttoned upto the neck, my uncle's normally severe face had a strange, withdrawn look to suggest that life was nothing but a trial. My cousins, who were huddled in a corner, averted their eyes when I looked at them. My effrontery could not be condoned.

The courtyard was filled with all the aunts in the world. Some rushed forward chanting a prayer and emitted a short, sharp breath over my head. Others discussed which sacrifice would be more propititious; a cauldron of *pilau*, or a black goat. I was lucky enough to have been found. There were too many stories of boys who wandered alone into the bazaar and never returned.

I didn't visit Kasur again for sometime. My eldest sister had moved back to Lahore and my parents no longer felt it necessary to make an annual trip. Then, one summer, my sister went to visit her mother-in-law, and her eight year old son fell ill.

My nephew, Javed, four years younger to me, was a shy, pleasant looking lad, who idolised me and ran every errand for me unquestioningly. Word came to my father that Javed was fretting a lot and could I come and cheer him up a bit. I, along with two of my sisters, was dispatched to Kasur by train.

We arrived in the morning. Javed was lying listlessly on a charpoy inside. He hardly registered my presence. By early afternoon his condition worsened; his fever was so high that the charpoy was brought out into the veranda. His eyes remained half closed and even though he was being mopped, his whole body was drenched in perspiration. Every now and then he would wretch, and throw up a green vomit. His mother cradled him and sobbed silently. Aunt Ruqaiya remained composed and kept chanting a refrain 'God is the curer' in a low voice, which was as dull as it was soothing. My eldest sister looked terrified because she could recognise that her son's condition was caused by cholera, a fatal disease in those days.

I felt helpless and inadequate and guilty because Javed was suffering and I was not. I sneaked out of the back door into the narrow lane. I stood there not knowing what to do. I resisted the temptation of going to the bazaar and sat down on the steps of a neighbour's doorway.

I must have dozed off for I was woken by a shriek followed by wailing. There were loud cries of 'Javed is no more — *Hai Hai Hai.*' I rushed into the house; my elder sister was knocking her head against the wooden post of the charpoy. She was dragged away; other women were beating their breasts and keening. I tried hard to weep but tears evaded me. The lane outside was now busy with traffic. I went upstairs and sat down amidst cans that smelled of rancid butter. The keening went on all afternoon.

Much later, when hundreds of people had gathered in the house, I was able to catch a glimpse of my nephew. His body had been washed and wrapped in white cotton. His nose had turned slightly crooked and he was several shades darker. There were rose petals strewn all over his body. The place reeked of roses. From that day on, rose petals would, forever, remind me of death.

I have never visited Kasur since, but the town has haunted me throughout my life. I remember it with affection and horror. The babbling aunts keep blowing benedictions over my eyes; the *dain* with the matted hair still beckons to me as indeed *Taijee's* angelic smile fills me with warmth. It's a place, which evokes a strong flavour of vetiver and fenugreek and — no matter how much I dismiss it — death.

KHADIM MOHYEDDIN

My father died at a bus stop. I had hoped that he would die quietly and naturally in his sleep. He did the next best thing. He died in harness, waiting for a bus to take him to the university where he was to hand over some papers he had been annotating. A man who was sitting on the wooden platform of his tiny kiosk saw him totter and collapse. He rushed to help, but by the time he was able to reach the prostrate body, my father was dead.

I wasn't around when this happened so I couldn't see my father's noble and serene brow in death. He had a fine, oval face and in his dark, wide-set eyes was a gaze at once penetrating and sardonic. He had a broad forehead and his nose had length and dignity. His chin was firm and the line of his mouth indicated that it would open in a broad smile.

My father was an inveterate walker. He walked with his head slightly bent because it had been ingrained into him that to walk upright would suggest a swagger, or hauteur, which was, culturally, not acceptable to him. Modesty and self-effacement were the two tenets his father had told him to hold on to, and throughout his life, he lived by these principles.

In all my travels I have met no one outside the musical profession who cared so intensely about music. I remember when he took me to Patiala, at the age of seven, and introduced me to Ustad Abdul Aziz Khan Beenkar. The Ustad didn't speak to me much, but he kept his hand over my head for what seemed a very long time. His tunic was as shabby as his surroundings. He played a few airs on his *Vichitra Veena* which didn't make any sense to me. When we left the little, dark room in which he lived and practised, my father mused that countless treasures would lay in store for me if I learnt to appreciate music. It took me a very long time to discover that he was right.

He was a passionate amateur (I use the word amateur in its true sense). He could accompany anyone on the tabla. His favourite instrument was the *Dilruba* which he could play reasonably well. He could strum a few strokes on the *Sitar* as well, but he preferred the sweep of the bow. (The *Dilruba*, alas, has not only gone out of vogue, it has disappeared altogether. My cousin Ayub, having inherited the love of this instrument from my father, is the only person in the country to possess one). The harmonium brought out a different mood in him. As his fingers ran up and down the scale he became less serious, almost flippant, and his mind wandered over to the romantic melodies and the comic duets from Urdu theatre. If no one was around he would sing to me a ditty like:

nikal nikal nikal ja
chatak matak latak satak matak atak latak ja.

I loved the sweep of the words and the staccato rhythm and would ask him to repeat the phrase. He would do so, but never without pointing out that the melodic structure had been borrowed from such and such a raga. He played none of the instruments with professional expertise, but he rightly saw no harm in a good try; and in the readiness with which he would have a shot at everything, lay a considerable part of his charm.

In the best years of his life — after he burnt his English clothes and joined the *Khilafat* movement — he wandered a great deal in and around what was then known as Poona, trying to acquire musical knowledge from the Gurus that lived in Maharashtra. He must have made some notes because I discovered, among his papers, a little black book, yellowed with age, in which he had put down more than a hundred and seventy five *bandishen* (songs set in ragas with the ascending and descending modes strictly codified), the date when he heard these renditions, as well as the rhythmic cycle which laces these compositions. All of this is carefully noted in his fine, mature handwriting. Sometimes he hears the same *Bandish* from two different composers, but in varied rhythmic cycles. Here he has devised a highly individual form of notation, which shows where the accents change even though the words are the same. I have gone through this notebook a few times, never without marvelling over the care and pain he took about setting each composition down. This little book is one of my dearest possessions.

In later years when he was in Lahore, known universally as 'Professor Sahib' (even though he was only a senior lecturer) he spent all his spare time in trying to enlist support to have classical music introduced as one of the subjects in the Punjab University. The authorities had, grudgingly, allowed it to be an optional subject for the F.A. Examination (the exam that enables a student to qualify for degree classes). My father was not satisfied with this. He wanted music to be a degree subject so that it could be taken up seriously by the students. The opposition came from the Muslims who thought music to be a 'Hindu Thing'. 'Professor Sahib,' I once heard a lawyer say to my father in the bus which took us from Model Town to Lahore, 'You are a thorough gentleman. Why do you go on about this raga business?' 'So I can remain a gentleman,' my father said without a moment's hesitation.

Towards the 40's, a small percentage of Muslim girls had begun to take up post-graduate studies which meant that instead of going to their own segregated girls colleges, they had to come and attend classes in the University campus, the very building where music classes were held. The guardians of Islamic morals pointed out that Muslim girls could not be allowed to tread corridors where *natch-gana* (singing and dancing) took place. After a meeting at Islamia College, a resolution was moved demanding separate premises for Muslim girls. Nothing came of it because the vociferous protestors didn't ever allow their own daughters to be foolish enough to take up post-graduate studies, anyway. The fact remained that not a single Muslim girl decided to opt for music when it was finally introduced into the curriculum. After partition took place, the first casualty in the university was music as a subject of study.

I wish I could say that my first appearance on the stage in a play written and directed by Khadim Mohyeddin was the beginning of my long and chequered career in the theatre, but that would be romanticising the story of my life. More than a decade would go by before I would tread the boards again.

I tried during my college years — for the inclination was there — to act for the GCDC (Government College Dramatic Club) but was turned away on the grounds (which I find as ludicrous now as I found it then) that debaters were not welcome. All my overtures were spurned by the secretary, a simpering fop who, in a St. Anthony school accent, told me that my credentials as a prize-winning Urdu speaker in declamation contests did not merit an audition. Years later, I saw this pompous prig coming out of Burberry's in the Haymarket, close to the theatre I was appearing in, and was much amused at the way he averted his eyes to avoid me.

I wrote to my father from Australia that I had decided to resign from my 'gazetted' job with the government, and go to England to study drama, not, I assured him, as an academic subject, but with a view to becoming an actor. I remember that I tried to intellectualise as much as I was capable of, invoking his love for the dramatic art and reminding him of the years when he tried to impress upon his students that plays come to life not on paper but on stage. My decision, I emphasised, was not the whimsy of a wayward mind.

Why I sought his approbation, I don't know — my cultural upbringing, I suppose — for I had made up my mind that even if he showed disapproval, I would go ahead. I knew that all through his academic career dramatic productions were a 'fun thing', a pleasant diversion that made the return to the sedate world of academia agreeable. I was aware that he associated the world of professional theatre with showmanship and a degree of crassness, which he abjured. In any case it was inconceivable for anyone in the early fifties to think of acting as a desirable profession.

His reply, when it came was sympathetic. 'I fear for you,' he wrote, 'and I shall pray for you.' He wished me luck and hoped that people's negative opinions would not turn me sour inside. I needed to be strong and I needed to be prepared to withstand disappointments.

Of his years in England I know very little. He knew some of the songs of the twenties and one of them, 'I want to be happy', amused me a great deal. He sang it in a tenor's voice, a bit like Rudy Vallee. When I was small and had learnt the word 'pudding', he told me that 'Yorkshire pudding' was not really a pudding. Apart from this, the only other bit of knowledge that he imparted to me was that his favourite department store in London was Marshall and Snelgrove. His dressing gown, which used to be brought out of the big trunk every winter, bore the label 'Marshall and Snelgrove' in italicised lettering. The two words seemed to me to epitomise England.

Amongst his books was a tiny album with black and white photographs of buildings with charcoaled spires, but there were three snapshots which fascinated me: one in which my father is stretched out on the grass reclining on an elbow. It must have been cold, for he hasn't taken off his overcoat. His Homburg lies in front of him. Behind him stands a girl in a knee length dress with a cloche hat over her bobbed hair. She has a beaded necklace, which reaches down, well below her waist and she stands as though she is all set to launch herself into a Charleston. She is pretty and she has the insouciant smile of a ringmaster's assistant. My father's quizzical smile suggests that it is not his idea to be photographed.

In the second snapshot, the same girl, this time, hatless, has her right arm around my father's waist. She has a perky smile which, it is my guess, has been switched on at the photographer's request. My father, in a different suit, looking rather dandified with spats over his shoes, looks resigned to being encircled. He seems to be saying that in Rome you must do as the Romans do. Was he conscious that his inquisitive children would look at this snapshot with great interest?

The third snapshot doesn't convey much. The girl is sitting in the side car of a motorbike, facing the camera, while my father, his Homburg on his head, sits on the pillion, looking straight ahead. There is a third man who stands at a distance.

Who was the girl? My sisters thought she looked funny because she was a Memsahib. I thought she looked enchanting. One of my sisters, my father's favourite daughter, who was fond of reading English novels, and therefore, an authority on all matters relating to England, declared that her name was Jane and that she was our father's landlady. My desire to be in England, as a growing lad, was fanned by images of pert, bob-haired landladies, who made you feel weak at the knees by their impish postures. One look at the landladies, when I arrived in England, was enough to convince me that Jane couldn't have been one.

After we became friends and smoked each other's cigarettes, I once asked my father about 'Jane'. Smiling, bashfully, he told me, in between pulling at his hookah, that her name was Edith Brookes, and that she was a member of the touring company of 'Chu Chin Chow', the hugely successful West End musical that ran in London for years. His eyes registered a look of such wistfulness that my next question — what she meant to him — died on my lips.

Affluence eluded him all his life. He lived a hand to mouth existence and was perfectly reconciled to it, if only because he knew that he had chosen a line of work that did not offer any financial rewards. He never listened to any 'get rich quick' schemes and never filled out a lottery ticket or a racing card throughout his life.

It was with great pride that he told me the story of how his father, a school master and a magistrate of a small town near Ferozepur, had turned down a largesse, offered to him by no less a dignitary than Howe Sahib. G.D. Howe, a terse Scotsman, was the commissioner of land revenues entrusted with the responsibility of distributing vast tracts of land that had fallen under the British tutelage after the end of the Sikh rule in the province. Howe Sahib, on one of his tours, was so pleased with my grandfather's efforts to introduce the teaching of English in his school, that he sent for him and told him that he had decided to bestow upon him, 35 *murrabahs* (square miles) of land near Jhang. My grandfather, my father recounted, went down on his knees, 'Sahib', he beseeched, *'Hum pe itna zulm na keegiay'* (do not inflict, such a heavy punishment on me). He pleaded that a man who was familiar with only two instruments, pen and ink, was incapable of looking after lands. Besides, he entreated — and here my father chuckled — his children and grandchildren would become wastrels. They would become *aish parast* (luxury-loving) and this he could not afford.

It was an act of supreme courage, my father said, because nobody dared to displease Howe Sahib. Howe left the district, but not before awarding a plot of land on the outskirts of Sheikhupura, to my grandfather. My farther inherited one third of this plot, as was his due. He could have sold it and made a bit of money, but it would have entailed a heavy amount of administrative work to have his portion demarcated officially, and he couldn't be bothered to spend endless hours pursuing petty officials of the department of the Registrar of Lands. Innocently, he gave his land to a contractor who offered him a pittance every year.

I remember this contractor well. He would arrive once a year with a canister of *ghee* and *gur*, wrapped in a home-spun material. 'Salams to the landlords,' he would announce before settling down in a chair on the verandah. (My father cringed at being called a landlord). He would then take off his turban as a mark of supplication and say, 'Sheikh Sahib, what can I say? We have been undone. The untimely rains ruined the crops. I have brought you whatever I could. As God is my witness I have not kept a penny for myself,' and he would hand over an envelope to my father. Sometimes the script began differently: '*Maliko*, (respected owner) what can I say? Too much rain has ruined us...' My father would say, 'Don't you think you should keep something for your self?' The contractor would stand up, hold my father's hand in his two hands and declare that if he touched a penny of this amount, he would be unable to face his maker, on the day of judgment.

The contractor cheated my father every year. The money my father received was always less than the agreed amount. My mother—and, at times, my sisters —would talk about the chicanery of the contractor, but my father told them that they knew nothing about how weather conditions affected the crops.

He was careful with whatever few pennies he earned. He would have liked to have been extravagant, to travel and to entertain, but he had to restrain these tendencies. He had five daughters, and the responsibility of having to find suitable husbands (as well as sufficient funds for their dowries) weighed heavily on his mind throughout the middle years of his life. He had a restless spirit and every now and then he would have a renewed enthusiasm for travel, for breaking away from what he considered to be his placid existence. He would announce that he was leaving for such and such a place, but frequently, at the last minute, abandon his plans. For a day or two there would be a complete hush in the house while he had an inward tussle with his inquietude.

As a rebellious teenager I must have added to his pains. My growing up process was no better than that of any other pimpled youth. I became insufferably surly. The man, who in my childhood I thought to be God, now struck me as a petty bourgeois. I considered his values of goodness and moral purpose to be specious and meaningless. I defied him in every way, coming home late and adopting an insubordinate manner towards him. He was baffled. He tried to apply psychology, asking me to describe what was eating me up. I responded with a hostile silence. When this didn't work, he became the stern pater, which alienated me even more.

He must have discussed my boorishness with Professor Sirajuddin, one of my English teachers because I was asked to report to the professor not in the staff room, but at his bungalow. Sirajuddin was a man who could be as droll as Archie Rice when not teaching. He had a ready wit and was fond of drawing upon a vast fund of Punjabi fables. With trepidation, I arrived at Professor Sirajuddin's house. He was affable and charming, he lamented that being such a gifted student I didn't take enough part in the college activities. He boosted my ego and walked with me all the way to the gate to see me off. Then, as I took my leave, he said, 'I don't know what your definition of culture is, but let me tell you something: whatever parents do for children is nature, but what children do for parents is culture.' Remorse filled me like hot liquid surging through my veins. I felt ashamed to face my father. He sensed this, and to ease the situation, asked me quite casually, if I could give him a hint or two about Ezra Pound whom he found to be quite abstruse. I realised that though I carried Pound's *Cantoes* with me everywhere, I didn't really understand him at all.

In spite of hearing tales of horror, we in Model Town, didn't experience the internecine fighting that went on everywhere in the city during the time of partition. Almost quietly, imperceptibly, the Hindus and Sikhs left their residences. One sultry afternoon I saw one of our neighbours, a retired engineer, emerge from the corner house (that belonged to a Sikh, an ex-army captain), with a rolled carpet. He threw it on the road and toed it all the way to his house. The ex-army captain had left all his belongings in the house. He had come to see my father before leaving. 'If God so wills I will be back one day and take my stuff. If not, it is all yours,' he said, and with tears in his eyes, he embraced my father.

When I told my father about the brazen theft of the carpet, he became colourless. The dire changes of history that took place in 1947 made him somewhat embittered. It was not in his nature to become sour, but he no longer believed in human kindness. During his afternoon walks he would gaze from object to object as though they would help him find a source of love that would replace his lost faith. He became more at ease with people who cherished their own privacy, thus defending his. He became testy. My mother suffered his testiness with ascetic quiescence and a withdrawn silence that had no accusatory colouring to it. This irked him so much that he exploded every now and then, but his explosions were like bubbles that subsided within a few moments, leaving him contrite.

Whatever it was that caused him anguish, he was unable to share it with my mother, his sole companion in his later years, a simple woman whose undying devotion to him was not enough to compensate for her lack of intellectual and musical sensibilities. He would often rush to Jamshoro to spend a few days with his favourite daughter whom he regarded to be a kindred soul. In her company he listened to music — and reminisced. He was unabashedly partisan to his middle daughter, much to the chagrin of my other sisters.

He was not an easy man to know. His own innately guarded nature that was full of seeming contrarieties 'affectionate and aloof, good-humoured and testy, expansive and reticent' stood in the way of an easy traffic with his fellowmen. He bore his grief in privacy. I shall never forget the day when, after listening to a particularly moving rendition of raga *Poorya Kalyan* by Shrimati Bai Narvekar, he left the room and did not come back for quite some time. I found him standing behind the door and sobbing quietly. In spite of all his complexity he was a man of great kindness.

I believe I only got to know him in the last few years of his life, and to know him was to love him. His modesty, his humbleness, his conviction that an understanding of literature maketh a man, his child-like delight in music, his belief that people must not be told off even when they were wrong, are qualities rare amongst men. When my rising fame on the London stage was dealt a heavy blow in the sixties, he wrote to me a consoling letter ending with '.....Ideals might lead to disillusionment, but without ideals there is no life. Khadim Mohyeddin.'

EAT YOUR HEART OUT

As far as I am concerned, you can keep your Shane Warne. The best leg-break bowler I ever came across was Saleemullah. He was the youngest of three brothers, all of whom were cricketers. Bowlers I should say, for I never saw any of them bat, although Saleemullah once helped me correct my stance, and in so doing demonstrated a few imaginary strokes on both sides of the wicket. Saleemullah's elder brothers were thick-set and heavy-jowled, but he was slim and tidily built. The brothers wore caps of different kinds, but Saleemullah always wore a fez which he never took off even when he bowled.

We used to live on Rattigan Road, a narrow lane that stretched from the Parsi temple to the boundary of the Lahore Veterinary College. There was a turning a few yards away from our house, a square with an open compound in the centre, where Maula, the cowherd, kept his two cows under a home-made shed. (Eventually, Maula would lay claim to the entire square, because one of his ancestors, a holy man, was buried in that hallowed ground, but I leave that story for another time). There were a few houses that stood, cheek by jowl, on one side of the square, including Saleemullah's, and it was outside his house on the kutcha street that Saleemullah and his brothers bowled to the likes of us. There was only one wicket installed at the bowler's end. There were no wickets at the batsman's end, only a crate or two or a discarded, broken down chair or sometimes even a charpoy made to stand upright with three lines drawn heavily, in chalk, on the ground in the middle.

Saleemullah's brothers — I cannot recall their names — were fair like their Kashmiri ancestors. They always wore two or three days growth of beard. Saleemullah was darker but neat in appearance. He had a lovely action, his left arm stretched obliquely across his forehead as he approached the bowler's crease, and he brought it down elegantly as he released the ball which nearly always hit the same spot before curving and breaking sharply. You could place a coin where the ball landed; nine times out of ten it would hit the coin. His wrong 'un was not so much a googly, but a ball that did not break. It was as though the ball decided at the last minute to go straight instead of left.

He bowled for an hour or so — the elder brothers were up and down seamers, who bowled to us at half their pace — and then picking up the one wicket and the bat, which had no rubber grip, only a black twine on the handle, they withdrew into the house.

Twice a week, there used to be a cricket match at Maula's compound. I was fascinated by these matches. Teams arrived, dressed in white, and dumped their gear in or outside the cowshed. Maula would provide a couple of extra charpoys on which they sat and bantered, swearing and cursing with a freedom which shocked and thrilled me at the same time. One of us would be sent to knock the wickets into the ground (there were no bails) and then, amidst raucous laughter and more swear words, they walked into the ground which didn't have a tuft of grass.

The home team's captain was the dashing Pasha (later known as Anwar Kamal Pasha, the highly successful movie director). I don't know how, but he always managed to put the visitors in first. Even when he lost the toss, he would look at the opposing captain imperiously and say, 'You would like to bat first wouldn't you?' The opposing captain dared not do otherwise.

The main reason for letting the other side bat first was that Pasha wanted to bowl the first six or seven overs and disappear. Rumour had it that he had several liaisons and he used this time to visit one of them for an amorous rendezvous. He was a medium fast bowler, but on that dusty patch the ball didn't fly about. Now and then he would hit an uneven spot on the ground and the ball bounced awkwardly for the batsman. This delighted him no end and he would chuckle flagrantly over the discomfiture of the batsman. He got more wickets out of bravado than ability.

Pasha was a very handsome young man. He had a shapely head with wavy hair, a Ronald Coleman moustache and a well-proportioned body. He was short-tempered, but laughed a good deal as well. 'I'm nearly home, you ill-begotten so and so....' He would shout to his mother from the road approaching his house. His mother, sitting on a low stool smoking the hookah, feigned displeasure, but glowed inwardly. Pasha would make sure that he used the shocking words only when his father was not around.

Pasha's father, Hakim Ahmed Shuja, a man of considerable literary ability, was one of the most prominent personalities of Lahore. He was a bigwig in local administration and many people called upon him. He had written a few plays in the mode of Agha Hashr, and he loved regaling his visitors with the year he played the female lead in *Yahoodi Ki Larki* (The Jew's Daughter), a Hashr play, which borrowed freely, from *The Merchant of Venice* and *The Duchess of Malfi*. Hakim Ahmed Shuja had learnt, probably from my father, that I had played the part of a Chinese girl in my school production, so he had a soft spot for me and would often make me sit beside him. He wore round glasses and his eyes beamed goodness. I loved being in that household. The lady of the house, Pasha's mother, was outwardly stern, but soft as marshmallow inside, and her daughter (whom I'd always remember as No No Nanette) was an eighteen year old sylvan beauty of exquisite grace. Pasha hardly ever spoke to me. Occasionally, he bestowed a smile on me.

When he returned to the match from wherever he had gone, Pasha would immediately put on his pads, sometimes only the left pad, and walk on to the wicket. One of the batsmen would, naturally, withdraw in his favour. The fielding side made no objection for they knew that it was Pasha who provided the post-match refreshments.

From the first ball he would threaten the bowler, dancing down to the middle of the pitch. He would let forth a vigorous expletive if he missed, but if he connected, the ball would go sailing into the front garden of the Principal's house. One of us would rush after it and retrieve it, but not without receiving a scolding from the gatekeeper. Pasha would relish the hit with an angelic smile, followed by a highly imaginative invective.

Saleemullah and his brothers never played in any of these matches. They were a devout family and it injured their pietistic feelings to be exposed to what they regarded as profanity. His brothers might not have been much sought after, but Saleemullah was always coaxed by Pasha to join in. My view was that he refused because he thought that he might be asked to take off his fez while bowling.

But there was one match in which Saleemullah played; in fact he captained the team. Pasha, for some reason, was not to be seen anywhere. That day, Saleemullah did what I have never seen in my entire life. He bowled half a dozen men round their legs. His leg breaks were devastating, pinpointingly accurate. The ball would pitch, the batsman would shape up to meet it, and be bamboozled. The ball would dart in like an arrow. Not long ago, when I

saw Warne bowling out Gatting in a similar fashion,
I thought of Saleemullah and his fez.

Next day, at school, I boasted about Saleemullah. He
is the best ever, I said. My classmates wouldn't
believe me; they cited Amir Elahi, whom they hadn't
seen either, as the greatest. What did I know about
spin bowling, they scoffed. What did I know about
cricket, they sneered. What did I know about cricket!
I, who had measured the 22 yard space between
wickets a hundred times. I, who knew what a no-ball
and a wide ball was. I, who knew how to signal a
boundary. Why, oh why, did my father choose to put
me in a school which only had philistines? I wanted
to gouge their eyes out, but they were bigger and
heftier.

Even my friend, Om Prakash, a roly-poly boy, with
wide nostrils, said he could hit Saleemullah with
impunity. I couldn't argue with him too much for
fear that he might refuse to let me ride his brand new
bicycle. I didn't even know how to ride a bicycle
properly. Well, I could, but I didn't know how to get
off or get on and I needed his bike, desperately.
Alright, I said, squirming with frustration, you come
to my place and I'll take you to him and I'll put a
paisa on the ground and then you watch.

Om Prakash came the same afternoon and I took him
to Saleemullah's house. He and his brothers always
came out of their house at a certain time. There was
never any need to knock at their door. That afternoon
no-one showed up.

I have never been a confident cyclist.

LUDHYANA

Noon Meem Rashed once told me that on the rare occasion when he chose to take part in a Mushaira in Delhi, he was asked pointedly how he would like to be announced. 'Rashed,' he said, 'but if you want to be particular, Noon Meem Rashed.' The man who had been deputed to introduce the poets in a flowery language, reminiscent of Khwaja Mohammad Shafi, was the achkan-clad, pan-chewing, Shakir Dehlavi, a distant grand-nephew of Nawwab Sail Dehlavi, 'Rashed?' he enquired, somewhat bewildered, 'Rashed, from where?'implying that poets whose names had no appendage were not truly welcome in that particular Mushaira.

Badayun, like Rudoli and Barabanki has never produced a poet who does not insert his ancestral town into his name. When it comes to Badayun, we only think of Fani and, to a lesser extent, Shakeel, but there are countless Shakebs and Irfans and Kausars. Rashed Sahib once observed poker-faced, that the mysteries of Badayun's poetic heritage are known only to Badayunis—as indeed that of Rudoli to Rudolvis.

Iqbal was the first redoubtable poet to break away from the tradition. Miraji, Rashed and Faiz followed him. Iqbal decided to be known as Iqbal and he got away with it—in India, at any rate. In Iran, people still refer to him as Iqbal-e-Lahori (though strictly speaking he should be called Iqbal-e-Sialkoti). Other renowned poets of the era remained firmly attached to their cities; Riaz was always Riaz Khairabadi; Jigar was Moradabadi, Josh was Maleehabadi, and Firaq was Gorukhpuri.

Even before the middle ages, poets of Persia used the name of their birth place as an appendage to their pen-names. Urdu poets of the subcontinent followed the pattern. The 'progressive' poets of the thirties discarded the practice but some of them—Sahir, Majrooh—continued to remain loyal to their birthplace.

If Sahir was not a Ludhyanvi would he have written differently? Ludhiana was what the colonialists called a '*moffusil*' town. It had an intermediate college, a government school, a hosiery industry, a few congested bazaars like you found in every growing town in the Punjab and, of course, the 'Civil Lines' reserved for the 'Sahibs' who, in the evening, lounged in armchairs under a whirling ceiling fan in the middle of their lawns, and sipped gimlets.

I went to Ludhyana with my college cricket team to play against the now degree college. The college didn't have our rooms ready. Actually, the team wasn't meant to be staying in rooms but in a dormitory with 22 beds arranged as in a hospital ward. Unfortunately, the dormitory had been occupied by a visiting contingent of scouts.

We parked ourselves along the railway platform until Raj Baldev, the ever-resourceful all-rounder of our team, made it possible for us to move into the waiting rooms. There were two of them; one exclusive to the first and second class passengers and a large, general waiting room, which had a few sleepy inmates. Raj told them that we had been quarantined and that we were waiting for the official doctors, who were arriving from Amritsar to examine us before deciding where to send us. The passengers hastily packed their belongings and made way for the furthest end of the platform. We moved in and unrolled our hold-alls.

The skipper of our team had already moved to the first-class waiting room, where his man-servant (the skipper belonged to aristocratic parents who wouldn't dream of sending their offspring on a long railway journey without his personal servant) had made his bed on the cane divan. When I went to speak to him about Jal Daruwalla, I found him lounging in that huge cane chair with double-layered wooden arms that swiveled out to allow you to put your feet up. The position that you assumed in this chair, with your legs wide apart was not unlike that of an expectant mother about to deliver a baby.

Jal Daruwalla was an awkward young Parsi who suffered greatly because although he was past seventeen, his face did not show any signs of a beard. He was a harmless spinner who batted number ten only because the number eleven batsman, Ghafoor, was an even poorer batsman. I had gone to tell the skipper that Jal was on the verge of tears because he was desperate to go to the loo but wouldn't, because he felt the toilet in the general waiting room was too filthy for words.

The skipper had a soft heart. He sent his servant to bring Jal in. Jal's face was blotchy and he was sweating, but when he returned from the toilet in the first class waiting room, he was smiling and full of gratitude. The skipper told him to bring his luggage over and settle down in one of the vacant lounging chairs. Daruwalla said he couldn't. If anyone deserved to be there, it was I who had come to his rescue. Thus it was that both of us lodged in the cooler, cleaner, plushier surrounds of the first and second class waiting room for the next four days.

We lost the cricket match, an annual fixture, but won the debating contest. Honours were not even because cricket was the real glamorous event. I still can't forget the bizarre manner in which Raj, our all rounder and main hope, got out. He had taken a swipe at a ball which flicked past his bat towards the third man. He ran, but the batsman at the other end, Siddique, was so engrossed in fixing the *nara* (cord) round his waist that he didn't even look up to see what had happened. Desperate, Raj ran back towards his crease and made it, thanks to the wayward throw from the third man which went in the direction of the square leg boundary. It was here that Raj made his real mistake. He ran for the additional run, but Siddiqui had made up his mind to stay put and stay put he did.

In the mid-forties Ludhyana had no architectural feature that I can recall. There wasn't even a clock tower. The bazaars were woefully devoid of any characteristics. The small tailoring shops and haberdashery kiosks belonged to the Muslims; the rest of the commerce was in the hands of the Hindus. I remember, in particular, the milk stalls where huge vats of milk simmered and bubbled. Sikhs, young and old, stood around gulping large copper glasses filled to the brim with milk. The Sardarjis who owned the stalls wore singlets and Samurai buns, instead of turbans, on their heads. There seemed to be an easy mingling of the three communities. The tensions between Muslim and Hindus that had become palpable in cities like Lahore and Lyallpur were remarkably absent in Ludhyana.

Sahir Ludhyanvi grew up in this city. And so did that peerless satirist, Ibn-e-Insha. If I had known it when I visited that city, I might have looked at it differently.

SMUDGER

I was once admitted to a hospital in London because I was stricken with quinsy. The only other occupant in the ward was a freckle-faced 11 year old lad, who had a weak heart. There were other beds, but they remained unoccupied for the duration of my stay.

This was in the golden days of the National Health Service, when hospitals had more beds than patients and you could, actually, choose your hospital. I would have been quite happy to go to the one in St. John's Wood where I lived, but the girl I was going out with in those days, insisted that I should go to Hampstead because the hospital there was within walking distance to her flat and it would be convenient for her to visit me. She hardly ever came, which taught me a thing or two.

You don't feel depressed or ill-tempered if you have quinsy (an abscess in the region around the tonsils), you just feel a peculiar loss of appetite because you know you won't be able to get any food down on account of the hurdle that stands between your mouth

and your oesophagus. Drinking any liquid is equally
wearisome. I used to fill an eye dropper with water and
insert a drop on the side of my mouth hoping it would
by-pass the lump. I would usually grimace and squirt
my eyes during this futile exercise. It made the young
boy, my ward companion, chuckle a great deal.

He was a comely lad with close-cropped hair and
piercing eyes. I have rarely come across an eleven
year old with sharper intelligence or a sunnier
disposition. His mother had died and he lived with
his grandmother, a sturdy Cockney lady, his sole
visitor. His name was Ashby. I once made the mistake
of calling him Ashby-de-la-Zouche and he winced at
my lack of originality. It was obvious that he had
had his fill of being dubbed as a town. I apologised,
and he said, 'Oh you can't help it. No one can.....' But
he forgave me with a heart-warming smile.

I owe a great deal to Ashby for acquainting me with
some of the oddities of the English language. It was
he who told me that to 'put up or shut up' means to
tolerate. 'When you put up with someone, it means
you can stick him,' he went on to say. 'Ha Ha!' I said,
'that's daft. Stick him like what? Stick him in the back?'
'No, silly,' he laughed, 'when you stick someone like
that it means you hate him, but to say you can stick
him means you like him,' 'So,' I said 'you stick me, I
stick you?' 'Yeah' he beamed.

I had no idea how serious his condition was until he
told me one day, quite matter-of-factly, that he had a
hole in his heart. 'They say I'll make it. Make what?'
He said and grinned, 'They say a lot of stupid things

like every cloud has a silver lining. Clouds don't
have linings.'

He wasn't bitter when he said this. He didn't know
what bitterness meant. The only time he ever
twinged with an inner pain was when the night
nurse, tucking him in, cooed, 'Now be good.
Remember worse things happen at sea.' This was her
pet phrase.

'Silly moo,' Ashby said after the nurse had left. 'Why
do worse things happen at sea than on land?' Then
as an afterthought, he said, 'What are these worst
things?' 'Well, Moby Dick, perhaps.' I tried to be
flippant. 'Aw, come on, it's naff. It's like saying 'all
other things being equal. They always say it when
they go over me. What other things? And being equal
to what?'

There he had the better of me. I could only marvel at
his acute sensitivity. He confided in me that it only
served to disappoint him when people told him to
cheer up. He usually felt pretty cheerful anyway.
Years later, I read a story in an American magazine
about a lugubrious insurance agent who feels so
maddened by his over-solicitous neighbour, trying
to jolly him up, that he plots to murder him. I thought
of Ashby.

The rougher edges of his Cockney accent had been
smoothened out by his schooling or his own efforts.
He didn't drop his aitches like his grandmother; nor
did he add them to words in which the aitches
remain silent. You could trace the Cockney lilt in his

speech, but not the full range of undulating Cockney sounds.

Sometimes I wondered if it was his affliction that gave him a kind of wisdom unassociated with boys of his age. Some of his observations were truly amazing. I had no answer when he asked me why we have to change our clothes during the day when we wear the same pair of pyjamas night after night.

He often used words that I had never heard of. All I could do was to register real surprise and this delighted him no end. 'Hey smudger,' he once said to me and I looked at him quizzically. A 'smudger' meant a friend, a mate; 'brass monkeys' meant cold. 'How come?' I asked and he assured me, 'It is brass monkey's weather, don't you know?' I would learn later that in Cockney lore the racks of cannon balls on board a warship were called brass monkeys. Perhaps it was a sailor who first said that it was cold enough to freeze the balls off a brass monkey.

Other words he taught me were: Rosie Lee (rhyming slang) which meant tea and 'Kate and Sidney' which, of course, was steak and kidney. It certainly evoked the image of a dish more appetizing than the canteen steak and kidney 'pud', which tasted like cat food mixed with chewy stodge.

When I came back to the ward after my operation, Ashby looked after me like an angel. He sat by my bed in case I needed a drink or a tissue. The two nurses who alternated their duties chided him. 'Is he paying you a lot of money?' they said flippantly. He remained unnerved. He left my side only when it was time for his grandmother's visit. After she left, he put the bunch of grapes, which she had brought for him, on my bedside table. I was so touched I nearly sobbed.

I had no idea why he had taken a shine to me. Was it because I had been to a drama school and he idolised actors? Or was it because I laughed with him and didn't try to patronise him or treat him as a little boy? It could have been all these things or none. His affection was so unalloyed, so wholehearted that I felt a pang of guilt for not being able to offer him the same amount of unbridled love.

As I got better, his condition took a turn for the worse. He spent most of the mornings in an inner sanctum going through a series of tests and was only brought to the ward late in the afternoon. His face looked flushed and hollow, but he still smiled at my feeble jokes.

When I took leave of him he didn't cry or snivel. 'Goodbye smudger, will you come and see me?' he asked, his eyes ever so alert. It was I who snivelled. 'Of course I will.'

Within a day or two, I got a two-week spear-holding engagement with the Derby Rep. When I returned to London I went to the hospital. The ward was full of some old patients, but Ashby was not to be seen. I went to the reception. The matron at the desk informed me that the 'poor boy' had gone to his maker.

My 'smudger' had, at last, made it.

MUSIC AS I KNEW IT

On the occasion of the birth of a son, his only son, my father, a reticent man threw caution to the winds and held an all night musical soiree. The peerless Ustad Malang Khan played the *tabla* until the early hours of the morning. He refused to accept any remuneration.

In our family lore the celebration of my birth in Lyallpur became more and more romanticised as I grew older. When I was five, my eldest sister, not averse to fantasising, remembered it as a lavish evening when hundreds of people listened, enraptured, to beautiful music. When I was about nine, she once showed me off to her friends as the 'Prince of Wales' whose birth was marked with a glittering reception featuring the 'best of musicians'.

I learned what actually took place from my father years later, when he and I had struck on equation at last. In his typically modest manner he told me that when the midwife announced the birth of a son to some of the inmates of the *mohalla*, his dear friend and neighbour, Sardar Jaswant Singh, felt that the event called for rejoicing and that there ought to be an impromptu concert of some kind. He sent word to Ustad Malang Khan and gathered some close, mutual friends. Malang Khan, one of the most outstanding percussionists of his time, lived in Lyallpur in those days and knew my father quite well. He arrived along with a few of his pupils who were joined by some amateur singers of the *mohalla*. Sardar Jaswant Singh sang a number in *Raga Bhopali* that he had learnt from my father; my father gave his rendering of a composition in *Malkaus* that he had picked from Fateh Din, the tailor. There was a singsong, but a great deal of *tabla* playing. Malang Khan was so happy for my father that he decided to use the occasion as a marathon solo session, much to the delight of my father and some of his chosen friends. The Ustad also improvised some intricate syncopation in the rhythmic cycle of ten beats, my father recalled.

If the *tabla* wasn't my father's first love, it was certainly the first instrument he learned to play. He was besotted with music at an early age. He used to sneak out of his house and go to the vicinity of Kasur where some itinerant folk musicians had settled down. He cultivated their friendship and learnt from them the rudiments of percussion, enough to be able to accompany them with tolerable competence.

My grandfather became alarmed at his son's disappearances from home for long hours. It wasn't difficult for him (being an honorary magistrate of sorts) to find a sleuth, who soon learnt about my father's whereabouts. Grandfather, accompanied by the sleuth arrived on the outskirts of the town and found his young son providing the beat for the singers on a *ghara* (pot of baked clay). He was told to leave at once; his ears were boxed and he was warned about visiting the domain of the musicians. My grandfather, like his father, was a highly respected teacher of Persian, who looked upon music as a libertine pursuit.

But my father had been hooked. He never went back to the *dera* of musicians, but he kept his passion for music alive for fifteen long years. When the longing became unbearable, he gave up his *sarkari naukari* (a government job), much to the horror of his relatives and his community, and left for Maharashtra in search of a musical guru. (In the early twenties of the last century, no one left a secure government job, especially a job that carried a pension!)

For more than two years he lived in and around Poona, picking and absorbing musical knowledge not only from musicologists but singers, and drummers, composers of theatrical songs, and tinkers and tailors as well. He learned to play the harmonium fluently and could accompany accomplished classical singers. His study of ragas earned him the respect of many professional musicians, like Ustad Jhande Khan.

Emperor Akbar set up a remarkable precedent when he offered a prominent place in his court to the great musician, Mian Tansen. Since then, it became a practice for Rajahs, Nawabs and other minor rulers to have a retinue of musicians attached to their courts. It was part of *noblesse oblige*. The classical music in

India flourished largely owing to the patronage of these 'Rajwaras'. The musical *Gharanas* and their upholders thrived because of the munificence of the princes and the princelings.

The British abhorred our classical music and scarcely acknowledged it except in disparaging terms. In the 150 years, before the subcontinent became independent, the professional musicians survived mainly because of the sustenance received from the ruling princes. The art of classical music may not have spread outside courts, but it was handed down from one generation to the next. Those who did not find favour or employment in a Princely State lived in cities and towns, eking out an existence as the tutors of courtesans. I am, of course, talking of Muslim musicians.

Middle class Hindu girls learned music — like they learned to crochet — because it improved their marriage prospects. For the kind of learning they needed, there were *Mahavidyallahs* (music-learning institutes). *Mahavidyallahs* and *Sangeet Ashrams* were established in most major cities of India in the twenties. Hindu boys and girls joined them to learn *bhajans* and *geets* and, in some cases, classical singing. The well-off families engaged music masters to equip their daughters with a small repertoire of songs. The study of music was a taboo not only for the Muslim girls but boys as well.

Johnny Patrick, a highly respected name amongst British musical arrangers, once told me that it takes a violinist at least a year to be able to play the instrument by reading notes, five more years to qualify for a professional orchestra and six hours a day minimum for the rest of his life to play well. When I mentioned to him that this was precisely the case with our musicians, he said, rather patronisingly, 'Ah, but they don't have any score to study.' His tone suggested that our music was a fanciful pastime that could not match the eloquence of Western classical music. 'Music,' he went on to say, 'entailed a study of counterpoint and polyphony, descant and duplet, not to speak of the diminished seventh and the dominant seventh. A musical system in which one note is joined to another in a linear way could not be taken seriously.'

Patrick was not alone in holding on to the impression that our music hasn't got the weight and the depth of a Beethoven symphony or a Mozart concerto. Many of our own educated people feel the same way.

Music does not become profound or weighty simply because a treble melody is sung—or played—above a basic melody (descant). In the metrical system of our percussion the duplet is a naïve and almost elementary feat. The *tabla* player can not only play a group of two (chords or strokes) in the time of three, which is what duplet means, but a group of five or even seven, in the time of four. The prosodical language of the *tabla* is so rich and complex that few players are able to master it in a lifetime.

Ustad Malang Khan was one of the greatest experts of this language. He spent five to six hours a day working on unusual mathematical permutations of our established *taals*. His mornings were taken up by teaching scores of pupils. He never took a holiday (none of our musicians ever did) and there was no Christmas or Easter break. My father had a very high regard for his technical virtuosity. He remained devoted to Malang Khan's performances. It was only in the last few years of his life that he developed a partiality for the younger *tabla* player, Allah Rakha Khan. Of the two, he felt, that Allah Rakha Khan had the sweeter touch.

My father left for Lahore soon after Malang Khan moved to Delhi to join the musical ensemble of All India Radio. In Lahore he did not arrange or sponsor musical concerts as he did in Lyallpur, because his passion had taken a different turn. He was now spending all his spare time setting about the task of persuading the University of Punjab to open a department of music. He helped in the formulation of its syllabus and wrote textbooks for its courses. (It is regrettable that the Punjab University library which once prized itself in keeping archives, doesn't stock the two volumes of *Rag Sikhsha* (learning of ragas) that he wrote specifically for the university students.

My father could scarcely contain his excitement when the University at last announced that music would be a part of its curriculum. Initially, the study of music, an optional subject for the degree course, was confined to the theory, but thanks to the untiring efforts of his friend and colleague, Jeevan Lal Mattoo, the practical ability – vocal as well as instrumental – was also included. It was one of the happiest days of his life. He celebrated it by inviting Jeevan Lal

Mattoo and Shyam Lal Zutshi, the two music examiners, to go and see the famous Calcutta based Kathak dancer, Leela Desai, who was on a professional tour of Lahore. And he took me along, much to the chagrin of my sisters.

The performance took place at the Regent Cinema on Mcleod Road. A make-shift stage had been put up in front of the cinema screen which had been covered with a backdrop of a sylvan scene of swans and lotus flowers. The theatre was packed. It was the first time that I attended a professional performance and I felt a curious excitement.

Ms Desai arrived on the stage to tumultuous applause. She was a vivacious black-eyed beauty and her dancing was nothing like what I had seen in the movies. The aesthete, Jeevan Lal Mattoo, remarked that she had a rather limited repertoire. My father felt that she could do with a better drummer. My opinion—I was nine years old at the time—was not sought, but I thought she was the most beautiful thing I had ever seen. I still remember her radiant, flashing eyes.

If that was one of the happiest days of my father's life, then the day the music department was closed soon after the establishment of Pakistan, was one of the saddest. The clergy condemned music in no uncertain terms and declared that under no circumstances would they allow young minds, especially university students, to be polluted by a 'Hindu' practice.

The Government of Punjab, who controlled the affairs of the University, remained silent. The University administrators, who ought to have taken a stand, cowered. My father wrote a strongly worded letter of protest, but it went unheeded. Indeed, the newly appointed Vice Chancellor of the University, Omar Hayat Malik, a mathematician of some reputation, issued an edict that all sciences, henceforth, were to be taught in conformity with the teachings of Islam. The circular was only distributed to the departments of science. He, obviously, thought that it was the sciences that needed to be Islamised.

I don't know how the others reacted, but the circular puzzled Dr. Nazir Ahmed, a zoologist by profession, but a man with an extraordinary perception of Punjabi and Persian mysticism as well as music. How zoology and botany—or chemistry, for that matter—were to be taught to comply with the new mandate was anathema to him. When he approached his friend, Sufi Ghulam Mustafa Tabassam, with the quandary, the genial Sufi had a ready answer: 'Tell your students that animals should no longer be studied by their structure, but by the order in which they accepted Islam.'

The newly-established Radio Pakistan in Lahore also came under a cloud for broadcasting music that was infidel in name and, it was alleged, character. Overnight ragas like *Shiv Ranjini*, and *Saraswati* were proscribed. Musicians were bewildered, they didn't know what was kosher and what was not. I was sitting in Noon Meem Rashed's office, trying to write a publicity note for a programme meant to explore the legends behind the songs that village women sang while working their spinning wheels, when a producer known for his flair for pedantry, came in and said he felt that the time had come when all the ragas should be given new Persian names according to their moods. He had prepared his list but he would bow to Rashed Sahib's superior knowledge of Persian.

Rashed took off his glasses and stared at the nervous looking producer like a seargent-major eyeing a callow recruit. Then, replacing his glasses, he said, 'Rajah, you have missed your vocation. *Tum footpath pay logon kee hajamat banaya karo* (you should be shaving people on the footpath).' When the producer left in a huff, we had a good laugh conjuring up names like *Mai Angabeen* for *Madhavanti*; *Khoobroo* for *Lalit* and *Barg-e-Hunar* (my feeble attempt) for *Gunkali*.

I was told in the 'Duty Room' of Radio Pakistan (this was the place where you heard all the gossip) that the great ZAB, the Radio chief, addressing a meeting of programme producers, had stressed that they should only concentrate on raga *Aiman*. It was the greatest of all the Muslim ragas and it revealed new dimensions whenever you listened to it, he was supposed to have said.

I doubt if Zulfikar Ali Bokhari, who knew his music, made such an asinine remark, but I know for a fact that the daily feature 'Pakistan Hamara Hai' (Pakistan Belongs To Us), that was launched soon after the inception of Radio Pakistan, always included Iqbal's poetry set to raga *Aiman*. Hameed Naseem, the main producer of the programme never stopped telling the cast (of which I was a member now and then) that the true implication of the Persian word, *Aiman* (meaning august), was security and well-being. 'It's like finding a shaded spot in the midst of a scorching sun,' was the metaphor he often employed.

So the maestros of the day sang *Aiman*; and almost every *ghazal* and *geet* was composed in the illustrious and august *Raga Aiman*: No one dared to point out that in scale and structure they were all playing the *Raga Yaman*, which had been sung in India for thousands of years and which is probably as old as the Hindu *Shastra*s.

Bare Ghulam Ali Khan read the writing on the wall and left for India, where he was revered. (He may not have had a contretemps with ZAB, as was rumoured, but the fact remained that ZAB was not enamoured of his art). Roshan Ara Begum, the peerless singer, perhaps the finest jewel of the Kairaina *gayaki*, migrated to Pakistan and settled down in Lalamusa, where she tended more to her buffaloes than to her musical scales. After a few years she was persuaded to make some recordings for Radio Pakistan, but none of her renditions had the verve of her pre-partition work.

The rejection, the outright condemnation of *raga*-based classical music was condoned by the government and those in authority because music was the last thing they wanted to think about. But it would be ridiculous to suggest that every bureaucrat and official was anti-music. Many thinking people in the cities felt that unless something was done., the upholders of classical music would vanish altogether. When the Arts Council was formed in Lahore, the governing body had some enlightened souls who insisted that training in classical music should be included in its list of activities. The affable (and knowledgable) Feroze Nizami was appointed as the head of music.

Feroze Nizami may not have created any outstanding pupils, but anyone who took even a three month training course, under his supervision, developed an affection and a reverence for music throughout his life. I remember hearing an unusual composition (in raga *Shudh Kalyan*) from a lady doctor at a social gathering in Cricklewood in 1956. I complimented her and asked her to sing some more. She said, quite innocently, that it was the only 'song' she knew. She had learnt it from Feroze Nizami. As she mentioned his name tears swelled up in her eyes. She told me that she bitterly regretted not having been able to continue with her music lessons.

Institutions like the Arts Council can (sometime) create a musicologist but rarely turn out a singer of great stature. The reason is obvious: our music and its vocalisation is not for the amateur. An *atai* (one not belonging to an established family of musicians) can only have a passing acquaintance with a *raga*, because he doesn't have the family support to explore its core. There is no one around to guide him about holding a note, sustaining it, and keeping it buoyant without turning it into a lament. An hour long tutorial will not do. The process involves constant work everyday, hour upon hour, and it can only be accomplished in a *gharana*. I have heard the most skilled amateurs (including Shahid Ahmed Dehlavi, perhaps the most conspicuous amongst them all) and found something missing in their performance. You may call it an inability to hide their technique or an absence of a laid back confidence; I call it panache.

Ustad Salamat Ali Khan (of the *Sham Chaurasi gharana*) was by far the most towering musical genius that flowered in Pakistan. In the two decades — the fifties and the sixties — India with all their musical conservatoires, their state patronage, their Malik Arjuns, Jasrajes, Bhim Sen Joshis, etc., had not been able to produce a classical singer of the eminence of Ustad Salamat. We did not give him the recognition he deserved, but he kept growing in stature, entirely because of his own dedication. His range was truly staggering. I once complimented him on his incredible facility to glide from one octave to the other and he said, modesty, 'You get it if you work at it for ten hours a day, maybe a little more.'

Salamat Ali Khan's exposition of the allegro was as breathtaking as his mature and thoughtful unfolding of the adagio. And his sense of *layakari* (rhythm) was extraordinary. He first wove the *raga* with melodic threads of rich colours dropping a pearl here and a pearl there; then in the rhythmic work on the *raga*, he made exquisite necklaces out of the scattered pearls. Our standing in the world of music took a severe blow when he became paralysed.

In a society where public posture has always been different from private thinking, classical music has lived a palsied life. The covert patronage that it received could only mean that its practice was confined to certain pockets. In their own way, the descendants of the Tilwandi *gharana*, the Patiala *gharana*, the Agra *gharana*, and the offspring of Bhai Lal Mehmood kept the torch burning, but the hearts of their male children, though nurtured in the musical discipline, were not in it. You only have to listen once to the progeny of Ustad Fateh Ali Khan and Ustad Latafat Hussain to realise that they possess neither the technique nor the depth of their ancestors. With the odd exception, our *sitar* and *sarangi* players are mediocre; there is not a single *sarod* player, and since the demise of Shaukat Husain, we haven't got a *tabla* player of any real stature. The great maestro of *tabla*, Ustad Tari, has taken up residence in America. *Tanpura*, the most essential of all instruments, has disappeared completely. Ustad Salamat Ali is no more. Ustad Fateh Ali is ailing. There is a flickering light in the form of Ghulam Hussain Shaggan, but classical music, as I knew it, is gone.

SHADOWPLAY

My reading habits are desultory. I read several books at the same time. I keep a pile of books on the table next to my wing chair in my study, and a smaller pile on my bedside table. There are many nights when I find sleep hard to come by and even such titles as 'A History of Moral Philosophy', fail to put me to sleep. I used to fret about this but now I get out of bed and come downstairs to my study to pick up whatever book lies on top of the pile, and open it where the book mark is. All these books are wonderful, imaginative and exciting. Eric Fromm's 'Man For Himself,' a work that identifies the crucial link between psychology and ethics that underpins all our actions, made me wonder why I did not pursue psychology, a subject I took my honours in, along with my bachelor's degree. Macintyre's History of Moral Philosophy From Homeric Age to the 20th Century, is about ethical ideas that we employ, and what lies behind our ethical decisions. It is a well-argued book but I felt that it did not turn me into a better human being perhaps because of my inherent incapacity to accept moral self-righteousness as a yard-stick of human relationship.

But by far the most astonishing — and intriguing — book of the year 2006, is Clare Asquith's 'Shadowplay' which paints a vivid and striking picture of the complexities of religious politics in Elizabethan England. She unfolds the mysteries about the abstruse hidden references in Shakespeare's plays so brilliantly that it is one of the most compelling books I have ever read.

Ms. Asquith sets the scene from the day that Henry VIII forbade actors to interpret scriptures or to dramatise matters of doctrine. Censorship of the stage, she tells us, arrived for the first time in England in 1543. Shakespeare grew up in a Catholic family that remained defiantly Catholic in an anti-catholic era. There were Catholics on both sides of his family. His relatives and acquaintances suffered appallingly, for their faith and beliefs. During his early years a wave of anti-Catholicism spread throughout England. The queen's agents and commissioners kept on confiscating Monastic lands around Stratford. Heavy fines were imposed on those who showed their loyalty to the Pope. Sometimes they were evicted from their homes and tortured; many families went underground.

When Shakespeare was 17, all the lively, inventive productions of the 'Mystery Cycles' that had been staged for centuries around the feast of Corpus Christi, were banned. He also saw that access to the printing presses was permitted only to literature that debunked Papacy.

Clare Asquith presents well-researched and documented accounts to prove that the monarchy (and those who manipulated the monarchy) commissioned playwrights to write new versions of morality plays replacing Lucifer with the Pope, and the seven deadly sins with the Roman Catholic Cardinals, monks and friars. Elizabeth's spymasters lined up 'good government playwrights' to write stridently Protestant drama. London audiences were not moved by these propaganda plays; they preferred to flock to the theatre where they could savour the coded references to the glory of their faith.

Ms. Asquith's book, as Antonia Fraser has observed, is a riveting literary detective story. She traces — and unravels — Shakespeare's coded messages step by step, from his earlier plays to 'The Tempest', his last work. She tells us that Shakespeare worked out a set of simple markers, basic call-signs that would alert his audience to the entry point they needed to decipher the hidden story. The master key to the hidden level, she emphasizes, is so simple that it is easy to miss. There are the terms 'high' and 'fair', which always indicate Catholism and 'low' and 'dark', which always suggest Protestantism. (The modern Christian distinction between high and low church goes back to Pre-Reformation days).

One of the most poignant examples of the 'high-low, dark-fair' image that she cites is the scene in Hamlet in which Hamlet compels his mother, the queen, to compare her late husband with the villain she has chosen to wed. The old Hamlet was a sun god:

> 'A station like the herald Mercury.
> New lighted on a heaven kissing hill
> Could you on this fair mountain leave to feed
> And batten on this moor...'

Hamlet's coded language here is that Elizabeth, the Queen of England, had swapped the high ideals of Catholicism for the base and dark Protestantism. (A moor was a pun on the dark looks of Claudius and low-lying land, the opposite of the fair mountain).

Towards the end of 16th century there were few English Catholics of any means who had not considered going into exile. The number of Catholics who had left England ran into tens of thousands. Ireland was rebelling against Protestant England and the new Philip of Spain was preparing another Armada. 'No one knew for certain', Miss Asquith points out, 'whether dissent or loyalty could prevail'. The regime's spy network was so strong that people dared not discuss things openly.

It was in this climate of seething hostilities that Shakespeare produced, arguably his greatest work. According to Ms. Asquith, Hamlet is a man who, more than anyone else, embodies a covertly disaffected group of what 'we would call England's intelligentia'. She is convinced that Hamlet is based on Sir Philip Sidney, an intellectual giant who epitomized the very best of Elizabethan England, and whose writings remain 'profoundly secular despite his strongly religious nature'.

Sidney has been traditionally portrayed as the quintessentially Protestant hero, but Ms. Asquith's research shows that he was a discreet Catholic fellow-traveller. He died mysteriously at the age of 32. In describing Sidney his biographers usually quote Ophelia's description of Hamlet:

> 'The courtier's, soldier's, scholar's eye, tongue, sword
> Th'expectancy and rose of the fair state
> The glass of fashion and the mould of form
> The observed of all observers'

Sidney died when Shakespeare was 22, but his disciple, Greville, who had taken upon himself the mission of fostering the cult of Sidney, was known to Shakespeare and he could well have supplied him with a string of details linking Hamlet with Sidney.

Ms. Asquith describes these links graphically: Sidney had a habit of jotting down ideas on notepads in the oddest circumstances. 'He was wont even while hunting to take a tablet out of his pocket and write down his notions as they came into his head'. Hamlet does exactly the same. As the ghost leaves him in the first Act, his instinct is to take out his *tablets* and note that 'one may smile and smile and be a villain.'

There are other close similarities. Sidney was prone to melancholic lethargy alternating with bursts of energy. Hamlet too, is subject to sudden demonic fits of rage alternating with manic bursts of energy. Sidney was loved and admired by his countrymen and Hamlet was loved of what Claudius calls 'the distracted multitude'. Like Sidney, Hamlet is sent away from his country by a treacherous king to be killed.

She argues that by the time Shakespeare came to write Hamlet he had become increasingly dominant in expressing his indignation at the folly of England in choosing rabid Protestantism. William Cecil, Elizabeth's Secretary of State, policy maker and key advisor, had died. Shakespeare could now take a stab at him by portraying him as Polonius.

When she dissects the world's most famous soliloquy ('To be or not to be') she finds that it is a debate about the morality of revolt. The momentous decision for Hamlet is whether to risk damnation by taking life — a mortal sin in the eyes of the Catholic Church — and by taking life to escape the persecution that would be inevitable in the fiercely anti-Catholic Tudor era. Seen in this light, the speech addresses other significant, unanswerable questions of Shakespeare's time: the oppressor's wrong, the proud man's contumely, the law's delay, the insolence of office etc etc.

What matters to us is not who Hamlet is modelled on—or Polonius, for that matter—but what the play conveys to us. And it certainly moves us today as intensely as it has, generations of playgoers, in the last four hundred years. Shakespeare dwells upon all the ethical and moral issues of his age and expresses (in a divinely written speech) the agony of a thinking man. The question he asks still haunts us in our age. Is it moral to rebel against a tyrant? Is it a duty?

It is hard to believe that Shakespeare's entire dramatic energy was spent in countering Protestantism or that his soul purpose was to write drama glorifying Catholicism. No man who takes up a religious cause can create a Hamlet, an Othello or a Lear. If Shakespeare had written to propagate a cause, his conflicting characters would have been his mouthpieces and not so sharply delineated and individualised.

Ms. Asquith is far too astute an analyst to suggest that either. Indeed, when she examines Ophelia's relationship with Hamlet in which a subtle exploration of spiritual issues of the day is integrated with a failed love affair, she writes that the 'Get thee to a nunnery' scene 'typifies the delicacy with which Shakespeare blends the political and the universal'.

Nearly everyone of Shakespeare's fellow dramatists underwent some form of danger ranging from imprisonment, exile and even death. The imprisonment—as in the case of Kyd, the author of

'Spanish Tragedy' — was accompanied by torture. And yet Shakespeare who, in hidden language, activated 'the call of the resistance' and pleaded for 'the cause' in nearly all his plays never fell foul of the authorities. The reason, she says, is that Shakespeare's dramatic structure and his motives become a drama of soul, and its protagonists (following the hidden code of England's post-Reformation vicissitudes) become so multi-faceted that they universalize their struggles in resonant language distilled from centuries of humanist Christian thought.

Shakespeare's cautions artistry was so great that his hidden language remained undetectable to succeeding generations who accepted the official version of English Reformation. The subterfuge was essential if he and his work were to survive. He was writing in a climate more dangerous, more oppressive than anything experienced by his predecessors His greatest concern was that the true history of the age would never be told. He needed to find a new method of writing, one capable of recording the whole unhappy story of England's political and spiritual collapse against the background of a regime for whom the slightest topical reference was justification enough to imprison a playwright.

As a proof that Shakespeare pleaded for the cause of the recusants in most, if not all of his plays, she offers a clue that lies in a strangely insistent passage written by the editors in the first Folio published in 1623, which asks the reader to look beneath the surface of the greatest universal plays to something hidden below.

Ms. Asquith is of the view that when Shakespeare realized that even being the favourite court dramatist, he had not been able to exert any influence on the monarch—James 1 who had succeeded Elizabeth—to bring about a change in the official anti-Catholic policy, he gave up playwrighting and retired in Stratford. From now on he would only produce ordinary drama.

Even if you do not agree with her arguments, 'Shadowplay' (steeped in scholarship) is one of the most original and compelling works on Shakespeare. As a result of Clare Asquith's findings, Shakespeare's dramas begin to take on a significant new dimension.

OH THAT DYLAN THOMAS

My friend, Akram Kazmi, whom I hadn't seen for yonks, rang me the other day to say how much he liked the piece I had written on the film scene in the fifties, not so much for what it contained, but because of the Dylan Thomas quotation at the end. 'Do you remember how we used to read Dylan Thomas...? Oh that Dylan Thomas,' he kept saying.

Akram Kazmi and I used to walk from the Psychology Department of the University, situated opposite the Lahore museum, to the Coffee House not too far away. I used to go there religiously to soak up the irreverential, intellectually stimulating conversation for which the Coffee House was renowned. Kazmi used to accompany me, more to indulge me than to follow any serious pursuit. He was a few years senior to me and he had 'seen the world'. He was the most laid back creature I had ever come across; his premature grey hair was a substantial witness to his world-weary outlook. When listening to 'April is the cruellest month...', he would cock his head to one side; his eyes would narrow behind his thick-rimmed glasses, and a half smile would play upon his lips, suggesting that he knew exactly what it meant.

One of his friends, who had just acquired rudiments of logical positivism (he was reading philosophy), would occasionally intrude and rattle off names like Muir and Whitehead. Kazmi, realising my irritation during such interludes, would quieten him down by pushing over whichever slim volume of verse I might have placed on the table (in those days it was either Auden or Eliot) and command me to read, 'Here I am an old man in a dry month'. He would declaim the opening like of 'Gerontion' in his appealing, rustic accent, implying that the poem was about him, making me ache with an indescribable pain because I had not yet begun to shave everyday.

Kazmi's ploy didn't always succeed. The philosophy student would sometimes intervene and proclaim the superiority of Ezra Pound. I didn't know much about Pound and though I had read a few of his cantoes I didn't understand them and was, therefore, unable to contribute towards the conversation. The philosophy student knew as little about Pound as the rest of us, but he used terms like 'logocentrism' and the 'stability of meaning'. He was fond of telling us that Pound did not employ reason in language. Kazmi, who had a healthy disregard for the philosophic analysis of language, would evoke an almighty oath and burst forth into 'And death has had no dominion', thus making it clear that, as far as he was concerned, no poet could equal Dylan Thomas. Even after listening to my rendition of

Rashed's *'Ittifaquat'*, set in Raga *Malkauns*. (I fancied myself as a composer in those days), on the slopes of Lawrence Gardens, Kazmi would first mutter and then intone, 'It was my thirteenth year to heaven.'

I arrived in England in 1953, with a letter for J.B. Clarke, one of the bigwigs of the BBC. Armed with the letter and the brazenness of my years, I went to the Broadcasting House in London. The heavy entrance doors led to an imposing reception hall where I was made to cool my heels. Everyone and everything moved silently. Upon a nod from one of the receptionists, the sergeant-at-arms would move from his position by the huge column and, with guest in tow, disappear into the inner sanctum. Suddenly there was a commotion. The heavy doors swished about and a cherubic looking, fat man walked in, totteringly. He was humming loudly. The receptionist, who had stopped working, looked up and smiled affectionately. The man was whisked off at great speed. Visitors waiting patiently looked at each other. 'Ah yes,' said a man who had lowered his newspaper briefly, 'Dylan Thomas,' to no one in particular.

I told my classmates at the Drama Academy the next day that I had seen Dylan Thomas and immediately went up in their estimation, not because of my encounter (there had been none) but because I had had access to the Broadcasting House. John Gray, (in our estimation, tipped to be the next John Gielgud) who knew chunks of Thomas by heart, suggested that we should all visit the 'Buxton', a club in Soho, where Dylan Thomas spent his evenings. Not everyone could gather courage, but John Gray and I and Geoffrey Slater (my Boswell in those days) went one evening to the Buxton. We had a few florins between us. Luckily, we were joined by Kay Double-day, another classmate, a plumpish American girl, who always wore black tights and hooped earrings. We welcomed her heartily because we knew that with Kay around we would no longer have to sit nursing our half-pints: she was rich—and generous.

Dylan Thomas was sitting on a stool by the bar. He was dressed in a faded tweed jacket and baggy trousers. His collar was crumpled and his hair was tousled. Two or three people stood around him; they looked like actors by their deportment. A distinguished looking man (whom I recognised to be Louis MacNeice) stood slightly apart; he had a pipe in his mouth which he kept lighting from time to time.

We had hoped for pearls of wisdom—or a mighty tirade against the iniquities of the world, for which he was famous. None was forthcoming, only chuckles and conspiratorial whispers. Once or twice we heard 'rage, rage' in his booming, melodious, Welsh voice. We thought we were in for a treat, but he mumbled something incoherently. 'Do not go gentle into that good night,' began John Gray and continued. He spoke it beautifully. We were sitting not too far from Dylan Thomas and I think, or like to think, that he heard his poem being recited for he waved a podgy hand in our direction. And that was all. Our hopes were dashed. Kay declared that Dylan was a slouch.

A few days later I read that he had left for America on a lecture tour, and within a few weeks, the news was flashed in all the newspapers that he had died — of alcohol — in an American hospital.

Dylan Thomas died at the age of 39. No poet in recent history has generated such a quantity of gossip, or reminiscences — or criticism. He was not just a poet, he was a star. He was a rebel against society as well as a great romantic figure that all could recognise — from Tokyo to Toronto.

Before his lecture tour to America, Dylan Thomas's main source of income was radio. He was greatly in demand as a 'reader'. Some producers rated him as the best all-round reader of verse. He took part in discussions as well. Once he appeared with Edward Shanks, an elderly poet who didn't care much for his verse. Shanks said he had shown a book of Thomas's verse to a friend, who called it a disaster to English poetry. Thomas retorted, 'You've stolen my thunder Shanks — I too was asking a friend whether he knew you, and he said, of course I know his verse. Is he still alive?'

John Arlott, the greatest cricket commentator I have ever known, was, as everybody knows, a fine poet as well as a wine connoisseur. By the end of 1945, Arlott was a talks producer at the BBC. He handled dozens of readings in a programme called 'Book of Verse'. Thomas was a regular reader in this programme. Arlott wrote:

> He would stand, feet apart and head thrown back, a dead cigarette frequently adhereing wispily to his

lower lip, curls a little tousled and eyes half closed, barely reading the poetry by eye, but rather understanding his way through it, one arm beating out a sympathetic double rhythm as he read.

Not many people are aware that Dylan Thomas was greatly in demand as an actor on BBC Radio. Louis MacNeice, who was on the BBC's staff as a writer-producer, employed him frequently. He appeared in many features and once played the lead in an allegory called *In Parenthesis*. A minor member of the cast was Richard Burton, who was then doing his conscription service in the RAF. Years later, Burton wrote:

> I worked with Dylan a few times or several and once for instance a director said to him, 'Dylan would you take the words Mam! Mam! And scream them for me, you understand that you are dying in No Man's land, and you hear the Royal Welch sing. I will give you a cue light and then scream for me woodjew — there's a good chap, and the green light flickered and Dylan, short, bandy, prime, obese and famous among the bars screamed as I have never heard, and we were all appalled, our pencils silent above the crossword puzzles, and invisible centuries gone atavistic, hair rose on our backs.

Rumour had it that he screamed without taking the cigarette out of his mouth. Dylan Thomas never took himself seriously as an actor. 'I know and the birds know that I am only a fat little fool ranting on a cliff,' he said during a student interrogation.

Thomas made three trips to America, each one more lucrative than the first. He ran through the money as fast as it appeared. Like most people of his ilk he was always short of cash and whenever he was down and out he would write to a benefactor or benefactress urging him/her to see him through 'in order to pay bills, in order to leave Laugharne, in order to start again, yet again...' Marged Howard-Stepney did more for him than anyone else. She was giving him money against the wishes of her advisers. Thomas wrote to her, 'My dear Marged, you told me once upon a time to call on you when I was beaten down...' He then changed it to verse: 'You told me once to call on you/when I was beaten down,' but not satisfied with this he amended it again:

> Once upon a time you told me I remember in my bones
> that when the bad world had rolled me over on the
> scalding stones, shameless, lost as the day I came I should
> with my beggar's cup howl down the wind and call your
> name and you, you would raise me up...

She provided him with a house and a fireplace where his slippers could be 'warm as toast'. He lived in this house for a while, but then moved on after turning the place into a dosshouse.

Thomas's famous remark (when asked what brought him to America) about his insatiable desire to see naked women under plastic mackintoshes had endeared him to university students throughout the United States. 'I am no grey and tepid don smelling of water biscuits,' he said and the undergraduates howled with laughter. He was the darling of American campuses. Students and dons flocked to see him. He disappointed them frequently because of his inebriation. At times he had to be carried to the stage, and yet when he began to read poetry it was as though angels were holding him up. Many people including eminent scholars have written that they had never heard anyone like him.

Dylan Thomas, the performer, has always fascinated me. He became a legend in America not because of his poetry, but because of his performance of poetry, and as an impromptu speaker in front of a large audience. He gauged the mood of each audience and never read the same selection at more than one place. Reading at the Poetry Centre in New York he introduced William Plomer's 'The Flying Bum' by saying,' I should explain that "bum" to an Englishman does not mean what it means to an American. "Bum" means "fanny" and "fanny" doesn't mean to an American what it means to an Englishman though geographically it's quite close.' The American audiences in the early fifties were prudish beyond description, but Thomas flattened them. The response was sensational.

I have always enjoyed reading doggerel and Thomas was particularly good at that:

> *He can write a poem to a human*
> *Being when every bloody line I write*
> *Is about loving one woman.*

He obviously meant Caitlin, his wife, with whom his love/hate relationship has become the subject of scores of essays. In his work hut at Laugharne, he scribbled many half poems written in his darker moods. My favourite is:

I do not admire them the little thank yous
Crying, cringing, abominable hyenas
Ashamed even of their own
acknowledgement,
Who whine outside the ashbins
For further titbit.
They should be put in a sack and drowned
Yelp cringes and all
In a sea of self-pity
Why do you mingily snarl outside my window
Despicable rodents?
Is it for me you are the self-appointed accusers?
Down with you sulphurous ones
My own degradation is enough.

In America his manner, in conversation, in interviews, even in letters he wrote to different people in England, became more and more self-deprecating. He was not writing any poetry and this must have irked him a great deal. His capacity to spin words and make a lovely rosary remained as alive as ever. In a letter to a friend in San Francisco he says:

How could I not have written when every week of the piggish year I mean to write with all my heart?... Either I hang by my whisky toes thinking of nothing and lust, or sit big-headed in the wet earth, thinking of turnip poems; and time sails by... I fall in love with undesirable, unloving, squat, taloned, moist, unlovely women and out again like a trout... I write poems to hide them before I can find them... and next week I shall be thirty seven horrors old...

His *Collected Poems* was published a year before his death. The book was greeted as a major event and most critics were full of praise. Philip Toynbee called him the greatest living poet in English, even though he thought his language was often mannered and 'occasionally that of a charlatan'. Stephen Spender wrote the definitive review, to my mind:

> The romantic characteristic of Dylan is that his poems contain the minimum material which can be translated into prose. Words are related to one another like the colours of a painting, by the exercise of that sensuous word choosing faculty of his imagination which cares more for the feel of words than their intellectual meaning.

Dylan liked the review so much that he wrote to Spender to say that no other critic had ever attempted 'to set out, plainly, the difference between the writing of poetry from words and writing of poetry towards words'.

The 'writing towards words' is a prowess which has enchanted me all my life. I love Dylan Thomas's poems because they are lovely to read. He knew it; he said more than once he wrote for the ear and not the eye.

Akram Kazmi was right when he said, 'Oh that Dylan Thomas.'

MUST THE KING SUBMIT?
THE KING SHALL DO IT

As a cricketer, my reputation in England grew when I made 64 not out against a Police XI at Imber Court. I used to play for the stage XI, but teams like TV Travellers and 'The Thespians' often invited me to play for them.

In the fifties and sixties, actors in England were devotees of cricket, not so much because they were temperamentally drawn to it as because they tended to be more free in the afternoons than members of other professions. We played charity matches which drew a fair number of spectators because our team included a star or two. Before he became a Lord, Olivier once came to play in a match in Henley-on-Arden. Unfortunately, his back rebelled, so he umpired for a few overs, exchanged a few coarse jokes with the bowlers, and left.

I once caught a glimpse of the great Gielgud coming out of the gates at Lord's. He had a straw hat on and he was wearing an MCC tie. Later on I learnt that he

had never been a member of the MCC. How could he
then be wearing the club tie? Perhaps I hallucinated.

In 1994, Sir John had turned 90 and was still working.
Tributes from all parts of the globe were showered
upon him. Miles Kington, the foremost satirist of our
times, wrote a hilariously funny piece on Gielgud's
cricketing prowess. 'It is not often realised that
Gielgud was a keen cricketer in his earlier days,' he
wrote, 'His fielding was ineffectual but remarkable.
His reflexes were unexpectedly speedy and if the
ball came towards him he would instantly lean away
from it and make a dramatic gesture in the other
direction as if fainting, or falling in love...' On one
occasion when the team had appealed loudly for a
run-out which had not elicited any response from the
umpire, Gielgud stepped forward and declaimed
impassionately:

> *Oh man of stone, look now upon the crease*
> *And tell me where you saw the grounding of the bat.*
> *No, never was that bat on the hallowed ground...*

And much more in the same vein. The umpire was
quite unmoved, but the batsman promptly burst into
tears, admitted he had been run out and walked back
to the pavilion. It is probably the last time in the
history of cricket that there has ever been a standing
ovation for an appeal.... I later asked him how he
had acquired the knack of improvising in
Shakesperean style, but he said it was a speech he
had prepared and memorised for moments when he
could not remember his lines. He had used it in *Julius*

Caesar, Macbeth and *The Merry Wives of Windsor* and no one had ever spotted it except his fellow actors'.

For many of us Gielgud was the voice of Shakespeare. We were in awe of him. Every actor that I know, or know of, tried to do a Gielgud. I do not remember any rehearsal of a play—be it for stage, radio or television—during which someone didn't let fly with some Shakesperean lines in Gielgudian tones.

My favourite Gielgud, when I dried during a rehearsal was, 'What must the king do now? Must he submit? The king shall do it. Must he be deposed? The king shall be contented.' Never was there an occasion when someone else in the cast didn't chip in with 'Let's talk of graves, of worms and epitaphs,' invoking the Gielgudian tremolo.

A line like 'Let's talk of graves...' has Shakespeare written all over it, but there are countless other phrases that he wrote which we use or quote in our everyday conversation. We do it so often that it is almost unbelievable that the phrases were not used before Shakespeare. How did people get by without them?

Shakespeare's images and metaphors have entered our speech and our psyche far more than we realise. I am not talking about 'to be or not to be' and 'tomorrow and tomorrow and tomorrow,' but how many of us would recognise 'out of house and home' or 'with bated breath' to be Shakespearian? Even

'what the Dickens' has nothing to do with Charles
Dickens. It comes from Shakespeare.

Some of his phrases are so familiar we think they are
proverbs. Some, through over-use, ('household
words', for instance) have become *cliches*. They are
still in common usage because they are so expressive.
Here are some of the expressions which most of us
assume are just everyday English:

1. With bated breath
2. Tower of strength
3. Filled with milk of human kindness
4. Budge an inch
5. Out of house and home
6. What the Dickens
7. Seen better days
8. At one fell swoop
9. In the mind's eye
10. For goodness sake

> 1) 'Shall I bend low and in a bondman's key,
> with bated breath and whispering humbleness
> say this—Fair Sir...'
> Shylock (*Merchant of Venice*, Act I)

> 2) 'The king's name is a tower of strength.'
> Richard (*Richard III*, Act V)

> 3) 'Yet do I fear thy nature, it is too full of the
> milk of human kindness to catch the nearest
> way.'
> Lady Macbeth (*Macbeth*, Act I)

4) 'I ll answer him by law. I'll not budge an
inch, boy, let him come and kindly.'
   Sly (*Taming of the Shrew*, Act I)

5) 'He hath eaten me out of house and home.'
   Mistress Quickly (*Henry IV*, Part II)

6) 'I cannot tell what the Dickens (meaning
devil) his name is.'
   Mrs. Page (*Merry Wives of Windsor*, Act 3)

7) 'True is it that we have seen better days.'
   Duke Senior (*As You Like It*, Act II)

8) 'What all my pretty chickens and their dam,
at one fell swoop?'
   Macduff (*Macbeth*, Act IV)

9) Hamlet: 'My father — me thinks I see my
father.
Horatio: 'Where my Lord.'
Hamlet: 'In my mind's eye, Horatio.'
   Hamlet, Act I

10) 'For goodness sake, consider what you do.'
   Wolsey (*Henry VIII*, Act III)

It is an incredible fact that these expressions are not
found in recorded English before he wrote them
down.

THE HERO MUST LOOK WELL-FED

We are a fat people. Nobody minds this. Fatness is a symbol of prosperity, well-being, status and authority. Nearly all our august personalities are fat; even our movie stars are fat, with large posteriors and well-rounded, shiny cheeks.

Many years ago, I was cast to play the lead in a film. It was the first film for a director who had been a cameraman all his life, and he was anxious to do everything properly. He arranged for me to meet my leading lady well before the start of the film. We were meant to be engaged to each other in the movie and it was vital that we liked each other, he said. The meeting was to take place in the actress's second floor apartment in Karachi. The director and I arrived at five in the afternoon. The door was opened by a squint-eyed youth, who took one look at us and scampered downstairs.

The leading lady, now a star of many movies, had made her name in a television commercial, in which a man sang his desire for a cup of tea. A girl (our leading lady) appeared, crinkled her nose, pouted a little and, coquettishly, suggested that he should drink, 'Lipton'. The crinkling of the nose and the alluring smile that accompanied it, had shot her into stardom.

She was bulkier than I imagined. Dressed in 'bell-bottoms', very popular at the time, she had painted her nails on top of last week's paint. There are very, few sights more off-putting than a woman's hands with corrugated layers of nail polish. Coyly, she introduced me to her mother, who was sitting at one end of a long settee. The mother paid scant attention to me, but beamed at the director, who called her 'Mummy'.

I sat down awkwardly in a corner. The director, noticing my reticence, turned to 'Mummy' and began to praise me, which added to my discomfiture. After a while, he turned to me and came out with some well-chosen phrases in praise of 'Mummy's' daughter. Mummy's expression never changed. I thought he was going overboard.

Tea arrived. There was a wide assortment of eastern and western confectionery. The director took a few pieces on his plate. I was offered some. My food habits were stricter in those days; I refused politely. The director, who had, by now, decided to play the matchmaker, began a new game. 'You must make him eat something,' he coaxed the leading lady. Then he got up, picked a plate, placed a *pera* (a sickeningly

sweet marzipan without almonds) on it and gave it
to her saying, 'Let us see if he spurns your offer.' She
approached me, held the *pera* between her fingers
and pouted in the manner of her tea-ad. I declined,
murmuring something about having had a rather
heavy lunch. 'Maybe, he doesn't like our local sweets'
she said, and put it in her own mouth. I was then
offered a piece of pink cake with crusty sugar icing.
'No, thank you,' I said for the umpteenth time.

'Mummy' who had been guzzling contentedly,
suddenly shrieked, 'Thank you, Thank you *kia karta
hai–kha na*' (stop saying thank you — and eat). The
game went on. She would hold a cookie or nougat,
crinkle her nose, wait for my refusal, and then eat it
herself. 'I shouldn't eat so much,' she said to the
director flirtatiously, 'from tomorrow I shall go on a
diet.' 'Mummy,' a mass of mis-shapened flesh,
weighing about two hundred and ninety five pounds,
chuckled like a cockatoo. She had the kind of voice
you could cut a piece of hardened cheese with. It
saddened me to note that it wouldn't be long before
our leading lady became as gross as her mother.

When we left the apartment, eventually. I said to the
director. 'She really ought to shed a few pounds, don't
you think?' 'Oh she's alright,' he said and then,
hesitatingly, as though not to offend me, he
continued, 'I think you should fill yourself up a bit.
The "hero" must look well-fed.'

TENNESSEE WILLIAMS

In later years, with his French cut beard and a reclining, intellectual forehead, he looked like a benign academic from Sorbonne, but when I met Tennessee Williams in New York he had a cherubic face with shiny, pink cheeks; the thick moustache that he wore sat incongruously on his lips.

He came into my dressing room offering a limp hand. His companion, a man with a creased face, who looked very much like Burgess Meredith but wasn't, said 'Mr Tennessee Williams was very keen to meet you.'

Williams smiled, more with his eyes than his mouth. He made none of the customary remarks that visitors usually make when they go backstage after a performance. He sat down, wearily, on the battered divan which occupied most of my dressing room. Rumour had it that John Barrymore once slept in it. (His companion chose to perch himself on a stool). He accepted a drink and asked me if I liked New

York. When I told him I did, very much, he said he
wasn't sure he did, any more.

He didn't talk much except to say that Forster was
lucky to have found me. By way of polite
conversation I asked him if he was working on a new
play and he nodded rather enigmatically. It was
obvious that he didn't want to talk about it. I thought
it would be foolish of me to make small talk. After a
few silences, during which it occurred to me that I
would never be able to dine out on the story of my
encounter with the Tennessee Williams, his
companion stood up. 'Come along,' he said, 'Let Mr
Mohyeddin (he pronounced it as Mo'yeddin
accenting the second syllable heavily) rest'. William's
eyes smiled, 'Oh' he said, heaving himself up, 'She is
a misery, She won't let me be.'

I was used to such 'camp talk'. In England, actors,
even those who were not homosexual, enjoyed
referring to each other as 'her' and 'she'. In America, I
was to discover later, the camp slang was the sole
prerogative of the coteri of gays.

The cultural watchdogs of America resented
Tennessee Williams. In the wake of his twin
Broadway triumphs—The Glass Menagerie and 'A
Streetcar Named Desire'—Time magazine accused
him of creating works that were 'basically negative
and sterile'. The reason for this off-handed dismissal
was obvious: 'Time' (owned by rabid conservatives)
had learnt that William was gay. Being gay was akin

to being highly depraved in the post-war years in America.

America produced many fine playwrights in the post-war era, but the two names that dominated the scene were Arthur Miller and Tennessee Williams. They not only wrote good plays, they were box-office draws as well. In the sixties it was generally believed that Williams wrote strong parts for women and Miller wrote strong parts for men, a false assessment, in my view, as far as Williams is concerned, because he has written excellent parts for men as well. Stanley (A Streetcar Named Desire), the Gentlemen caller (A Glass Menagerie), and Big Daddy (Cat on a Hot Tin Roof) are just some of the roles that any actor would give an arm and a leg to play.

'Cat on a Hot Tin Roof' is a play that was not allowed to be performed in London until the office of the Lord Chamberlain, who censored every play, was abolished. It is about a self-made Southern millionaire who refuses to believe that he is dying of cancer. His two sons vie with each other for Dad's money. The women in the family are gold-diggers as well. The younger son is an alcoholic, an All-American football hero who would rather share his bed with another All-American football hero than his attractive wife, but when the wife announces that she is pregnant, he is greedy enough to acquiesce in the falsehood; he must now sleep with her to support it. Along with 'Death of a Salesman' this is one of the greatest American plays of the 20th century.

In 1955, when the play was produced on Broadway, the formidable, Elia Kazan directed it. He did everything in his power to shroud the character of the alcoholic ex-footballer in mystery so that his homosexual leanings would not be visible. Kazan had come out of the McCarthy inquisition, unscathed, — the price for betraying friends and fellow-travellers who had left-wing leanings — and he was not prepared to be denounced for directing a play about homosexuality. Ken Tynan has written an account of how Williams was badgered to alter many of the key phrases in the play in order that the motives for the hero spurning his wife remained vague. And indeed all the initial reviews of the play insisted that the reason why the hero refuses to co-habit with his beautiful wife were mysterious. It was not that the reviewers couldn't fathom the reason. They fathomed it only too well; it was their prudery that prevented them from mentioning a subject which was considered to be a taboo.

Tennessee Williams' remark that the 'Theatre is a place where we have time for people we would kick downstairs if they came to us for a job,' is well worth a thought. In a novel or a short story the characters you cannot empathize with, skip away from your consciousness; on the stage you cannot escape them unless you choose to walk out of the theatre. You may decide that you want to have no truck with such unsavoury people, but they hold your attention — sometimes fascinate you — and rivet you to a spot for the 'two hour traffic on the stage.'

Williams made a seminal contribution to the theatre. He had the remarkable ability to identify himself with men and women. His vivid language, complex characters and rich emotional texture has captured the world's attention. His plays have been performed — in translation as well as in the original — all over the world. He has been an incalculable influence on the theatre. He is one of the few playwrights whose plays are in constant revival. Today he is more popular than ever.

I rate Tennessee Williams as one of the best playwrights, not just of the 20th century, but of all time. He created characters who live on the extremes of life, the social outcasts; people whose lives are marginal. He went beyond realism and discovered in the voices of these outcasts a means of creating a new sort of theatrical poetry.

LEELA LEAN

Nobby Brabham had a bad leg and he limped as he walked, much in the manner of West-End actors simulating the gait of gout-ridden aristocrats. Nobby was not an aristocrat, but he dressed, talked, and entertained like one. He was a charming host who could have become a little too fond of his own assets, but was kept in check by his plain and sensible wife, Esther, who was an aristocrat, but extremely down-to-earth.

The Brabhams lived in a smart town house near Lancaster Gate. They were childless and they entertained frequently. I was introduced to them by a successful West End actress — I shall call her Henrietta Ince — who had made a reputation for playing suave ladies in drawing room comedies. Henrietta and I met when we were both appearing in Oxford in different theatres. When our respective plays were transferred to the West End, more or less simultaneously, we began to see more of each other. She had known Esther since the time when Esther, in an attempt to de-class herself, had accepted the job of a wardrobe assistant in the same theatre where Henrietta was playing the lead in a Lonsdale comedy. Esther became Henrietta's dresser for a while. Rumour had it that Nobby went backstage with a bunch of roses to pay court to Henrietta, but was so smitten by Esther, when he encountered her outside the dressing room, that he gave Esther the flowers and asked her for a date.

Apart from Henrietta, who was a regular invitee, Esther's chic dinner parties were attended by a rich variety of people: diamond merchants from Antwerp, Central European counts (Esther's parents were from Austria), art critics, county judges, dress designers and Lofty Wickham-Flint, a cherubic, wavy-haired man given to wearing flamboyant socks, who always had an appropriate remark for every occasion. He was Nobby's business partner in some ways.

I don't think I ever met a more amiable man. Lofty was not a politician, but his perception about politics and political personalities was astute. It was through him that I first learnt about the shenanigans at Cliveden. He happened to be at the poolside when the Pakistani Field Marshall, according to newspaper reports, frolicked with Mandy Rice-Davies in the swimming pool.

Wickham-Flint invited me (and the Brabhams, of course) — Henrietta was on tour — to spend a Sunday at his place. He lived in a beautiful Georgian house near Amersham. We were greeted by three or four friendly dogs who accompanied us into the hall, and not finding us very interesting, disappeared. We walked through the spacious hall into the morning room with lovely French windows which revealed the lush green undulating Buckinghamshire landscape. There were comfortable chairs all around, but the main feature of the room was an exquisite Regency chaise-lounge on which sat, cross-legged, like a high priestess, Leela Lean, with a golden ring in each one of her toes. One or two guests sat close by, listening to her with rapt attention as though they were receiving benediction. There was a pause as we were introduced. The spell was broken; positions were shifted; courtesies were exchanged. Leela Lean did not move an inch. After a few minutes a different circle formed itself around her.

She had been the legendary Leela Madkar about whom it had been said that apart from the Khajuraho temples, the only other thing worth seeing in India was Leela Madkar. Her long hair that reached well below her waist, her Mogul-miniature eyes and her perfectly sculpted nose had made her into the darling of portrait painters. David Lean, the great movie director, on what he described as a 'spiritual work-out' tour of India, must have been taken in by this quintessence of oriental femininity. He wooed her, pursued her (Leela would later confess that he hounded her, but the remark was made when she had become embittered), allowed himself to be photographed everywhere with Leela ever so slightly leaning upon his arm, and soon the fabulous Leela Madkar became Leela Lean.

All of this I had heard from friends in India and England, including dubious stories about Madkar: the wealthy business man, who was callous and never gave Leela the care and succour that she needed; the Maharashtrian gentleman who was heartbroken when he heard of his wife's waywardness and took refuge in an *ashram*. It was generally believed that Leela swept Lean off his feet and that, well before he took his return flight from Bombay, he had knelt and popped the question.

When I got to know Leela, I realised that it was not Leela, the flirt, who used her wiles to 'make a catch of the century' as one Indian newspaper put it. David Lean was an unusually handsome man with ascetic features and a winning smile. He had gone through a couple of marriages which had turned him into a bit of a misanthrope. He needed a new experience, an Eastern lady, who would not assert her individuality, a decorative woman who would be submissive and stay content wherever he chose to lodge her. It was Lean who swept Leela off her feet, brought her over to London, parked her at Basil Street Hotel in Knightsbridge, and then went about his work.

David Lean was a big name in those days. He was in New York or else he would have been at Lofty's country house that afternoon. The Oscar he had received for his *River Kwai* had meant that big American money was now at his feet. He had not yet embarked upon his career of reclusion and visited the likes of Wichham-Flint in his wife's company (a practice he was to discard within a few years). People, naturally, flocked to meet David Lean's Indian jewel. Leela seemed to revel basking in his glory.

She talked hurriedly with a very slight stammer; at times it was difficult to understand what she said because she ran some words together like 'Davidhateslondon'. She had the kind of accent much sought after by stand-up comics. Nobby and Esther stood around her, absolutely fascinated. When luncheon was announced she asked me to sit near her. She wasn't going to be hurried.

She spoke to me in chaste Hyderabadi Urdu. It was an agreeable surprise to learn that her Urdu was devoid of any trace of Hindi. When 'DavidandI' were in India every movie star had asked her to introduce him to David. It had become quite tiring for him. Even the great Dilip Kumar had approached her. She would like me to meet David. She had seen me in the play that I was appearing in at the time, but wanted to see it again because David hadn't. I felt flattered. She was dressed in a smooth grey saree. The rings on her toes glistened. She had liquid eyes with long, eyelashes.

Lunch was a long drawn-out affair. Wickham-Flint was renowned for his excellent cellar. The lull between courses was filled with conversation brightened by some excellent vintage stuff. Leela left before the dessert because she had to go and meditate. Everyone tried to persuade her to stay on but she was firm.

A few weeks later, true to her promise, she came backstage with the great man. He was courteous; she chattered and he listened, smiling benignly. I stood, a towel wrapped around my neck, until David Lean insisted that I sit down and stop playing the host. The gist of Leela's talk was that David had been interested in filming Forster's masterpiece for a long time. Lean suggested that I approach Forster about it. I mentioned that as far as I knew, Forster was deeply suspicious of Hollywood and its output. Lean said he had heard about it, but Leela insisted that Forster's reservations would become ill-founded once he realised that David Lean would be tackling his work. 'Whydon'tweaskhimtolunch?' she enquired.

Lean, in a tone of voice used for recalcitrant children, explained that one did not invite an eighty year old, secluded Cambridge don to lunch. I became familiar with that tone later on, because he adopted it whenever actors mishandled their props, or an over zealous assistant did something wrong. Leela, suitably chastened, sighed and said the ways of the West were strange. This pleased her husband because it strengthened his notion of Indians as an unspoiled, slightly muddled, deviously spiritual people. I was on guard all the time. I wanted to know what Lean thought of me as an actor at the same time as I wished not to appear too overwhelmed by his presence. I had spent sufficient time in penury and wasn't therefore, susceptible to accepting the newly bestowed status of celebrity without being wary.

Leela Lean understood that I was in awe of her husband and was unable to give her the attention she commanded. She turned the conversation to the Pinter play which had just opened and how hard she found him to swallow. Her husband interrupted her. 'Come on,' he said, gently. 'We can't stay here all night. The man has things to do.' She got up, but not before inviting me to lunch. 'Can we?' she asked him. 'He is not a secluded don.' 'Yes darling,' he said with a winsome smile.

Lean's visit created a bit of a stir backstage. After he left everyone in the cast wanted to know what he was like. Was I going to be in his next film? Did he say when he was going to begin shooting it? Everyone assumed that because of his beautiful Indian wife, my connection with David Lean was firm and solid.

It took a long time for the lunch to transpire. In between, I had a chance to see Forster. I told him about Lean's visit and interest, but Forster good-humouredly said it was simpler to say 'No'. He had already told me about the overtures Hollywood had made towards him and how he had found it difficult to tell them he was not interested. He was sure his work would be distorted and he didn't want that.

The invitation for lunch came through Maud Spectre, who was David Lean's casting director. When I arrived at his hotel suite, Leela opened the door and greeted me with a Hyderabadi salaam. She apologised for the delay; David had to go to all kinds of places in Europe and America and, much against her wishes, she had to tag along. As usual, she spoke breathlessly.

She was dressed in a *farshi gharara* and a short sleeved, fitted *kurta* which showed her excellent figure to perfection. The *dupatta* was an accessory, flung across her neck. Her long hair hung loosely; a tiny diamond sat upon her nose. She was barefooted; this time only two silver rings adoring her toes.

She perched herself on a big settee for a moment before settling down, cross-legged, as she had, at Wickham-Flint's house. She said she couldn't relax if she sat like an *Angrez*. Ideally, there should have been a *takht* with bolsters all round. 'That what I 've been accustomed to,' she said with a sad little smile. 'And a *paandaan*?"I said jokingly. 'Oh yes, yes, yes,' she perked up. 'I have one, but it is only a travelling *paandaan*, given to me by Nawab Sahib Chhattari. I had such beautifull proper *paandaans* in Hyderabad.'

I tried not to look at her, in case I betrayed my infatuation. There was a small *tanpura* resting in a corner. She told me she carried it everywhere. She couldn't live without her morning practice, *riyaz*. We talked of music and ragas. She talked of the great musicians she had hosted in her house in Hyderabad. She interspersed her discourse with a few well-known Urdu verses, misquoting them slightly.

David was nowhere to be seen. He was doing preparatory work on *Lawrence of Arabia* in those days. He must have been held up in a script conference, she thought. When David worked, he forgot all his appointments. Lunch was ordered; she was a vegetarian but I could have whatever I fancied. I declined politely and had to make do with an insipid celery and carrot cutlet.

The afternoon lingered 'as it malingered'. She was now reclining on the settee on one elbow. I was still expecting David Lean to turn up any moment and so, exercising a great deal of self-restraint, refrained from any flirtatious remark. She sensed that my self-composure was hollow and, with a deep throated laugh, got up to announce that it was time for her meditation. I took leave of her. She told me that David was going to cast me in 'Lawrence'. She had suggested this to him but David had taken the decision without any coaxing from her. David never listened to *sifarish*, she said. I mustn't become hoity toity and turn it down. I needed to work with directors like him. She asked me to promise that I would accept whatever I was offered.

I saw her only once before I arrived in Akaba for the filming of 'Lawrence'. This was at a premiere to which she had invited me. She never spoke to me on that occasion. She and David were surrounded by movie moguls and film stars. Some starlets stood around her as though she was royalty. She was decked up in jewels. She wore a black velvet cloak over her saree; her hair fell over the cloak like a silken waterfall. She looked gorgeous.

The filming had not yet begun when she landed in Akaba. We were all living in tents. There was only one bungalow other than a few ramshackle army barracks, and that's where the Leans were lodged. A big marquee had been installed not too far from their bungalow as a 'mess'. We all ate there together in the evening. The Leans would sometimes deign to join us. Leela had given up wearing jewellery. Instead she wore flowers. The flowers were flown in especially for her from Amman and her maid threaded them into bangles and earrings. People bowed to the majesty that she invoked and she bestowed gracious smiles on everyone. When I developed a virus of some kind she prevailed upon David to have me moved to the spare room in their bungalow. She tended to me, caringly. I learnt a bit about her. Her devotion to religion was absolute. She had been hungry for love ever since her childhood, but she had never got it. People professed to love her but that was not the kind of love she hankered for. Her mother was an extraordinarily beautiful woman; compared to her she was a plain Jane.

Soon we all moved to a gruesome location in the middle of the desert. Leela went back to Amman. David was now fully immersed in his work, but in the evenings he was spending more and more time with his continuity girl, who assumed a new authority within days. Previously, she carried her own portable stool; now a prop man carried it for her.

After a few gruelling weeks of work I, along with two other actors, was sent to the only posh hotel in Amman to recuperate for a weekend. Leela got to know of my visit. She was staying with some American friends in a luxurious villa. I was invited over and the American hostess never allowed me to return to the hotel. Leela was back to wearing long earrings, silken sarees and golden rings on her toes, but there was a pinched look about her, and her eyes remained hooded most of the time. She began to say something in Urdu once or twice but the hostess intervened, 'Hey, no shop talk.'

I wasn't able to talk much to Leela during that weekend, because the hostess monopolised me. She was one of those ebullient Americans who thrive on hobnobbing with people from the world of show business. Leela may have regretted inviting me over because her eyes were sad when she said goodbye to me the next morning.

I learnt from a postcard sent to me by the American hostess a few days later that she had gone to India, indefinitely.

Three eventful years rolled by very quickly and I found myself in New York preparing for a one-man show which took me to the library a good deal. As I left the library one late afternoon, it began to pour. Everyone knows that it is easier for a camel to pass through a needle's eye than for you and I to find a cab in Manhattan when it rains. I cursed myself for not carrying a mac and for not wearing a hat. My hair was dripping wet as I waved frantically at every passing yellow cab. A taxi eventually pulled up near me; the door at the back opened and I heard someone say, '*Ah-yea*, I'll drop you,' Murmuring thanks, I got in quickly. He was a thick-set man with a round, chubby face and darkish, tortoise-shell glasses. He introduced himself, 'I am Aslam Khan, the brother of Dilip Kumar.' He knew who I was. He would drop me wherever I had to go, but if I wasn't too tied up could I not come up to his apartment, which was very close, and take some refreshments. He was civilised and persuasive.

His younger sister, Farida, and his brother, Ahsan, (both of whom I was to meet frequently in Bombay in a few years time) were also staying in the apartment. I spent an agreeable evening. All three of them came down to find a cab for me. 'By the way,' said Ahsan, putting his hand on my arm, 'I met a lady here who talks very fondly of you. Her name is Leela.' Farida remarked impishly that ladies were bound to be fond of ZM. "I didn't know that she was in New York,' I said, embarrassed for no reason whatsoever. We agreed to meet soon, as we parted.

It gave me a bit of a start when I received a phone call from Leela Lean a few days later. Why had I not been in touch with her? Had I forgotten? Had I become too important? She knew I had been in Manhattan for quite a while. She had seen the Khan clan who had told her about my whereabouts. She had swallowed her pride and was ringing me up herself. 'Cometomorrow'.

She was living at the Hamilton, a small hotel off 5th Avenue. It had a narrow, dark lobby, not too unlike the Basil Street Hotel in Knightsbridge. David was obviously partial to a bit of gloom. The suite she had been installed in was comfortable, though not plush. The *tanpura* rested in one corner, the silver framed photograph of her Guru, the late Maharishi someone, stood on a tallboy. She was dressed as ornately as I remembered: bracelets, diamond-on-the-nose, toe-rings, earrings, all complementing a burgundy and cream saree. 'You look ready to be painted,' I said.

In between cups of coffee and stale pistachios, she rambled about her long stay in India, the trips she made from north to south. At times she felt she found a meaning to her life—when she woke up and walked barefooted on the grass or when she sang a few phrases to herself as the sun was going down, but most of the time she felt uncomfortable; she no longer felt at home with friends she had known for ever because they had begun to distance themselves. She belonged to the glamorous world of Hollywood and 'showbiz'. She wanted to be accepted for what she was, but this was not possible. They wanted to hear scandals about Rock Hudson and William Holden, and she couldn't tell them any.

It was Sam Spiegel, the arch manoeuvrer, the real force behind 'Lawrence', who plotted her return. Spiegel knew instinctively that Leela would fit in well with his plans for the grand opening of the film in America. A bedecked oriental beauty on the arms of Lean was exotica of the highest order. He began to make phone calls to her. When, eventually, she asked David whether it would be a good thing for her to return, he said, 'You know what farce openings are. Come if you can stand being monkeyed around.' But Spiegel insisted; in fact he said he would come and drag her out personally if she became silly. 'And don't worry about David, he is English-shy. Of course he wants you to be here.'

It had been a long, unending spree, days spent in getting dressed and browsing in antique shops, evenings taken up with sitting on silken settees, her feet tucked under her, soaking up the admiring looks of men and women. And then the night of the Oscars, 'the fanfare, the ballyhoo, the limousines, the Spencer Tracys, the Pandro Bermans, the jingbanglot'. The glitz of the Oscars and the opening had won off. David was away; he hadn't shown up for weeks.

It was not till our second meeting that I told Leela why I had been hesitant in making contact with her. I didn't want to run into David who, I felt, was sure to imagine that I was after a job. 'I might as well tell you,' I said, 'My visit to you in Amman must have caused him some displeasure because he cooled off towards me and I stopped getting the nod from him to join him at his table for dinner.'

She laughed bitterly. 'He was muchworsetome.' She had tried to plead with him, tried to explain that it was her friend, Lueen, who had insisted upon my stay in her house, but David was convinced it was a conspiracy to undermine him. 'David is a big sulker.' And he could be sadistic.

I saw quite a bit of her during that autumn. She did not finish her toilette until mid-day. When I suggested we go out for a meal, she declined. Later on I realised that she was being cagey. She had the comfort of staying in a hotel but that was it. The modest stipend given to her through one of David's secretaries was barely enough for the special dry-cleaning of her sarees. If she wanted extra money, she had to ask his secretary, who bluntly told her that she would have to check with David first. She didn't like doing that. The same secretary probably kept a record of who she went out with. She could get a limousine, but she would have to inform the secretary where she was going. Sometimes she would be so overwrought that she would sit cross-legged on the floor and quote Ghalib: *Kis din na hamarey dil pe aarey chala kiye.* Her propensity for mis-quoting had not diminished.

Once or twice, upon my insistence, she picked up the *tanpura* and began an alap of *Asawari*, a difficult raga at the best of times. It was evident that she was tone-deaf for she repeatedly went off key. She had a passion for music, a deep-throated voice like Gangubai Hangal, but no musical sensibility. I admired her absorption though. She would flick off an imaginary tear as she put away the instrument.

In New York, she moved about in a social circle of well-heeled Jewish doctors and stockbrokers and their heavily bejewelled wives who all lived in individually designed homes in Long Island. They were all anxious to learn about the real significance of *mantras*. She was the ideal person to satisfy their curiosity. Besides, she could tell them tittle-tattle about Jose Ferrer and Anthony Quinn. Oddly enough, the wives didn't resent their husbands' unconcealed fascination for her. They adored her because she was totally unaffected by American opulence. The husbands doted upon her because she didn't wear her femininity as a weapon. Leela was their icon.

She never talked to me about my work or myself so I never discussed it with her. Usually, she chattered, desultorily, about Nawab Sahib Chhattari and Bahadur Yar Jung, and other noblemen of Hyderabad, who had been her admirers.

She was not daft and, often, her opinions of plays and personalities were astute. She would stop abruptly and sigh as a mark of full stop. If, at such moments, I got up to take my leave, she didn't try to stop me, but looked at me with those hooded, lambent eyes. She could fall in love with me, she would say teasingly, but it would only make me run away.

This always made me a little uneasy because she saw quite a few other people to whom she was equally attached. Did she say this to all the others? She was not promiscuous by nature; it was just that she gave herself wholeheartedly to anyone she thought would love her with all his spirit; bodily love stayed in the inner crevices of her soul as something shady, an act of darkness. Once when she snuggled close to me, as I parted, I found that her bracelets and rings and ear-chains were like pincers cutting into my flesh. I observed (in jest, I thought) that it must take her hours to remove that armour plate, and tears rolled down her cheeks. There was a time, she said when she never had to do it. Her Indian maid would, slowly and gently, undo each ornament —and massage her feet while doing it.

I returned to New York after more than a year to learn that she had been removed to a single room. David had rented a place for her in Los Angeles. She had gone there but had felt miserable. People had been nice to her; at least two of Lean's admirers, George Cukor and Fred Zinneman, excellent directors both, had invited her over a couple of times, which restored her dignity for a day or two; otherwise she just sat around waiting for the sunset. At last she became defiant and insisted that she be moved back to New York, but this time a different minion could only arrange a single, poky little room.

She had begun to neglect her appearance. She had become moody and languid. Sometimes I could see that her brain was drumming its fingers and looking around for something to do, but then apathy set in. She looked an ex-B movie star, sliding across her room in a faded, chenille housecoat. It was her rich, black, shimmering hair and her mysterious eyes which prevented her from looking frumpy. The once pampered lady of leisure who had spent her life cruising antique shops and enjoying long, sumptuous dinner parties, was reduced to eating yesterday's potato salad. Her *pooja* brass gods and goddesses occupied the windowsill. She was anxious to peel off life's accessories, but was torn between living and not living. David only spoke to her through one of his assistants. After years of pain and disillusionment she was teetering at the edge of despair, but she didn't moan. 'Why don't you go to India?' I suggested. But India only meant a daughter who was married with children. The thought of living with her daughter in a tiny two room flat and playing grandma, sent a shiver down her spine.

Why did she choose to exist as a more or less discarded mistress? She must have known deep down that David was never going to come back to her. There had been gossip about his dalliance with his new secretary. I think she hoped that there would be a large enough settlement to enable her to live in the style and manner to which she had become accustomed—a hotel suite with room and maid service. She didn't want a home; she wouldn't know how to run it. She didn't know how to get into a subway or drive a car. There were people still willing to pick her up and drop her back, but she did not go out as she used to. Perhaps she didn't want word to reach David that the abandoned, suffering wife was seen cavorting.

Her stammering had become a bit more pronounced, but she was determined not to become morose or religious. A new devotee, a part-time teacher in Bronx, brought her freshly cooked vegetarian food three or four times a week. He was a shiny looking man with a balding head and he was quite content to worship her from afar.

It was during a rehearsal in London in the late seventies, nearly fifteen years on, that an actor I normally avoided because of his feigned uncouthness, informed me that he had a message for me from Leela Lean. She had invited him that evening and she had asked him to bring me along.

She was ensconced in a lavish suite at the Grosvenor House Hotel. Had a settlement been made? I wondered. The large sitting room was full of young people from the subcontinent: long-haired painters, plain earnest looking girls, research students, out-of-work actors and a Maharajah who was having his palm read by a bulldoggish woman. Leela hadn't lost her knack of drawing people to herself.

I went looking for her in the pantry. She looked at me and shut her eyes as if I had betrayed her in some way and she couldn't bear to see me. She looked wrinkly and frail, her hair had greyed and her once moist lips were partially cracked. Then she took a step towards me and held my hands, her fingers were gnarled. She was dressed in all her finery.

It was not a setting I cared for, so I left soon after. As always she didn't try to stop me. She looked perfectly at ease with her surroundings. 'Come again', she said, 'and bringyourwifealong. I've heard a lot about her,' she stuttered slightly, 'b..beauty.'

I never saw her again. The cruellest blow she was dealt with was that she was evicted from her Grosvenor House apartment. The settlement may not have allowed for a large suite in a posh West End hotel. No one knew her whereabouts, not even the actor who kept tabs on everyone. Where had she gone? Which country? Which town? The lady who evoked lush, exotic landscapes had simply vanished.

Only last week I was walking along 5th Avenue when I thought of looking at the narrow façade of the Hamilton. It doesn't exist any more; there is a new plaza in its place. I felt a strange pang as I stood for a while looking at the glass and steel structure. I could have sworn I heard a few resonant notes of *Asawari*, albeit, slightly off key.

TALK IS CHEAP

I do not know when the honorific *Abul-Asar* (the most effective) was bestowed upon the poet, Hafiz Jallundhri, but in all the books and magazines which carried his poetry, he was never referred to without the epithet. When he appeared on my television show, (thanks to the ministrations of Ibne Insha, aided by that self-proclaimed maverick of film journalism, Ahmed Bashir), I asked him how long it had taken him to compose our national anthem. *'Abul-Asar'*, he inflected the words pointedly, 'does not take time once he decides to do something', reminding me, in no uncertain terms, that I had committed a cardinal sin by not mentioning his honorific while introducing him to the audience. It was a memorable lesson for me never to think that creative people were less priggish about the titles bestowed upon them than ordinary mortals.

Hafiz Jallundhri had a puckish wit; he had a vast reservoir of *Mirasi* jokes. I had hoped that his joviality would come across the screen, but it did not, largely because he chose to project himself as a 'saviour of the nation'. Most of our august personalities do, when they appear on television.

I don't remember how the conversation drifted, but he began to hold forth on our overwhelming dependence on Western medicine. As a result, he contended, our people wear an unhealthy look. The eminent poet was known for his predilection for *hikmat*. The comedian, Zarif, was another guest on the show and he launched into a scathing condemnation of *Hakims* whom he dubbed as quacks. Zarif did it only to bring down the poet a peg or two, but Hafiz Jallundhri rose to the bait. It was a banal contest; the comedian living upto his reputation for ribaldry, and the eminent poet stooping lower and lower, trying to be street smart in order to steal a laugh. He didn't win the contest, but he left no doubt in any one's mind that he had been brought up in a background which was, to put it mildly, shadier than Zarif's.

If you were to look at the inner working and the ritual of the 'talk show', you will find that it is the only format in which your favourite as well as your embarrassing, moments can occur within the span of a single programme. It is a form in which an unknown personality, sparring with the host (or a guest), can gain enough notoriety to become a television host himself. The trendsetter, Quentin Crisp, was right when he noted, that 'no matter how ignominious a person's public image, as soon as he gets on television he becomes a virgin in the eyes of the viewer'.

The talk show was reproduced rapidly over the years. In the digital age of multi channelism, the talk show is now more prominent than ever before. Even in our limited setup there are countless talk show hosts. We call them 'compares'. Every young man or young woman that I meet informs me, coyly, that he is 'comparing' a programme.

The talk show started out in America. It was the natural evolutionary step from the showbiz gossip columns and the radio shows of the forties. In the mid-fifties, the comedian, Steve Allen, introduced the format to the late night television schedules. At the time, such programmes were not considered worthy of being sponsored by the big advertisers. Allen's live talk shows made them, and the networks sat up and paid attention.

When the talk show reached England, it had a different complexion. In America it was a romp; celebrities revealing their secrets to a high spirited host in a boisterous, party setup. In England, the show was a serious affair, the guests were stiff upper-lipped famous personalities. The host did not project his own image.

John Freeman's 'Face to Face' was a paradigm of a tasteful television talk show. Freeman, whose image remained largely absent from the screen, relied on incisive, well-chosen questions. Gently, persuasively, he got underneath the skin of his guests. Thus Gilbert Harding, an icon of radio and journalism, shocked the nation not so much with his tears, but his propensity for homosexuality. (This was in the mid-fifties).

The main attraction of the talk show is the slow eradication of the aura of personality. The public is ever greedy to become privy to the private lives of the rich and famous. In television terms it was as big an event as the advent of the 'talkie' in cinema. People are avid about learning the secrets of their idols. What better entertainment could the producers provide? And talk is cheap. Parkinson, one of the greatest television hosts ever, describes the talk show as 'an unnatural act between two consenting adults'. The public never gets tired of watching this act.

Very soon, into the run of my own television show, I realized that our celebrities do not have the courage to bare their souls in public. Indeed their resistance to let the viewing public become privy to their private lives and thoughts was so strong that I had no recourse but to let them spout the half a dozen *clichés* with which they came armed. It was best to let them ride their hobby-horses. The high moral tone that they adopted soon betrayed their timorous vulnerability; the sham that they wore as a cloak slipped more often than they realised. Hafiz Jallundhri was not the only case. Once a famous movie star asserted that she disapproved of dressing immodestly, that she never went anywhere — even to work — unchaperoned by her mother, and that she only wanted to appear in 'good' films (her concept of a 'bad' film was the one which flopped at the box office), but what could she do? *'Hamaray to rate fix ho*

jate hain,' she said. This produced a big laugh. The
poor girl was blissfully unaware of the fact that she
had revealed the seamy background from which she
had emerged.

The chat show continues to remain the exclusive
domain of celebrities. Non-celebrities make their
contributions and, sometimes, make their mark, but
no one switches on to a show that does not feature
recognisable names.

All talk show hosts harbour the illusion that they
have a faithful following and that their own
personalities will prolong an otherwise ailing show.
After all, Johnny Carson kept his 'Tonight show'
running for 30 long years. They forget that there was
a multi-million dollar organisation with 17
permanent writers, 25 well-paid and sharp
researchers and a vast platoon of PR boys, not to
speak of the largesse doled out by the biggest TV
network in the United States, to keep the show afloat.

Here, in our country, it is not difficult for anyone to
occupy the host's chair in a talk show. Model girls,
car salesmen, laboratory assistants, school masters,
insurance agents, ingénues, unsuccessful movie
starlets possessing no other assets but the patronage
of an influential producer, often do. The trouble is
that once in the chair, they hope to succeed by using
the theme of survival that binds them to their guests.

PINO

I have not always been fortunate in the choice of my film roles, but I have been singularly fortunate in having opportunities to work with some of the most illustrious actors of our times. Peter Ustinov, who died a couple of weeks ago, was one such luminary.

Many moons ago, we were cast in a movie which, after three days of filming, came to an abrupt halt because the movie moguls in Hollywood — having seen the rushes — felt that the Armenian born director, Richard Sarafian, was no good and that he ought to be replaced. From a remote part of Kenya, we were flown back to Nairobi and lodged in the plush surroundings of a colonial hotel, to await the arrival of the new director. Peter Ustinov was given a suite next to my room. His sitting room had large French windows which he kept open. Whenever I went past he would call out, '*Ya effendi.*'

Apart from being a superb mimic, Ustinov had an uncanny feeling for the cadence of a language. He spoke several European languages fluently (and masterfully). His make-believe Arabic was just as good as his make-believe Japanese. From our respective positions — he, sitting by his writing bureau, I, standing in the veranda outside — we would conduct a conversation in Arabic, that is to say, gibberish which sounded like Arabic. I struggled after a while, but he would carry on as though he was born into the language. The banter over, he would invite me in for a glass of chilled Chablis.

There was an excellent French restaurant in Nairobi called Chez Marcell. Ustinov dined there almost every night. He often invited me. Never once did he allow me to pay for the meal, 'I am on a bigger allowance than you are,' was his pet answer.

He was a gourmet and the establishment knew that. No effort was spared in preparing the choicest meal imaginable. At times, he would pass me a tip, 'In doing your turbot, you'd be better off adding a few peppercorns to the poaching liquid.' I owe everything I know about French cuisine to Peter Ustinov.

The meals were a delight, but his conversation was hilarious. I would laugh until my eyes began to water. 'Now, now Carruthers,' he would say, in the manner of a Marlborough schoolmaster, 'Control yourself.'

Peter Ustinov was the wittiest raconteur I have ever come across. His observation of human foibles was so acute, his grasp over people's speech patterns so perfect, that he could turn the most mundane happening into a piercingly amusing incident. He could impersonate a dyed-in-the-wool American widow as perfectly as he could, a young Prussian subaltern, or a middle-aged Cockney plumber.

No wonder he was the darling of the chat show hosts. Every one of them, David Frost, Michael Parkinson, Russel Harty — not to speak of their American counterparts — sought to have him appear on their shows again and again. They knew that his presence would ensure high ratings. Once, on his return from the United States, he appeared on 'Aspell'. How did you find Los Angeles this time? asked the suave and debonair, Tim Aspell. 'Very droll,' Ustinov answered, 'Even the more reputable newspapers now carry small ads like "Receive obscene phone calls from guaranteed nude ladies", 'They don't!' said Tim Aspell, in mock disbelief. 'Ah, but you forget,' Ustinov went on, 'that a high-spending city like Los Angeles has to cater for every taste with civic blessing. The ad is underlined with the announcement that all major credit cards are accepted.'

When the audience stopped laughing, he reclined in his chair and, with an impish glint in his eyes, said, 'It is no doubt understood by those who find release in such diversions that this little freedom is included among all the other large ones in that composite concept on behalf of which all the lethal missiles are ranged and the bombs are primed.'

You and I would find it difficult to speak with such exquisitely modulated facility, even if we have crammed such a speech. Peter Ustinov could articulate, with utmost ease, the most abstruse concept. Of all the eminent after-dinner speakers, he was the only one, I have ever heard, who never fluffed. I do not recall any moment when he, in order to connect one thought with another, 'ummed', or resorted to those commonly used words: 'I mean to say' and 'sort of'. Cerebration could have been his second name.

During the long intervals when a scene is being lit, actors normally have a snooze, play backgammon, have mild flirtations with the continuity girl or the leading lady's stand-in. Ustinov and I found a different diversion. We wrote carefully drafted notes to each other — he, in his capacity as an irate Governor of the North West Frontier Province, and I, as the arch enemy of the *Farangi*, the elusive, Faqir of Ippi. His letters lie in my writing desk in England. (Someday I must dig them up and reproduce them). The Governor's lofty tone and his vacuous sanctimoniousness had an underlying satire that would have done Michael Faryn proud. Each one of his notes had a newly designed monogram, and one or two delightful illustrations. Only Wintertton, the much-lamented film critic, could do better illustrations.

Friendships formed on film locations don't often last, but ours did. When his new play 'Beethoven' opened in Birmingham, I invited him to be the sole guest on the magazine show that I produced for British Television. He was aware that my slot did not get massive ratings, but he thought it would be churlish to refuse a friend. My programme was devoted largely to the attainments—and frustrations—of the new Britishers.

I do not think he was trying to please me or establish his credentials as an upholder of the cause of minorities, when he declared that there was a salutary skepticism in the air, and it was perhaps time to examine the history of prejudice to which small nations became victims. 'We live in an era in which pompous politicians attempt to continue the time-honoured hypocrisy which permits selfish policies to be propounded in expressions of high-mindedness.'

He was a caring man who knew that the West was pursuing a course that could only lead to more misery for the Third World. In his historical work on Russia, he writes, 'Today, of course, everything has been done to eradicate the traces of colonial presence, or rather to replace that presence, with another, the skyscrapers of large commercial interest eager to help the Third World help itself. Unfortunately, in doing so they create privileged classes within these new countries, leaving the underprivileged where they had been for long... The fact, is that emerging nations imitate much of the foolish symbolism of Imperialism, military rituals, awful national anthems and the like, in an endlessly paradoxical aspect of how the new freedoms are used, and not without the painful absurdity.'

He angered many people in America because he frequently debunked the United States' avuncular devotion to the cantankerous and mischievous policies of Israel, in which the voice of an ancient people is shrill and unmusical. He was particularly severe about American imperialism. 'If by imperialism we mean enslavement, not merely physical, but mental and economic, then it is very far from being dead.'

Ustinov (playwright, novelist, director, ambassador for UNICEF) was a movie star of some magnitude, but his heart was in doing humanitarian work. In Kenya he would often gather a bunch of sniveling, barefooted children, and amuse them for hours by reproducing the sound of almost every musical instrument through his mouth. They called him 'PINO'.

CHARMS FLY
AT THE MERE TOUCH
OF COLD PHILOSOPHY

In our part of the world, poetry is not so much recited as hammered. The readers (as well as most poets) thump out each line as if it stood by itself, irrespective of the rhythm of the following line or lines. The temptation of stressing and pointing out the rhyme is too strong for them to resist. The rhyme should be heard clearly, but if the phrase does not require any pause, the reader should go on to the next line without one.

The fault lies partly with the false notions we have about our system of scansion. We think that because the lines rhyme we have to intone them if not to sing them outright. Poetry reading has become akin to the rhetoric that emanates from the pulpit. This probably mesmerises some listeners, as sermons do, but it demeans the colour and music of the words which the poet has, intuitively, (or consciously) arranged as the vehicle of a particular experience.

Poetry does not sound better or more meaningful if you were to scan it technically. Most people, when they set out to recite poetry to a gathering, confuse the inherent rhythm of a poem with its meter. Rhythm is the actual movement of the words and this is rarely in agreement with the beat of the meter. The expressiveness of the verse depends upon the variations of the rhythm and the artful use of inflections. Naturally, you cannot disregard the prosodic arrangement.

Prosody is an immense and abstruse subject which, in the case of Arabic/Persian/Urdu, has been made more perplexing by long-winded terminology (*Hazaj –Mussadas–Akhrab Maqbooz*, for instance) to describe a certain type of meter. The meter itself is made up of words like *Maf'ool*, *Mafa'eel*, *Mafa'eelun* and their derivatives.

After a little bit of practice even a layman can learn the rudiments of this methodology. The permutations of *Maf'ool*, *Mafa'eel* can help him identify the prosodic nature of a couplet. If, however, he wants to learn why a certain title has been assigned to a meter, he has to be cognizant of the medieval, grammatical jargon: *Vatd, Akhrab, Kharam, Ushtar*, etc, Arabic words related to elisions.

The prosody pundits have made sure that no one understands the form of a meter unless he first comprehends the syntactic structure of elision. This is one reason why most people fight shy of studying the grammar of our poetry. The result is that today, apart from scholars, very few people can perceive the metrical language of a couplet.

The great 18th century wit and poet, Insha Allah Khan Insha, did try to simplify the system. He suggested that the entire mumbo jumbo of scansion could be reformed by substituting three words: *Gul, Saba* and *Chamanee*, which, he demonstrated, were capable of scanning not just the ghazal but all genres of Urdu poetry. He was not taken seriously.

In English too, the study of prosody is pretty daunting. The words you confront are: iambs, trochees, anapaests, dactyls, etc. In English poetry, the basis of all verse is the distinction between long and short syllables. A particular meter is characterised by a variety of 'feet', or recurring groups of stressed and unstressed syllables. Prosodists use the sign (-) for long syllables and (¡) for short. There are short-long (¡ -), long short (¡), short-short-long (¡ ¡ -), long-short-short (- ¡ ¡) with the inverted v sign, that is ^, indicating a pause. Here is an example:

```
U —   U —      U —   U —     U —
Among| the mount| ains by| the wint| er sea
```

The notation only shows me the stressed and the unstressed syllables, but if I were to read it as a musical score, giving full weight to the long syllables, I would be bleating like a parson. However, that is not the issue. The point is that even the above line cannot be properly read, as it is scanned, because prosodists differ about whether the line I have quoted is trochaic (long-short syllables) or not. My advice to a reciter is that he should give a wide berth to prosodists.

In English poetry the line-end is most easily seen in the two kinds of couplet, that which stops at the rhyme and that which runs over into the next line. Keats combines the two methods in the same poem:

> *...Upon her aching forehead be there hung*
> *the leaves of willow and of adder tongue...*
> ....
> *Let speargrass and the spiteful thistle wage*
> *War on his temples. Do not all charms fly*
> *At the mere touch of cold philosophy?*

This method allows the reader to vary the position of the pauses in such a way that the rhythm is always fresh. The fact is that each poem has to be treated differently. Pope's heroic couplets, which do not allow for enjambment (running over), has to be read differently from Dylan Thomas' 'Love in the Asylum'.

The first duty of a reciter is to understand and respect the poem he recites. If he is serious about his work he should try to train himself as to speech and voice; only then will he be able to develop a perception about phrasing, tone and clear, well-formed sounds. A training in rhythm is also necessary as well as the precise and rapid articulation, correct pronunciation and a range of tone and timber. A capable reader of poetry must give the effect of spontaneity and ease. Laboured speech kills the subtlety of fine poetry.

There are readers who seem to think that pauses of any length may be made to express their own sense of what is dramatic irrespective of how the poet has written the verse. You hear (and see) many examples of this during *Muharram* when there is a surfeit of poetry-reading sessions both on stage and screen.

Robert Speight, who was one of the finest readers of poetry it has been my good fortune to hear, made an astute point in his introductory remarks to one of his recitals: a reciter, he said, could never pass on, by vocal sounds what was in the poem unless his voice could interpret all that he heard in a silent reading. I have always found this to be a very useful tip. A good poem does create inner stirrings and, on occasions, when I have been able to externalise whatever I have felt in a silent reading, the result has been more than satisfactory.

Poetry contains words that vivify and give life. I am, of course, talking of good poetry, for there is an awful lot of bad poetry not only in English but in our own language and, I dare say, in every language. Once we have learnt to discriminate, we find that the finest art of elocution is in the speaking of poetry which, in turn, makes us realize why Mathew Arnold said that 'Poetry is nothing less than the most perfect speech of man'.

THE PEACOCK DANCE

I remember reading a stage direction in a Kalidasa play that said, 'enter peacocks dancing' or something like that. It is hard to believe that actual peacocks marched on to the stage—though if seals can be trained, why not peacocks?—so I assume that actors performed the dance in the guise of peacocks.

There are moments in a Bharata Natyam or a Kathak recital when the dancer executes a few steps simulating a peacock. The word *mayur* (peacock) occurs in every third *thumri* and when the accompanying singer intones it, the dancer takes it as a cue to walk mincingly.

It works well in the framework of a Kathak tapestry, but an entire ten or twelve minute piece, devoted to the antics of the peacock, palls. The only thing common between a peacock and our male dancers (or female, for that matter) is that they both have indescribably ugly feet.

The peacock dance has been a part of the standard repertoire of lesser male dancers for a long time. They performed them in 'variety programmes'. Invariably, the background music was a pastiche, depending on whether the dancer belonged to Bengal, Punjab or Oudh. I have been exposed to innumerable enactments of this dance, but I have never once seen a dancer from the South perform it. The South Indians stuck to their classical numbers except for the god-like Ram Gopal. He was the only deviant. I did not see him as the *mayur* but I did see him perform the dual role of a snake and snake-charmer, and he was magic.

Rafi Anwar had been trained under the tutelage of the mercurial Ram Gopal. He knew his *Tillanas* and his *Shabdams*, but he realised, after migrating to Karachi, that in order to eke out a livelihood, he would have to teach a mish-mash of dancing styles. Occasionally, he gave a public performance of a shortened *Tillana* to the accompaniment of a poorly recorded musical score, but, mostly, he presented his peacock dance.

Rafi Anwar may have left everything behind when he migrated from India, but he had brought with him his peacock costume. It had been made by a genius of a designer. The plumage was held on to the dancer's body by a concealed belt, which had a spring at the back. At the appropriate moment, after he had strutted on the stage, and moved his neck forward and backward like a rooster on the prowl, he would arch his body as though he had lost interest in his surroundings and, ever so subtly, pull the catch on the spring. Magically, the concealed tail spread out like a fan shimmering with iridescent colours. The applause was instantaneous.

Other dancers, whose costume had not been designed by a true craftsman, wore a kind of parachute outfit with a cord which they pulled to create the fan effect. The late Faqir Hussain Saga, whose only forte was 'the peacock dance', told me that there had been times when the cord did not work (*engine hee nahin chala*: 'the engine did not start'). He had a back-up device, which was to shake the tail feathers and use his left arm to prop them up.

Ghanshyam's 'fan' worked, but the colours were not gorgeous. Perhaps the costume had worn out when I saw him dance. The Ghanshyam School of Dancing — husband, wife and daughter all taught — was a modest outfit near PECHS. They had a few girl students who preferred learning to performing. Once every six months they staged a public performance. All the three Ghanshyams performed, but the *piece de resistance* was Ghanshyam's peacock dance.

You might think that in the earlier years there were only male dancers around. That is not so. The participation of women in the performing arts, dance in particular, is not a new phenomenon. Long before Rafi Anwar and Ghanshyam, there was Azurie. (Panna and Amy Minwalla entered the field many years later.)

Azurie's dedication to the discipline of dance was so intense that she fought every opponent — club going executives,   municipal   officials,   provincial governmental authorities—like a scalded cat. They felt cowered and left her alone largely because she spoke to them in her rat-a-tat, Anglo-Indian English, which they could not understand but which they took to be a command of some sort. She ran her dance school with impunity. Her students were well-heeled ladies, mostly.

'Madam' Azurie, as she liked to be called, had arrived from Bombay where she had lived and worked in the movie world. Like her contemporary, Khurshid (Tani of 'Tansen' fame) she had achieved a status of stardom, which she was unable to maintain in Karachi. She lived in a sparsely furnished apartment. Her only valuable possession was a large album on her table. I once asked her permission to look at it, but she insisted she would take me through it herself. Sandwiched, in between glossy enlargements of her dance poses, was a stark photograph in which she stood in a plain white sari against the background of a cremation scene. There was a tear in her eye when she told me that she had been an 'acting star' as well.

Dance took a severe hammering in our country almost a quarter of a century ago. It was declared to be a 'Hindu thing', which had no place in the monolithic Islamic state. (The humble non-religious 'peacock dance' vanished as well.) Those who had always felt that we must not own up to anything un-Islamic were delighted. The debate, throughout the eighties, was no longer about what we had inherited as our 'culture' or what, indeed, was the 'culture' we adhere to, but about how to root out the insidious 'foreign' (and therefore anti-Pakistan) elements which had crept in. Since it was feared that the slightest whiff from across the border would annihilate our 'ideology', the performing arts were confined to horse and cattle shows, and the fine arts, to calligraphy — at an official level, that is.

But, privately, we held pop concerts and disco soirees at which the courtesans of the day danced lewdly. Sometimes even classical dance recitals were staged. The cultural contradictions continued to operate throughout the 'dark decade'.

Way back in the fifties some worthies wrote in the Urdu press that our 'culture' begins from the day that Mohammad Bin Qasim landed in Sindh. It was this thinking that led a Lebanese diplomat to confess that since arriving in Pakistan he had learnt that Islam was born on the 14 of August 1947.

Seminars on 'culture' are fussy, time-wasting procedures. We shall not resolve anything, unless we understand that what constitutes our 'culture' includes a relish of pursuits that become forbidden from time to time. If this leads to a kind of hypocricy, then that, too, is a part of our cultural make-up. No matter what the strictures, we shall always derive a thrill out of atavistic pleasures.

DANCE: THE BUGBEAR WORD

Whatever our reservations about encouraging dance as a worthwhile artistic pursuit, we are not averse to deriving pleasure out of it. Publicly, we denounce it; privately, we enjoy watching it. It is this kind of dichotomy that has shaped our woolly attitude towards aesthetics as well as ethics.

We claim that dance is an integral part of our heritage. We even support, officially, a few dance troupes (for the sake of our representation in international cultural festivals), but we make sure that they stick to performing the half a dozen numbers — choreographed ages ago — that pass for folk dances. (At home we prefer to have the same dances performed by men only). This remains to be our public posture. In private, however, we drool over what the colonial rulers dubbed as 'nautch', that lascivious entertainment, which Kathak dance had been reduced to, during the British Raj.

In the Indian subcontinent, it took hundreds of years for dance to acquire a set grammar, which led to a codification of technique. In the south, it was in the temples that the art evolved its exacting standards. All codified classical dance was an enactment of the tale and glory of the gods.

Kathak, the dance of northern India, also developed, initially, as an offering to the gods. The art of story-telling was a part of all religious festivals. In the process of reciting the divine tales, the *kathaks* (story-tellers) began to enact their *kathas* (stories) through mime and dance.

Over the centuries, the practioners of the art of Kathak drifted from one place to another, looking for a centre where they could practice and perform in a conducive environment. It was not until the stable period of the Mughals that the art received the necessary impetus for its growth.

The refined taste of the Mughals was reflected in their patronage of music and dance. (Abul Fazl gives vivid accounts of these soirees.) The record of Mughal miniatures painted by innumerable painters is an eloquent testimony of their high regard for dance.

The various elements Kathak has imbibed, over different periods in history, has enriched the form considerably more than other classical dances. This is not surprising because Kathak is the only dance that combines both Hindu and Islamic influences. The Hindu influence gives it mythology, the narrative tradition; the Muslim influence gives it its brilliant virtuosity and its courtly elegance.

The religious content suffered a setback during the foreign invasions (12th century onward) that subsequently led to Muslim rule in India. The Mughal rulers, once they were sure of the wicket they had occupied, extended their patronage to the local fine arts in general, but music and dance, in particular.

Kathak now acquired a new vocabulary. The prayers to Ganesh and Vishnu, the enactment of the antics of gods and goddesses, were taken out of the repertoire and replaced by *Amad, Salami* and Persian ghazals. Only the Krishna theme was left in.

There are reasons for this. The Krishna of Kathak is no dialectician; he is warm, human, a mischievous child, a youthful lover, a cowherd, a flute player and above all, a prankster. His romance with Radha, the eternal Indian woman, his frolics with the *gopis* (handmaidens) became the theme of countless lilting songs. These songs, embellished over the centuries, enchant us today as much as they enchanted Akbar's court. No Kathak dancer can resist the opportunity of interpreting them.

Kathak is an amalgamation of poetry, spoken word, music, mime and rhythm. In Kathak the dancer adopts an upright stance unlike all other classical forms (Khuchipudi, Bharatanatyam, Orissi, etc.,) in which the dancer adopts a half-seated position with flexed knees. It is not concerned with covering floor space, its main concern is to create a soundscape of tonal variation through the combined sounds of *tabla* (or *pakhawaj*) and the *ghungroos* (ankle-balls). Standing erect, appearing to be static, the dancer produces changing accents in rhythmic patterns. Only the cognoscenti realise that the dancer, with the right shoulder slightly inclined, makes a constant but subtle movement to manipulate his weight.

Of all the artistic professions, classical dance is, perhaps, the most demanding both physically and emotionally. Every dancer worth his salt realizes this pursues it because it is the most ecstatic form of aesthetic expression celebrating the joy of life through the medium of human body.

Only one person in our part of the world took up this challenge and it is an unbelievable feat that, notwithstanding our disapprobation and apathy towards dance, we have produced a dancer of such peerless quality as Nahid Siddiqui.

The magic of Nahid Siddiqui begins to work when she begins to tap the floor with flat feet and slowly weave intricate rhythmic combinations into a given metric cycle *(taal)*. Not only the feet but her entire body becomes a percussion instrument. It would be true to say that she dances a *taal* rather than to a *taal*. The grace, the exquisite subtlety that she can bring to the shifting emotions during her *abhinay* (expressionistic work) is something I have not seen amongst the Indian dancers of her era.

In her *nritta* (pure dance), she always astounds the audience with her supreme control over the *laya* (tempo) and timing. Unlike other dancers, she does not have to check her hold over the tempo by repeating *toras* (short dance pieces) in between *toras*.

Her innate mathematical sense enables her to dance to any musical structure from any of the subsequent beats rather than wait for the *sam*, (the culminating point and the first key beat of the time measure). During *nritta*, a dancer is not expected to interpret emotions but wear a pleasant expression. Nahid Siddiqui positively radiates during her *tatkar*.

What distinguishes her work from that of other celebrated dancers is her realisation that creativity is not a rearrangement of known modules and formulas: it has to involve a new exploration of truth. She understands that basic emotions – anxiety, joy, longing, disgust, humility, despair – need not be expressed in the clichéd mode. In her experimental pieces she has shown that they can be interpreted, naturalistically, without flouting the Kathak tradition.

Her critics may pick on her for not beginning her recitals with *Ganesh Vandana*, or for not following the prescribed sequence of *Pramelu* and *Paran*, but they cannot deny that she can hold an audience spellbound with her remarkable presence, grace and precision.

We mustn't whinge about Nahid Siddiqui not having produced a worthy successor. Even if she had spent as much time in Pakistan as she did in training her young students in Birmingham, she would not have found a true devotee because no girl would have had the nerve to defy the strictures imposed by our society and take up classical dancing as a profession and a vocation. The irony is that even those who admire her for her utter absorption in her work and her total dedication to her art, dare not emulate her.

A DOLEFUL SONG

I am persuaded that there is absolutely no limit to the absurdities that can, by authoritarian action, come to be generally believed. Thus it is that we have come to believe that every serious or purposeful cultural programme on television—be it a 'long play' or a literary dissertation—must begin with a doleful song 'specially composed' for such an occasion. Every trite, ten or fifteen part drama serial now begins, and ends, with a second rate doleful song.

The special TV transmission to commemorate Faiz Sahib's death anniversary began similarly with Ms. Nayyara Noor, an accomplished performer, singing *raat yoon dil mein teri khoee hue yaad aiee*, a *qita* which marks Faiz Sahib's romantic and lyrical leanings, but does not characterise his approach to life and poetry.

Anyone with a modicum of sensitivity would tell you that the programme should have begun with a silver image of Faiz Sahib and, after an effective use of silence, (our television has not yet grasped the concept of silence), his voice should have risen either with *Hum khasta tanon se mohisubo* or *Nahin nigah mein manzil*. He recited both these poems with great feeling.

Faiz Sahib is often open to ridicule about his manner of rendition. Unlike most poets he was not in love with his own voice and often threw away his lines. There was hardly anyone he met who did not press him to recite his verse. Willy-nilly, he always obliged. Over the years his casual, lethargic way of uttering his own poetry became a second nature to him. But I remember that in a BBC studio, in Birmingham, he once read some of his best poems in a most moving manner, without those hesitant slurs which we exaggerate when we 'do' Faiz Sahib.

I hope, I am wrong but I don't think that PTV made any serious effort to record Faiz Sahib. People like him were kept away from television for fear that they might spread sedition. Now that he is no longer a *persona non grata*, the producer of the commemorative programme should have tried to obtain a decent recording of his recitals. His own voice in the beginning would have generated poignancy and prepared the viewer for the interesting journey that lay ahead.

Instead, the Faiz memorial transmission was reduced to the sameness which undistinguishes every other pretentious TV presentation. I didn't have the heart to take in what followed. When it comes to television, I am either lured or alienated, within the first forty five seconds.

Our acceptance of mediocrity on television is now so deeply entrenched that it would be almost impossible to rise above it. We applaud mundane observations and hackneyed jokes with spirited enthusiasm. Not only that: we punctuate the feeble punch lines with a fanfare. Nobody considers a joke to be worthy of attention unless there is squiggle of notes on the keyboard.

A squiggle here and a squiggle there and you have described most of our entertainment programmes on the box. It has taken years of dour bureaucratic planning to achieve this. The dictum was that the media must be mobilised to serve the interests of the state (we always equate the state with the administration in power); therefore it must avoid all topics which might give rise to contentious controversies. The bureaucrats decreed that apart from set slots for religious instruction there must be specific timings for soaps, music, drama, and current affairs which, until 9/11, remained a euphemism for 'official Kashmir policy'.

Within the framework, we have been juggling the same permutation with new, computerised titles, and a new jargon. Pop music now has a mystical flavour; popular drama has a surfeit of European and American locations; English-speaking ingénues prance on movie sets, condescendingly inserting Punjabi-Urdu in their spiel, and not so English-speaking presenters losing no opportunity to adorn their Punjabi-Urdu with subcontinental English.

A Mr. Toosi B.A. self-styled 'scientific' conjurer once came to our school and showed us several tricks (of which I only remember the pink litmus paper, first turning blue and then white). When he left, our teacher asked the class to write what we had seen happen. Nearly everyone wrote down something much more astonishing than the reality. We all thought we were reporting truthfully, what we had seen with our own eyes. This sort of falsification is true of our television programmes. We see with our own eyes only what we want to see.

Give any organisation power to generate beliefs and it will make, within 20 years, the majority of the population believe that two and two make five. All you do is to keep emphasising that it is the considered view of the authorities and that anyone who does not support this official doctrine has no chance to rise to any position of power. Admittedly, there would be detractors, but realising that the price of heresy is dear, they would succumb. So much for an authoritarian state, but even in a democracy governments tend to control thought.

This is one reason why there is no sustained creativity in a country like ours which, though at times, pretending to be a democracy, has always been an oligarchy. Conventional opinions rule our society. Unconventional opinions rule our sitting rooms and we know only too well that it would be futile to air them. When we do, we put our necks on the block.

The power of authority over belief in the present day is vastly greater than before. No one can deny, in face of the evidence, that it is easy to produce a population of fervent patriots. It ought to be equally easy to produce a population of sane, thinking people, but authorities do not wish to do so, since then it would be difficult to admire those in authority.

What we need are a few courageous eccentricities amidst us. I admire the letter-writer to an English newspaper who said that he had had his blood diagnosed and he found that Kashmir did not run in it. Eccentrics are non-conformists and are vital for the intellectual health of a society. We tend to confuse them with cranks. Cranks are a different breed that resort to lunatic logic.

There have been some notable cranks but none better than the one who asked Bertrand Russell to recommend some of his books as he was interested in philosophy. Russell did so. The man returned the next day saying he had been reading one of them and found only one worthwhile statement, and that, too, seemed false to him. Russell asked him what it was and the man said, 'You say on page 139 that Julius Caesar is dead.' When Russell asked the man why he did not agree, the man, drew himself up and said, 'Because I am Julius Caesar'.

AN UNEQUAL MUSIC

The best thing that can be said of contemporary fiction in hardback is that the jackets (or book covers, if you like) are exceedingly well-designed. No, I m not talking of pulpfiction, which sells the most, or crime fiction or science fiction which does nearly as well; I am talking specifically of fiction that passes through the portals of literature.

The thin, glossy art paper cover that ripped and frayed at the edges long before you had finished the book is a thing of the past. Jackets are now produced with a kind of paper that has the feel of a smooth mahogany desk.

But inspite of my partiality to attractive jackets, I give fiction a miss these days. It is because I find that as a traveller, nay pilgrim, on the path to literature, the going has become harder and harder. I want to follow the road but I keep stumbling because of the diversions.

What matters in literary fiction today is style and technique and certainly not the story, which only seems to be there on sufferance. It is like the Hollywood blockbuster of today in which the 'Special Effects' obliterate whatever threads of plot there might be. 'Writers seem to take up stories as if with a pair of tongs,' says Phillip Pullman, author of children's books, 'they are embarrassed by them. If they could write novels without stories in them, they would.' My sentiments exactly.

Novelists of today, those who belong to the higher echelons of the literary world, seem to ignore the fact that a story is a vital part of the way we understand the world – or a novel, at any rate. They feel that the reader will be captivated by the labyrinth of deconstruction, which they have craftily created. Any novel that makes a departure from this method is considered to be common and prosaic.

Two of the stalwarts of literary fiction today are Kazuo Ishiguro and Ben Okri. Both have settled down in England and both have produced works that have received a vast number of plaudits, confirming their position amongst the front rank of novelists. I would be pretending if I didn't confess that I found them to be tiresome. I gave them up after a few pages, though in the case of Mr. Okri (who won the Booker Prize with his *Songs of Enchantment*) I was aware that I was consuming refined and perceptive prose, but it was taking me nowhere except into more beautiful prose.

I gave up the struggle, unashamedly, because I felt that a kind of literary elitism was being foisted on me. Readers have been so conditioned that they feel embarrassed to admit that they find it hard to stomach the work of a literary giant for fear that it would betray their plebian taste. The fact is that a few read, and fewer enjoy, the novels of those who sit on the literary pedestal. We have allowed ourselves to be persuaded that a book with a story can't be quite in the same class as a book that leaves us to interpret what is unsaid.

I am not suggesting that I only enjoy reading those authors who write stories that can be read from the first page to the last. John Grisham, who sells in millions, is a smooth storyteller, but not much else. What I mean to say is that he doesn't open my eyes to anything much. He offers me a good tale which keeps me enthralled at the time, but is soon easily forgotten.

Too many novels today begin with a strong sense of displacement. I don't mind that so long as I am given information and not a mere literary knowingness. The problem with novels of deconstruction is that the writers expect me to weigh all the silences between the lines and I find that process to be tedious.

But it doesn't mean that I do not relish lustrous, perceptive prose. It is one of the greatest assets of Marquez (some people think he is even better in translation) but then Marquez is unique in that he never lets go of the thread of his story. Marquez has the ability to imbue the most humdrum and sedate happening with imagination, invention and humour, without ever slackening his grip over his taut and elegant prose.

For a whole year I avoided reading Vikram Seth's *An Equal Music*. The hype as well as the ecstatic reviews gave me an uneasy feeling that the book would bamboozle me with literary esotericism. Last week during an intensely hot afternoon—the power supply having been cut off—I picked it off my shelf in a self-punishing mood. Whatever misgivings I had were dispelled within the first three pages.

No musical critic, not even Shaw, has been able to write so articulately about a musician's relationship to his music. Every shift of the protagonist's (a violinist) mood and manner is like the ever changing pattern of a Bach Sonata. This in itself could have been a mere contrivance, but Seth, to whom music is dearer than speech, has woven a musical tale and a tale of music that is as beautifully crafted as it is expressed:

> 'From the moment a mere ten bars from the beginning, where it is not the piano that answers the violin but the violin itself that provides his own answer, to the last note of the last moment, where the cello instead of playing the third, supports with its lowest and most resonant most open note the beautifully spare C major chord, I am in a world where I seem to know everything and nothing'.

After he wrote *Golden Gate*, a novel in verse, which prompted Gore Vidal to say that it was the finest creative work to come out of America since the war, there has never been any doubt about Seth's capacity for poetic rhythms. In *An Equal Music* music informs speech and turns familiar rhythm sometimes into powerful blank verse and sometimes into a lyric:

> *Let our limbs be opposable at the opposite edge. Let our teeth be pulled but let us have baleen like whales, that our plankton love might grow, that we might ungnashingly plash and play.*
> *Grief and rue, grief and rue, break the erring heart in two.*

Like most great novels *An Equal Music* is a tale of unrequited love; it is about the love of a woman lost, found and lost again. It is a story in which the lovers discover that all their emotional distances can be covered with music and because of music. Seth delicately draws the parallel between love's leaps and plunges with the score of a fugue. When the final break comes and the beloved is lost for ever, the lover realises that music alone fills the chasm in the heart and the void in the soul.

It is a haunting, beautifully written work that taunts and tantalises and lifts you out of the mire of existence into an enchanting world. And it is a book that reminds me sharply not to be wary of contemporary fiction.

GAJAL

The English newspapers published in Dubai usually carry a full page advertisement announcing that the city is going to be offered a bonanza of ghazal singing. The one I saw had pictures of five singers (Jagjit Singh was not one of them) dressed in what today's coutouriers imagine to be a stylised version of an erstwhile Maharajah's outfit. Only a promoter could have had the gall to call them 'ghazal supremos', but that is how these minnows were billed.

It's a long time since ghazal moved out of the realm of a select crowd who listened to it not so much for its *tarz* (tune or melodic line) as for the manner in which the words were woven into the melody. In the 19th century, the high-class courtesan adopted ghazal as her chief artistic weapon and poetasters had a field day.

Originally, ghazal was a part of a musician's light-classical repertoire, which also included *thumri, kafi, tappa, dadra, kajri,* etc. Ghazal, like the other forms, was raga based, but, unlike the other forms it lay a great deal of emphasis on the written word. Music had to remain subservient to the emotional content of the word; each lilt, each trill, every musical phrase was conceived in order to bring out the meaning of the words, and create an aura of pathos. Pathos has always been regarded as the highest form of art in the Orient.

The professional singers who took to ghazal singing in the past did not have a high academic background, but they grew up in a culture where the language of the ghazal—the cruel beloved, the hapless rejected lover, the rose and the nightingale—was common currency. In any case, Zafar, Dagh, Amir Minai (the most popular poets among singers) were not difficult to understand.

Ghazal is the only form of literature, which was meant to be sung, but Muslim society did not really encourage singing. Consequently, singing (ghazal including) was confined to courtesans. It was an accomplishment they had to acquire along with etiquette, the art of repartee and coquetry. Many of them became famous as ghazal singers: Rasoolan Bai, Gauhar Jan, Kajjan Bai, et al. Akhtari Bai Faizabadi was the most renowned of them all.

Akhtari Bai Faizabadi was a striking looking lady. She had a strong (contralto) voice but her range was modest and her classical grammar was limited. Nevertheless, her presence and her ready wit made her into a star. As a minor poet herself, she must have sensed the thrill of poetic inspiration, but she chose, perhaps quite wisely, to render only those ghazals which contained a palatable dose of wistfulness: *'Naz wale niaz kya janen'*... *'Kya bane baat jahan baat banaye na bane'*...etc.

Excellent ghazals in Urdu are not always easy to understand. The shades and nuances of Persianised idioms, the alliterations and references to literary expressions of earlier times, elude the average mind. This is why the ghazals that become popular as songs are, mostly, specimens of mediocre poetry.

After partition, Akhtari Bai Faizabadi, who now preferred to be known as Begum Akhtar, became an icon. Today, in India, she is considered (quite mistakenly) to be 'the foremost exponent' of ghazal *gayaki* in the subcontinent, just as the Anup Jalotas, with an even more circumscribed technique, have come to be regarded as the doyens of ghazal singing.

Akhtari Bai Faizabadi's real contribution lies in making her audience believe that by attending her concert they had gained a higher cultural experience; she made them feel that they were connoisseurs of music as well as poetry. She did sing some less popular ghazals of Ghalib, but her musical realisation let the poetry down. But it is to her credit that she made the ghazal into an accessible musical form at a time when exclusive and restricted gatherings were confined to classical music alone.

Barkat Ali Khan (brother of Bare Ghulam Ali Khan) was one of the first classical singers to turn his energies towards ghazal *gayeki*. He became the envy of light classical singers. He did not have the cultural background of Akhtari Bai, but his innovative style gave the ghazal a fresh neo-classical dimension.

Classical music, like classical theatre, has always been the preserve of those who have a rarefied, cultivated taste. The 20ᵗʰ century saw a decline of the discerning audience. The pace of life did not allow for people to squat attentively — and patiently — on the floor, and listen to slow and gradual expositions of ragas. A ghazal would last five to seven minutes and its opening couplet about unrequited love would strike an empathic chord amongst the listerners. The ghazal thus became, in the latter half of the 20ᵗʰ century, everyone's favourite expression of deep feelings and desires. It was no longer confined to a courtesan's *kotha*. Thousands of people began to attend ghazal concerts in big halls and open air maidans.

I have no hesitation in proclaiming Mehdi Hassan to be the most outstanding ghazal singer of our times. It is not because of his enormous range, or his perfectly modulated voice, but because of the versatile manner in which he brings out the emotions of the poetry. He is the only singer who has learnt to render a poetic line correctly. More: he is the only musician to have dared to tackle subtle and stirring poetry and managed to imbue it with imaginative melodies. Of the many profound ghazals he has rendered, you have only to listen to two: Mir's *shehron mulkon mein jo ye Mir kahata hai Mian* and Iqbal's *la phir ik baar vohi bada-o-jam ai saqi* (both set in off-beat, uncommon ragas like *Charukeshi* and *Bhatiar*) to realise how perfectly his music interacts with the words.

The era of ghazal singing is nearly over. What you hear, nowadays, are pop-ghazals performed to the accompaniment of the keyboard and other electronic instruments. A ghazal needs to be sung to a harmonium, a *sarangi*, and a *tanpura*. Today, there is an assault of orchestration, which can only smother the voice and drown out the poetry. In their desperation to compete with 'remixes' and Western style 'bands', the ghazal singers of today resort to 'jazzing' up the concerts in an effort to give the ghazal the sound of pop music. The result is gruesome.

The Dubai audience is being promised a fantastic event. What they will hear is a gajal, India's tawdry answer to ghazal.

YOUR DEAL PARTNER

I like to think that it was my purblind, incurable innocence that led me to say yes to three dinner guests who asked me, in between port and cheese, if I could be the fourth for bridge. It was pure bravado on my part for I didn't know much about the game and only pretended that I understood the bidding. I made a hash of nearly every hand. If they had been less civilised, they would have thrown me out after the first few deals and that would have put an end to my twitching infatuation for the game. Instead, they kept saying, 'Rotten luck, old man,' and 'Hard cheese.'

This was way way back in the sixties. I was the week-end guest of Phyllis and Lewis Hawser in their gorgeous Hampstead home. The lovely Phyllis, sulked a bit when I took leave of her; I had ruined her evening, she said. She had hoped that I would sit with her and give her a real insight into the theatrical world rather than sitting down to 'boring old bridge'.

There are lots of people who find bridge to be a bore. I don't. I like its changing and shifting patterns; I like the sound of silent bells as they chime a nameless fandango in my head when I bring home an unmakable contract. Which is not very often, since I am an ordinary player and still fall prey to the temptation of gaining a trick by neutralising a high card held by the defenders — technically known as finesse.

No proverbial mother-in-law could stoop to the kind of bickering and sniggering that goes on when four people sit down to a game of bridge. The language heard in the Billingsgate fish market is chaste compared to utterances at a bridge table; the invectives which are bandied about and the imagery, relating to human anatomy, culled on the spur of the moment, is a marvel to behold:

> 'Did you have the queen of spades partner?' (The question is asked with icy politeness).
> 'Yes I did.'
> 'I think not. I think you chose to leave it behind in Mama's womb when you came out.'

Is there any game, indoor or outdoor, that causes such heated debate, such acrimony, such cantankerousness amongst friends? In the underworld, the bully-boss threatens to slit throats and everyone quails. Nobody even winces when such threats are made after a hand has been played. And yet, after raising their voices in anger, after screaming hoarse and foaming at the mouth, after swearing and cursing and thumping the table, the same four people get together the next week, or the next day, and begin another new session of bridge in the most jovial and amicable manner.

It is estimated that worldwide, a hundred million people play bridge regularly. The estimate seems to be inaccurate when you consider that bridge is now a required course in many high schools in China. Wang Zhiheng, an engineer by profession and a pretty shrewd player, informs me that most of the adult population of Jinzhou are bridge addicts. Jinzhou is a small provincial town and China's population exceeds one billion.

Bridge has been called the most intellectually challenging of all card games. It is said to require 'the logic skills of chess, the language skills of simultaneous translators and the partnership skills of successful marriage'. I find that last statement to be fatuous. (Is there a successful marriage and can the skill of partnership, an admirable trait in business circles, be applied to it to turn it into a success? A moot question that I might address in the future.) In my considered opinion, husbands and wives should not sit down as partners. A friend of mine does, and he gets such flak from his partner-wife that I wonder how he can find courage to share the same bed with her. Perhaps he doesn't.

The most apocryphal bridge story of the husband who pulled a gun and shot his partner-wife because she failed to lead the suit he had bid, (an unpardonable sin in a doubled contract) is often retold during a game, sometimes as a warning to the meek and thoughtless players. Incidentally, the judge acquitted the husband. As far as the story goes, he was a discerning bridge player himself.

So, if you do not wish to blow your domestic bliss, do not partner your wife; you partner someone else's wife—which is another way of blowing your domestic bliss. Bridge-playing married men end up in the doss-house anyway, but in order to avoid absolute hell, they prefer not to play with women as regular partners. Seriously though, intelligence and, to some extent, intellect are pre-requisites for the game of bridge. A modicum of logical skill as well as an elementary knowledge of psychology also helps to allow you to weave your way through 26 cards (your own as well as your partner's—known as dummy) in order to make the number of tricks you contract for. A greater degree of skill will enable you to prevent the declarer from fulfilling his contract. It is this tussle which keeps players so glued to the bridge table that they forget their appointments, their birthday dinners and, sometimes, their wedding anniversaries.

At a competitive level the bidding has now evolved into so many labyrinthine systems that they rival cryptography. Players exchange 70 to 80 pages of typewritten notes. The coach of the Canadian national team has created and refined a bidding system that requires his team members to memorise three hundred pages of closely typed instructions. At the most rarefied levels every card played is encoded with not one, but three, different messages to his partner.

It is ridiculous. I do not think that the great bridge wizards—Culbertson, Jacoby, Mollo—ever subjected themselves to such cramming exercises. I was glad to read somewhere that the most glamorous bridge player of our times, Zia Mahmood, relies more on judgment, technique and ability rather than the exactitude of a memorised system.

Since the advent of the game on the Internet, people don't set up games as they used to; they prefer to play on the Internet. True, you can now pit your wits against the giants and you can play against the computer itself, who will not protest if you have an argument with your wife for 15 minutes in the middle of a hand, but I find it to be all too inhuman.

I am not so sure that bridge is one of those rare competitive activities that reward age and wisdom, but I know that I will go on playing it, even as I know that I will never get to the top. There are supposed to be six trillion bridge hands and I know that of those that I am likely to come across, I will muff quite a few, but that is not going to put me off any more than the unnecessary tantrums thrown by those that I play with. I find bridge to be fascinating and fun and when I am able to manipulate a squeeze so that the lowly deuce of clubs becomes a winner, it is an ecstatic feeling similar to having executed a perfect *pas glisse*—or throwing your hat on the hatstand and landing it on the exact peg.

'Your deal partner,' you say, as you nonchalantly jot the score.

URDU MUSIC

There aren't many Renaissance men amongst us, Nayyar Dada is one of them. To the world he is known as an architect of distinction. I know him as a lover of classical music and a man who has a perspicacious eye for porcelain and vignettes — and a witty raconteur.

Nayyar Dada's spartan and meticulous taste is reflected in the salon he has set up in Lahore. The small café inside the salon is a delight. It has handpicked crockery and hand-woven upholstery, and a large alcove with some lovely, antique artefacts that come from Dada's personal collection. It also offers you the best coffee in Lahore.

But that is not all. There is music in the air. Not the piped music you hear in dimly-lit restaurants, but some real, chaste music, like Bare Ghulam Ali Khan's Kamod. Incidentally, Bare Ghulam Ali Khan used to be Inayat Bai Dheruwali's accompanist (on the *sarangi*) in his younger days. The interlaced phrasing of his *Drut* owes much to the *sarangi*.

The two upper rooms of Nairang Galleries — the name of Nayyar Dada's establishment — are devoted to the works of new painters. A raised platform gives access to a small library which houses books on music, painting, literature and criticism. Dada is pleased to see people browsing through the books. It matters not that they don't buy any thing. He has even placed a few chairs around so that serious browsers can be comfortable.

The rooms are spacious and ideal for musical soirees. I was informed that they were used not only for small musical gatherings, but book readings, seminars and lectures, as well. Dada told me that he had always wanted to create a meeting point of different creative mediums. He sensed that his own town-house was the ideal location so he decided to move to a smaller place. He has donated most of his own stuff: table lamps made of old Swati doors, delicately carved chairs and Victorian-Indian settees.

A section of the Galleries displays reproductions of renowned painters — Picasso, Matisse, Chughtai, et al. The reproductions are nicely framed and modestly priced at eighteen hundred rupees a piece. I thought of what I had paid for a print of Picasso's 'Woman in Repose' in London and shuddered. (A decent reproduction would have cost me as much as the price of a Persian carpet). I paid almost twice as much for the unframed print.

Dada calls it affordable art. He is convinced that if people hang these works on their walls, they will develop a better appreciation of art. He is all for replicating old art, old furniture, old artifacts and old designs. He describes some of the carvings and statues that are on sale, as 'hybrid original pieces that have a resonance of our past'. The past, he feels, must be carried forward, and used, rather than worshipped.

Lahore needs a place like Nairang Galleries. There are other art galleries, some better lit and better designed, but that is what they are—galleries. You go in, you walk through, you see the one painting (or a piece of sculpture) that really strikes you; you look at the price and either decide that you can't afford it or you wonder if you can haggle. In nine cases out of ten, you don't buy, but you wish you had.

The atmosphere in Nairang is different. You can sit down in the book section and look at the flow of traffic down below, or you just listen to the sonorous notes of Ustad Ali Akbar Khan's *Marwa*. No one will come pestering you. People wander in, have a cup of tea or a light snack, look at things around them and, sensing the atmosphere, lower their voices. This is something rare in our part of the world. In restaurants and cafes we tend to speak vociferously.

Many years ago, I was invited by that astute cultural analyst, Muzzaffar Ghaffar, to speak, informally, about my literary preferences at the Shakir Ali Museum, once the home of the great man himself. I liked the look of the place and mentioned in my discourse that its backyard could easily be converted into an open air theatre. The Museum could then offer two kinds of delights: fine art inside and theatrical art outside. My suggestions was received enthusiastically, but nothing came of it because Shakir Ali Museum (I think Nayyar Dada designed the house for the painter) was under the surveillance of the provincial government and governments need years of file-work before approving what they consider to be 'scatter-brained' schemes.

I heard that Nairang Galleries recently hosted a ceremony to launch a new book called *Urdu Mousiki* (Urdu Music). I am not going to quibble about the English spelling of the word moosiqui. Those who are aware of phonetics will tell you that, on the whole, the Urdu-ites pronounce the word as moo-seeqi, and those who belong to the 'land of the five rivers' pronounce it as mau-seeki. (Bear in mind that the letter q when it is transliterated into Urdu suggests that its phonetic sound is the hard k, which comes naturally to the Urdu-ites; the rest of the world has to make a special effort to produce that sound.)

Anyway, I was fascinated by the title. What is Urdu music? What, indeed, would I understand if I came across a book called 'Esperanto Music'? Music belongs to a region, a people, a country, but not to a language. Has the author written about the music of the Urdu-speaking people? Is it about vocal music in which the words are exclusively in Urdu? Or does he mean music preferred by the class of people known as 'Urdu medium'?

I remained intrigued until the book landed on my table. It turned out to be a bulky compendium of the grammar related to the prevalent *ragas*. It is, in fact, a precis (in Urdu) of the treatise written by Bhatkhande, Vishnudigamber, Thakur Nawwab Ali and a few others musicologists. Oddly enough, the 'poetry' associated with the *ragas* is mostly Hindi and Punjabi. Khalid Malik Haider, who has obviously spent years in the preparation of his book, hails from the Frontier and must be commended for his devotion to a musical system which has never been the prerogative of his province.

Urdu Mousiki is a larger than usual primer for students who wish to practise the ascending and descending scales of a hundred and thirty five odd *ragas*. Mr. Haider has taken pains to explain the intricacies of our music in the terminology of the western musical discipline; and here he fails, for the 'breves' and 'quavers' are not really equivalent to our *meend*, or *shrutee*. Also, it depressed me to note that he has been remarkably careless about the spelling of terms which are inherent in the musical jargon of the West. Aeolian is spelled as 'Aeollan' and 'dotted' as 'doted'. In the small section, headed 'Western Ecclesiastical Music', the word ecclesiastical is spelled as 'Ecclasstial'. The list is endless.

But full marks to Nayyar Dada for launching a book which has such an interesting title.

'WHY ASK FOR HAPPINESS'

He begins to play without the undue fuss - the fidgety manoeuvring of the posture, the tweaking of the knobs, the strumming of subsidiary strings, the chastening look at the percussionist to convey to him, but more to the audience, that his right drum is not quite in tune with the tonic. His tones are clear, lovely, and inexorable. He plays phrase after phrase, phrase upon phrase with such ease, such sublime skill that soon he becomes music itself.

I have rarely seen any of our musicians wearing old age so gracefully. His temples are grey, his head is bald and because his jowls are not drooping and his cheeks are now devoid of puffiness, his mouth and lips have acquired an ideal symmetry; his face is serene, composed, perfectly at peace with himself; his eyes contain an ocean of tranquillity, wisdom, profundity; he looks like a statue of Thesus I once saw in Hydra.

His intonation is perfect, so perfect it makes me shiver for fear I will never be able to hear it again.

He plucks the strings with consummate ease. When he deviates, ever so lightly, from the anticipated melodic line he closes his eyes. His head is perfectly still, his lips are half closed; he appears to be witnessing a celestial revelation.

From a beautifully modulated adagio he moves, imperceptibly, to a tempo in which he uses deeper, longer notes. I suddenly realise that we are in a different sphere. His *sitar* makes sounds which are gravelly, very rich and ineffably sonorous. There is a tingling sensation in my spinal cord; the world outside has thinned out of existence and I want to laugh with delight but don't in case I miss an inadvertant whisper or a dying fall.

The second section of the Alap (known as *Jor*) is like a stellar interplay, the stars having decided to shed their inhibitions. Now two, now three, the crisply enunciated dominant notes rise up from the well of his imagination, reach the sky and merge into a cascading tremolo that remains firmly under his control.

> He rises and begins to round
> He drops the silver chain of sound
> Of many links without a break
> In chirrup, whistle slur and shake

The Vilayat Khan concert that led me to make these observations was staged at the Royal Albert Hall in London, some years ago. I only saw a DVD recording of it last week. It was a stunning experience. Listening to sublime music relieves you of thought; time comes to a stop; seconds, minutes, hours slide along into a continuum; you are suspended into an exalted world of disbelief.

There are three kinds of audiences who attend concerts of classical music. The first kind comprises, almost exclusively, connoisseurs and is the smallest group in numbers. Mostly they are musicians, members of the musician's family, close friends and students of musicology.

The second group is composed of people for whom classical music has become a status symbol. They are well-heeled and well-dressed; they don't understand music, they are bored but they will keep on sitting and listening to, or giving the impression that they are listening to a high class musical performance. For them it is enough to be able to say, 'Oh I was at the Vilayat Khan concert last evening.'

The third type of audience is made up largely of unknowledgable and unsophisticated listeners; they come and go as they please and, given half a chance, they will not hesitate from talking loudly during a performance. They can number from a few hundred to a few thousand, depending upon the scale of the event. They are the 'public' or, in the parlance of musicians, 'the masses'.

This section, the bulk, responds not so much to knowledge or skill or subtlety, but rather to musical trivia, superficial gimmicks and even the demeanour of the performer on stage. The truly great exponents — Ali Akbar Khan, Fayyaz Khan, Amir Khan Indore valley — always disregarded this section. To have catered to their tastes was anathema to them.

Vilayat Khan remained oblivious to all three types of audience during this concert. He was not just drawing from a musical tradition whose reservoir of knowledge is deep but was contributing new ideas that resulted from varying interpretations of that tradition. Years of *tapassiya* (rigorous, meditative training) melted into the sweep of spontaneity as he soared above the realms of expectation.

It is perhaps not known to many people that Vilayat Khan, the scion of his *gharana,* was deprived of any serious training by his father, Ustad Inayat Khan, a doyen amongst *sitar* players of his time. I remember hearing him play *Poorya* on a 78 HMV disc. Inayat Khan died when his son was barely 11.

Sun-up and sun-down, the young Vilayat Khan practised. He was not the first child prodigy to have foregone the pleasures and exploits of a normal childhood. His instructors were uncles, cousins and other members of his *gharana,* many of whom may even have been jealous of his innate gifts. Only he knew that he must, one day, wear the mantle of his *gharan*a and so he immersed himself in the world of music until he emerged as a colossus.

Vilayat Khan has always interspersed his recitals with a sing-song interlude. He did so on this occasion with a delightful *bandish* (set composition) 'Achanak more ghar piya aye' (all of a sudden, the beloved arrived at my door). The word *achanak* is hardly ever used in classical *bandishes* and he accented it so craftily that the reading of the line became 'the beloved came to my door, suddenly'. His mellifluous voice had an impish ring when he rendered the refrain.

An interlude of this kind acts as a balm to the audience. They no longer have to keep their attention focused on the syncopation of dextrous combinations of rhythm and phrase. It also enables them to concentrate on the third and final section, which contains fast cross-rhythmic patterns, with a renewed intensity.

It is a tribute to the genius of Vilayat Khan that he chose to play *Hameer*, a *raga* which most of the great performers avoid because they feel that possibilities for unfettered improvisations on the *raga* are limited. This did not deter Vilayat Khan, for whom, in his maturer years, no *raga* was beyond his creative imagination.

A *raga* is rooted with its accepted form, dimensions and grammar, but the style, the mood and the emotions of the musicians will give it a unique identity. The truly profound exposition of a *raga* is like a moment gone by, never to be repeated or revisited.

Vilayat Khan's performance at the Albert Hall was an amazing evocation and celebration of our music. In his exquisitely crafted novel, *An Equal Music*, Vikram Seth writes, 'Such music is a sufficient gift. Why ask for happiness?'

THE MAVERICK

It didn't surprise me a bit to learn that a detailed study of Saadat Hasan Manto's life has appeared in India. (We, in our part of the world, do not have time to pursue such needless tasks). The definitive study of Ghalib has also been conducted in India. I am not merely referring to Kalidasa Gupta Raza's work, but that absorbing, exceedingly well-written life of Ghalib by Pawan Kumar Verma. The growing list of Indian publications on Urdu literature (albeit in English) is impressive.

You are probably familiar with the book but I have just finished reading *Manto Nama* written by Jagdish Chander Wadhawan and translated in English by Jai Ratan. The translation is literate and, at times, clumsy: 'There is more fame than money in a literary story whereas it is the other way round in a case of film story.' Or, 'In short where direct criticism of the powers that be has no place and is intolerable.' These sentences might carry some meaning for us in the subcontinent, but to those not familiar with our language, they convey an impression of sloppiness.

Having said that, I must confess I found the book well-researched and appealing. Wadhawan had obviously 'lived and breathed with Manto' before he set out to unveil the mystery of Manto's personality.

Saadat Hasan Manto was the youngest son of his father's second wife. There were eleven brothers and sisters. His father was a stern man and Manto spent his earlier years in constant dread of his father. Jagdish Chander Wadhawan, carefully, builds up the picture of a wayward adolescent who hobnobs with the rakes and layabouts of Amritsar in their slovenly environment, but is finicky about his own surroundings. In his house in Kucha Vakilan, the young Saadat Hasan, keeps his make-shift room meticulously tidy. He arranges pen, pencil, inkpot and paper neatly before sitting down to read or write. It is ironical that though his room is lined with books he fails in his matriculation examination twice and it is only with great difficulty that he gets a pass on the third attempt, in the third division.

This humiliation rankled Manto throughout his life. My acquaintance with Manto was brief. I only met him once at his apartment in Laxmi Mansions, in the company of two budding painters, Anwar Jalal Shamza and Moeen Najmi. Manto was in his cups (was he ever out of them?) and his talk was full of juicy, Punjabi expletives. He was ranting about Krishen Chander, 'that M.A., that son of a ... thinks he is a story writer. You don't become a story writer by passing an M.A. exam. He is a ...fraud. He doesn't know, nobody knows; only one man knows how to write a story - and his name is Manto'.

Ill health dogged Manto throughout his life. He contracted tuberculosis when he was barely 21. Apart from a congenital defect in his abdomen he suffered from pulmonary and respiratory diseases; he had chest pains that made him feel dizzy; he had to have his teeth extracted before he turned 30. In a letter to Ahmed Nadeem Qasmi, he says, 'I want to write a lot, but my listlessness, my constant tiredness keeps me under its grip and will not let me work. If only I could get a little peace of mind I would collect my thoughts which keep flying like moths in the wind … I will die one day uttering if only, if only….'

A lesser mortal would have wilted and spent the rest of his life doused in balms and unguents, but not Manto, who seemed to have been endowed with a demonic will to ignore his ailments. His sardonic sense of humour led him to observe that 'a perfectly healthy man who runs a temperature of 98.4, has nothing to his credit but the cold slate of his life'. Manto's body temperature was always one degree above normal.

Wadhawan describes the tribulations of Manto's trials — five in all — with candour. He doesn't become judgmental about the bigots who conducted the trials and condemned and penalised Manto; nor does he shower praise on the judges and magistrates who acquitted him. He concentrates on the physical hardship that Manto went through while embroiled in the wrangles of the courtroom.

One case in particular, concerning the story titled *Thanda Gosht*, was tried three times. It went from the lower courts all the way to the High Court. The lower court held Manto responsible for obscene writing and awarded him three months rigorous imprisonment as well as a fine of Rs 300, declaring that if the fine was not paid he would undergo 21 days additional rigorous imprisonment.

Manto appealed. The case was moved to the sessions court where, ironically, the judge, Inayat Ullah, generally thought of as a narrow-minded prig, made a priceless comment, 'If I punish Saadat Hasan Manto, he will say that he has been punished by an orthodox, bearded man.' He acquitted Manto with a smile and remitted the earlier fine imposed on him, in full.

The authorities were not pleased and they filed an appeal in the High Court against the sessions court's judgment. The case came up before Justice Muneer, who had the reputation of being an unbiased and a fearless judge.

Manto and his lawyers must have heaved a sigh of relief. The relief was short-lived. The honourable judge pronounced that the 'leanings of the writer' had to be taken into account and not his 'intentions'. A story could not escape from being obscene if the details of the story were obscene. A story was not like a book, which could be good in some parts and bad in some parts. He declared *Thanda Gosht* to be obscene, upheld the governments' appeal and reimposed the fine.

Justice Muneer sounds like a myopic literary critic of a vernacular weekly. Ignoring his remarks that a book can be good and bad at the same time—a bland statement if ever there was one—I am curious as to what he means by 'the details of a story'? Does he mean the 'incidents' that occur in the story, or the 'language' that some characters use, or the bits of narrative between dialogue? If a story is to be judged by its 'details' then nearly every story by Salinger and Updike is obscene. And how did the learned jurisprudent perceive the difference between Manto's leanings and his intentions? Justice Muneer's judgment was hailed as a landmark on the subject of obscenity. It makes me shudder.

Manto is not the only genius in the creative world to have drunk himself to death. Dylan Thomas, in England, and Meeraji, in India, come to mind immediately. Interestingly enough, both Meeraji and Manto died in their forties. Researchers may yet discover that self-destruction reaches its culmination when you cross the age of forty.

It is easy to say that Manto drank to drown his sorrows. The world has been full of painters and sculptors, musicians and actors, poets and playwrights who, like Manto, suffered from extreme deprivation—and humiliations—but did not take to drink. Drink to Manto was like a shield he wore to protect himself from his inner broodings. In the last few years of his life he was aware that he had lost his self-esteem. He began to borrow money unashamedly; he would accept a pittance for a story without a murmur and the pittance went out to buy cheap liquor. The degradation to which he had sunk made him loathe himself. There was only one way out: end his wretched life. He had been warned, repeatedly, that cirrhosis was eating him up and that if he didn't stop drinking he wouldn't live long.

During the few sober moments he had, he wrote, 'I am feeling so depressed. I wish I could do something. But what is that something? I keep pondering over it. I feel like writing so many things but there is no time for it. I don't know what to do about it.'

But he did know. He made frequent promises to give up drinking and, on one or two occasions, he did. Manto's sister told Wadhawan that he got his small room tidied up and sat down to write, 'after arranging all the paraphernalia on his table. Many days passed happily in this manner. We would sit down unobtrusively in his room taking turns one by one. One day he said that the method was leading him nowhere. He thought it would do him good to enter the mental hospital where nobody would come to meet him. After deliberating over it for a few days he entered the hospital. This was his own decision'.

The mental hospital in Lahore, the *pagal-khana*, was anything but a hospital. It was a prison occupied by derelicts and hardened criminals whose influential relations had had them certified as insane, a few schizophrenics and some decrepit outcasts. Manto spent sometime in the *pagal khana*. Urdu literature will forever be indebted to him, for it was here that the seeds of his superb work, 'Toba Tek Singh' germinated.

'Toba Tek Singh' is a story that is perfect in its balance and its structure. Manto's narration is artless; he doesn't waste a single word in the building-up of his story. The end is so moving that it makes you reel. It is a most scathing indictment of the senselessness that prevailed on both sides of the border in the wake of partition.

Manto's other stories on partition, that he wrote in Lahore, have a frenzied flavour. The fact is that apart from some trenchant sketches of celebrities and one or two penetrating short stories, Manto's literary output in Lahore didn't have the 'soul' of his earlier, memorable short stories. Perhaps it was because he felt restless in Lahore.

His decisions to leave Bombay for Lahore was not borne out of a religious feelings. Manto didn't have any roots in Lahore; he had only lived there for two years as a young literary aspirant. Besides he was not entirely sure that the partition was a good thing to have happened. His work had been rejected in Bombay and the thought might have occurred to him that it was because he was a Muslim.

Bombay was the only place he felt comfortable in. He had a fairly large circle of friends and admirers; he knew the byways of Bombay intimately and he had written some of his best short stories in Bombay. Indeed, he had achieved his fame as a towering writer of fiction while he was living in Bombay.

He arrived in Lahore in 1948 and, soon after, began to miss Bombay. He wanted to go back and wrote to

Ismat Chughtai about it, but nothing came of it. He
ran out of the money he had brought with him; the
lucrative job he had been promised with Gidwani
Pictures never materialised. He was down and out.

In Bombay his film earnings were two to three
thousand rupees a month (a substantial amount in
those days) and he picked up a tidy sum by selling
his stories and his radio scripts. He once worked for
All India Radio and had written nearly a hundred
radio plays. Barring one or two, all of them had been
broadcast.

He had become so adept at the craft that he often
managed to finish a whole play in one sitting. He
once sat down at his desk and announced to his
colleagues that they had only to mention a subject or
a theme and he would write a play on it there and
then. They were discussing the matter when a man
appeared at the door, 'May I come in?' he enquired.
'Well, here is a theme,' said one of Manto's colleagues,
'Why not write about it?' Manto inserted a paper in
his typewriter and began to click the keys. He
finished the play by late afternoon. It was later
broadcast under the title, 'May I come in?'

Manto should have been able to make some kind of
a living out of the newly established broadcasting
service in Lahore, but the doors of Radio Pakistan
were barred to him on account of a fracas he had had
with Zulfikar Bokhari in Bombay. Some producers in
Lahore Radio were Manto's well-wishers, but they
dared not offend Bokhari Sahib. Manto remained a
persona non grata for Radio Pakistan in his lifetime.

He wrote some film scripts but the movies turned out to be flops. In any case, the movie producers in Lahore were a different breed from their counterparts in Bombay. They felt more comfortable with hacks, who danced attendance on them, and didn't mind cringing for their money. Manto was too big a name for them.

It was not just financial worries that drove Manto to despair. Until partition took place, he had always been hailed as one of the stalwarts of the 'Progressive Writers Association'. Manto hated to be branded, and in some of his writings lampooned them. The 'progressives', *en masse* denounced him as a renegade and a reactionary. The reactionaries dubbed him as a licentious leftist. And the guardians of the newly found state's morals condemned him as a purveyor of filth.

Manto lashed out. He took swipes at all his detractors. The short pieces that he wrote, more for the sake of selling them for thirty rupees (which he desperately needed every day to slake his mounting thirst for alcohol) than for any lasting purpose, are insipid and slipshod; his wit is often blunt. Manto was well past caring. In his desperation he became reckless, and his writing suffered.

Manto did not keep a diary, but sometimes he recorded his inner most feelings in a letter:

> Since long I have felt in the words of Turgenev that I am the redundant fifth wheel of a carriage. I wish I could be of some use to someone.

He was a loving father and, from all accounts, a caring and loving husband. The realisation that he was utterly incapable of looking after the needs of his wife and three daughters must have galled him no end.

Saadat Hasan Manto was a maverick who, firmly, refused to go along with any party or creed. He remained a maverick throughout his short life. We should be grateful to Jagdish Chander Wadhawan for pointing it out to us so unambiguously.

'TO CYNTHIA, FROM HER COCKER SPANIEL'

Most well-to-do homes in Pakistan have a lot of mod-cons, ornate ashtrays, excellent crystal, expensive crockery, beautiful rugs, hideous paintings, ornate lamps but no books. I do not mean the obligatory *Encyclopedia Brittannica* — in a bookshelf provided by the publishers — but ordinary, real books. When I mentioned this, casually, in a speech delivered in Saginaw, Michigan, I drew a silent round of applause. The Americans who came to talk to me afterwards said that I had drawn an apt picture of many rich American homes.

A few weeks later, that suave opinion-maker, Gore Vidal, declared that Americans 'don't read much of anything. Reading even amongst the brightest students is dead'. Another major writer, Saul Bellow, predicted that the serious novel would be a marginal phenomenon soon. What Mr. Vidal would have said about our students, most of whom never read anything beyond the summarised version of their text books, is not hard to imagine. In America they still have libraries and more: they have Barnes and Noble.

The 'Used Books' halls of Barnes and Noble, one of the best laid out bookstores in the world, is where I spend most of my time when I am in America. There are rows of inviting bookshelves that give way to alcoves which are sitting areas with pedestal lamps and comfortable chairs, and though the color of the upholstery is somewhat faded, it is quite in keeping with the second hand books.

Unlike London, there aren't many browsers. (People have better things to do at 10:30 in the morning). I gather a few books and settle down in a wing chair to run through them. After an hour or two I feel a slight sense of guilt. I look around, but I never get an accusing look from any of the staff for not having bought anything.

I know where this feeling of guilt stems from. It goes back to my childhood when my mother and my two elder sisters would drag me along to go shopping for dress material. We would arrive at a cloth shop, be made to sit down, plied with sweet fizzy drinks in spite of protest—and then time would stop. For hours the salesman would unroll bolt after bolt; each fabric was touched, stroked, fingered; its merits discussed in whispers before the price was asked. The obsequious salesman would never mention the price but smile and say, 'Whatever you wish to pay, it is your own shop respected sister.' But when coaxed, he would mention a figure which caused hands to be raised to mouth in deep shock. Looks of utter disbelief were exchanged between my mother and my sisters.

After this dramatic interlude, my mother would make an offer which seemed to me to be ridiculously low. The salesman would swear upon his mother's grave that the price he had quoted was rock bottom; in fact it was below the actual cost price, but my mother would rise, sisters falling in tow. The salesman would implore her not to be hasty, but my mother would march off saying she would look elsewhere. We would walk out of the shop leaving hundreds of yards of material bunched up in disarray. I would die a thousand deaths.

The atmosphere inside a Barnes and Noble is not as funereal as in a library. The music that you hear, softly, is usually Mozart, Schonberg or Vivaldi – and it doesn't inflict upon you as in an elevator at Macy's. I rather relish the strains of the cello as I bend down to pull out a miscellany of mis-belief, misquotation and misconstruction and learn that though biologists and zoologists have continued to deny the truth of the belief that ostriches bury their heads in the sand to hide, we still believe that they do.

The books, on the whole, are in a good condition. A few paper-backs are dog eared, but the hardbacks have worn well. Some have the owner's name in them; a few have library stamps (I once came across a book called *The Story of the Life Of Caleb Smith–Told by Himself*, with an inscription, 'To Cynthia, from her cocker spaniel', written with a calligraphic flourish. Why did Cynthia choose to sell the book to B&N?) but mostly, they are unmarked.

The only complete book I finished while sitting in the store's snug armchair was a slim volume called *Writers Revealed* in which eight contemporary writers talk about faith, religion and God. Even as I write this piece, I chuckle over John Mortimer's memory of his father, an erudite, highly whimsical barrister.

Mortimer began to write in order to have something to read to his father who had turned blind. 'He never offered me any advice at all,' says Mortimer, 'except for telling me that I should never smoke opium because Coleridge had smoked it and it caused him to have terrible constipation. That was really the only bit of practical advice I can remember him giving me.'

One of my prized possessions is a highly engaging work on Victorian poetry and the rise of psychiatry. (The price had been reduced to $1.25, less than what you pay for a pair of shoe-laces). Ekbart Fass, the author, (a professor of Humanities at a Canadian University) focuses on what Victorian critics viewed as a psychological school of poetry related to early psychiatry, and rooted in what Wordsworth called the 'science of feelings'. The chapter on Swinburne, who was lambasted as 'publicly obscene', 'ravingly blasphemous' and 'the libidinous laureate of a pack of satyrs', is most revealing.

> For many loves are good to see
> Mutable loves, and loves perverse:
> But there is nothing, nor shall be,
> So sweet so wicked, but my verse
> Can dream of worse.

The computer may not be putting books out of business in America, but it certainly has reduced our libraries to a state of meaninglessness, because they are dismally stocked and hopelessly ill-kept. Whenever there is any talk of books, people lament that in this age of CD Roms and Online, no one has time to read books. I have, actually, heard some of our technocrats suggest, seriously, that what our libraries need is not books but computers and Internet facilities.

Such thinking frightens me. How can there ever be a substitute for a book, which you can read in a bus, lying in your bed or sitting on a rock by the sea? A book allows you to explore your imagination as you interpret the author's intention. A book offers us refined delights of being a part of something much bigger than ourselves. It gives us the purified exhilaration of nuances and undertone and equivocacy and contrariety; a book gives us imagination and imagination is happiness. A computer only gives us information.

PARSING AND KENNING

No one writes a better script for comedy than our newspapers. Thus yesterday morning; *"The Mongi Bandla police post was raided following public complaints that sub-inspector Basra invited call girls to his office. When army's team reached the ASI and a girl were found in an objectionable position."*

Pray note that the scriptwriter/reporter doesn't say 'immoral' or 'indecent' or 'indelicate'; he chooses the word objectionable because he thinks that it is the correct translation of *qaabil-e-itraz* (objectionable in police jargon). He could have followed it with 'posture' or 'state', but he prefers 'position'. He knows that the word 'position' relates to rank, social standing, status, etc., (much lauded and feared in our society). He picks this word to downgrade the inspector in front of the raiding party. Also observe how, without the help of any punctuation, he has suggested that the reach of the army is long. He is good at comedy.

There was rich material on the next page. Here, too, the scriptwriter creates humour by his arrant defiance of the established usage. '*A magistrate on Sunday granted bail to the police inspector after recovery of four stolen vehicles and illicit arms from his house.*'

With a broad brush-stroke, the scribe creates a mildly hysterical situation—one of the ingredients of farcical comedy. To begin with, we are not sure whether the stolen goods are recovered from the magistrate's own house or the inspector's. Then there is the issue of bail; would the bail have been denied if the goods had not been recovered? Sunday too, plays an important part; the magistrate is not harassed by too much work; he is in a relaxed mood; he grants bail.

The report goes on: '*Even this time he managed to secure his release within 20 hours as no departmental action so far been taken against him as yet.*' Does it confound you? It shouldn't, because all it means is that the inspector is good at getting a swift release and that his department has no intention of taking any action against him. The said inspector is some kind of a Clouseau who has formed a habit of getting arrested again and again. (Even 'this time' suggests that there have been other occasions in the past).

This is what happens when you show a complete indifference to nouns and prepositions and when you do not absorb the difference between an adverb and an adjective. It appals me to note that people who write in English do not know how and when to use a preposition. Above all they should know what determiners are. It is humble words like 'the' and 'a' that suffer most in their copy.

I am not suggesting that the cub reporters — and the seasoned ones — should become grammarians, but they must be required to reach the expected standard in writing a simple report. They simply have to learn how the language works. You can see for yourself that in the case of the ever-escaping police inspector, the reporter would have made some sense if he had written, 'Even this time, the police inspector secured his release within twenty hours of his arrest. No departmental action has been taken against him as yet.' By misusing that comprehensive word 'as' (adverb, conjunction, preposition, etc) he perpetrates a howler, and reinforces the view that the sole purpose of our English newspapers is to provide mirth.

There is another myth that I want to explode. It is assumed that those who write a kind of muddled language come from schools where the medium of instruction is Urdu. In the so-called English medium schools too, grammar lessons are considered to be old fashioned. Earlier this year, the Head of the English Department at Karachi University bemoaned that pupils do not get any grammatical instructions in our 'English' schools. Most of the teachers feel that in today's world it is a waste of time to impart knowledge about parsing and kenning.

'Parsing and Kenning' sounds like a firm of solicitors, but it isn't. While 'kenning' may be considered to be archaic and outlandish, you will not be able to write with any degree of confidence unless you can parse a sentence. Kenning is a metaphysical, compound word or phrase (used in Old English) that avoids using the actual name of something, for example, 'foaming fields' for ocean and 'fur pillow' for dog. Parsing means resolving a sentence into its component parts, that is, noun, pronoun, conjunction, etc.

I grant you that there is no earthly reason for a reporter to arm himself with a full glossary of grammatical terms. He doesn't need to bother his head with acrostics and acronyms and past past participles, but once he realises that there is no contradiction between grammar and freedom of speech, he might actually understand that a preposition expresses a relation to another person or element and not a figure of speech. He might also wake up to the fact that his writing is slovenly because his thinking is muddled. (The primary concern of grammar is clear thinking.) It matters not, whether he writes 'different to' or 'different from'; what matters is that he knows when a verb functions as a noun, how to modify a noun and how a word qualifies another word.

But then, where would I find my comedic material? This is what I collected this morning. It's so priceless I wish I had made it up:

> *Shagufta was married and had two daughters but her husband abandoned her. She married for the second time but could not bear child. Her husband insisted that she must have child. Later she wrongly told husband that she was pregnant and one day she had stolen the boy.*

The piece has a heading, 'Stolen Baby Recovered'. It defies comment.

SHIATSU

All taxi drivers are garrulous. The big, burly, heavily jowled driver, who drives me from Heathrow, to Finchley, is no exception. 'You must be tired,' he says heartily. I am pooped, and unable to breath through my nose because, as usual, the long 13 hour flight has blocked my nasal passages, so I grunt and mumble something to the effect that I feel like death, hoping that it might dissuade him from striking a conversation.

He is not discouraged in the least. 'Tell you what,' he says, 'you need Shiatsu. Believe me. You don't want any of your silly medicines.'

What is Shiatsu? I asked. Some kind of a soup? Perhaps I shouldn't have asked the question. He was now fully charged to enlighten me. Shiatsu, he pronounced it shy-at-so, was a healing system. He then went on to describe the number of ailments he had suffered from: eczema, constant headaches, chronic asthma, allergies. He had tried all kinds of medicines, herbal, homeopathic, the lot, and had all but given up hope when a mate of his told him to get in touch with the Shiatsu society.

They were very good to him. They told him that they could commence the treatment on the understanding that if there was no positive results within the first three treatments, they would not charge him anything.

He was a good storyteller; he knew how to build mini climaxes. 'At first I thought it was a bit of mumbo jumbo. My wife was dead against it. She thought I was going in for some kind of a voodoo. I must say I felt a bit cagey. No stethoscope, no prescription, no medicines, you know what I mean?'

But he had had his fill of pills and jabs. The steroids he had been taking had made him lubber-like. His headaches would make him dizzy for hours. He felt there was nothing he was not prepared to do or give up.

After the first treatment he had recovery from one infection which had been suspected by Shiatsu diagnosis. His energy level which had become 'worse than a dying rat' had improved. His 'airways' had been blocked for a long time so that he had been finding it hard to breathe, but now it was different.

As the treatment progressed, his headaches, which had plagued him on almost daily basis had gone, improving his temper and the quality of his life. 'My wife who had packed me off to the attic, looked at me one morning and said, "You better come back to your bed, Mush".'

He chuckled and I wondered how often he had told the saga before. From the jovial manner in which he went on it struck me that it made no difference to 'Mush' whether his passengers were attentive listeners or not.

Five treatments is all it took and in those treatments, spread over a couple of months, his sinus congestion and the accompanying pains had disappeared. Other changes in his health had taken place. His skin condition had improved, the amount of mucus he expelled had been reduced and, for the first time, in years, he was able to breathe through his nose. 'I am a happy man, a very happy man indeed,' he said. 'Here.....' he handed me a leaflet. He had, apparently, been appointed as a roving Shiatsu rep.

Not having slept too well, I woke up the next morning with a crick in my neck and a heavy head; my nose was still clogged up. I flicked through the Shiatsu leaflet. There was a picture of a sturdy, slightly out of focus, Japanese woman pummelling the backs and forearms of figures lying face down on the floor. Underneath the picture it said, 'Shiatsu is carried out on the floor with the client fully clothed.' I toyed with the idea of ringing up the society, but the thought of lying on the floor with my clothes on was galling.

I don't enjoy shopping in London any more. The reason is that I can never find anyone to help me. Oh, I don't mean salesmen who hover over you and keep saying, 'Are you alright?' every two minutes. I mean some one who can tell me what the price of an article is. Once upon a time, there used to be snooty salesman, in morning dress, in stores like Aquascutum and Burberrys, who advanced towards you and greeted you with 'May I help you Sir?' in deferential tones. And if you replied that you only wanted to have a look around, he turned away with his nose up in the air. Nowadays, you don't see him either.

I went to a department store (in our country it is called a departmental store) the other day looking for a converter plug so that I could use my electric shaver in America. I walked the entire length of haberdashery, but couldn't spot anyone. Eventually, I tracked down a frightened looking assistant and she said she didn't know where anything was because she was on loan from 'Lingerie and Swimwear'. I'd be better off trying to find someone in 'Small Electrics'.

I wasn't lucky there either. There was a man at the pay-in counter, but he was on the telephone having a heated argument about the department's ongoing shortage of medium sized carrier bags. After what seemed like an eternity, he put the phone down, took a handkerchief out of his pocket, wiped his brow and finding me looking at him, swallowed an expletive. Before I could ask him for a plug, he got on the telephone again, 'Martin, send Barney to Small Electrics,' he ordered. 'Someone will be here with you shortly sir,' and he disappeared.

I don't see many people shopping these days. The head of Saatchi and Saatchi thinks it is because women have become bored with brands. There are too many women who want something extra to persuade them to consume, he says. They want empathy, stimulation and emotional involvement and the ad. agencies are not giving them that.

The subject is now being debated in chat shows on television. One expert says it is because people are broke and can't afford anything. Others disagree. Women get stressed out if they don't go to the shops. But shopping at today's prices makes them stressed out even more, someone else says.

I can see a big future for the Shiatsu society.

SLEEPLESS NIGHTS

Long distance air travel is one of the most tiresome trials of the 21st century, unless you are one of those fortunate passengers who, as soon as the plane takes off, unlaces his shoes and goes off to sleep.

The first class traveller is spared the sight of the lumbering hordes of economy passengers as they trundle in; the business class passenger is not that fortunate. He settles down in his not so commodious seat and, flicking through the in-flight journal, watches the endless flow of harassed women carrying babies and pushcarts; panting men, wheeling and dragging their oversized trolleys. He can see the envy in their eyes, as they look at him, and he is embarrassed, for no real reason.

The business class, euphemistically called the Executive or the Club class, is really like the 'Inter' class that our railways used to have, (a compartment that had thinly padded seats instead of bare wooden boards). The 'Executive' traveller might take comfort in the knowledge that he is not amidst the riff-raff, but he is left in no doubt that he is a second class citizen, and that the half filled glass of bubbly that he has been offered, is not vintage Moet Chandon.

There are two categories of sleepers on a plane: those who wake up when the meal trolley is wheeled in, have a full four course meal down to the last grape (how any one can have the urge to tuck into a cold platter of beef three minutes after waking up, astounds me) and go back to sleep; and those who prefer not to be woken up.

I have still not acquired the knack of sleeping on a plane. I read instead, but there comes a time when words fail to make any sense. I hum; I try to recall the melodic structure of Raga *Devgiri Bilawal*; I multiply 367 into 93 and, failing to get the right answer, toy with the idea of becoming a Buddhist monk, but it's no use; sleep still eludes me. I decide to lie back.

All airlines today have resorted to 'state of the art' technology and installed a touch system panel embedded in the arm rest. The panel has hieroglyphic symbols. If you are an Egyptologist, you might be able to decipher what m ë l Ë ø stand for; a mere mortal cannot.

After a careful scrutiny of the panel, which has nine circles, I press the one that I think will recline my seat, but nothing happens. I press another which is meant to thrust forward the footrest, but nothing stirs. I look closely at the panel to locate the knob for the stewardess, but fail to find it.

The cabin is now dark except for my reading light. All around me are blanketed figures, most of them lying in foetal position. I walk upto the galley to find two stewardesses examining each other's nail-polish. Could someone please tell me how to change the position of my seat?

The matronly Swiss stewardess, who accompanies me back to my seat, has the air of someone who has a vast experience of dealing with retarded children. 'You want your seat to be pushed back?' she asks, with studied patience, I nod. She leans over and gently touches the top right circle. The back refuses to budge. She pats the back of my seat and tries again, to no avail. She now touches a knob in the middle which is meant to move the lower portion of the chair. When nothing happens, she looks at me, apologetically, and goes to have a word with the purser.

The purser arrives; he lifts the arm rest to examine a couple of wires. He fiddles with them for a while and then, puzzled, goes away to bring another steward. By now, the matronly hostess is also back. I get up from my seat to allow the three of them some space. They push and prod the chair, kneel down and peer into all the crevices. The newly arrived steward unscrews the entire right arm and discovers a packet of chewing gum stuck underneath.

The chewing gum has nothing to do with the operation of the seat, but how did it get there? They scratch their heads. The mechanic-steward says such a thing has never happened on this plane.

They suggest that I move to another seat. The only seat available in the cabin is at the very back next to a man, who, with mouth wide open, is snoring obscenely. 'I don't think that's going to be of any comfort,' I say, now resigned to spending the rest of the night sitting upright.

The three of them exchanged a few comments in German. The purser left to have a word with the captain. The matronly stewardess, her guilt about having doubted my ability for common sense writ large on her face, asked me if I would like to eat or drink something. She was sorry I had to go through the ordeal and assured me that the purser would be back with a solution.

The purser came back with the news that the captain had agreed to move me to the first class cabin. The stewardess would bring my belongings. Would I please follow him?

There are only three other passengers in the dimly-lit beige and burgundy first class cabin, and they are dozing off. My seat glides smoothly to become a berth, but by now I am wide awake. The night is nearly over and we are only three hours away from our destination. I really ought to catch up with some sleep.

But I can't. It's the wretched pillow. Every airline, even the one belonging to Singapore (with claims of providing the ultimate sophistication in travel comfort) gives you the same standardised 10" by 8" pillow. They may have Cashmere blankets and

Wedgwood crockery, but their pillow remains the same size and weight, a small pad good enough only for a pram.

It may be right for those who know how to fall asleep, but I am a tosser and turner and when, lying on one side, I try to fix it underneath a remote part of my neck, it slips and falls on the floor.

And then there is the lighting change. There is no doubt in my mind that at some clandestinely held conference in Mycenae or Mysore, all airlines agreed that the darkened cabin during an eleven hour flight must be turned into a fully flooded jeweller's shop precisely at a time when I have, at last, succumbed to a state of stupor.

I open my eyes to the smell of freshly baked croissants. There is a sharp pain at the back of my neck and a dull, thudding sensation in my head. A freshly made-up hostess approaches me with a winsome smile, 'Good Morning Sir, did you sleep well?' Oh yes, thank you, I have had yet another sleepless night.

DO NOT BELIEVE WHAT YOU READ

Unlike other dentists, the one I have discovered in Karachi is a caring soul and deeply sympathetic to my discomfort. At the slightest twinge from me, he stops whatever he is doing—drilling or scraping or tapping the back of my teeth with lethal looking weapons—and waits, placidly, until I regain enough courage to allow him to continue.

It has not always been so. When I first settled down in Harborne, the nearest dentist was a man named Willoughby-Ouseley, so I had to be registered with him. (This was at a time when dentists too, could be acquired as part of the National Health Service). On one of the walls of his waiting room was a plaque which read, 'Breathe deeply and evenly and slowly. Lifting your feet off the footrest can relieve tension and anxiety.' It didn't matter how evenly or deeply I breathed, once I was made to get into that reclining chair, which only the dentist could manipulate, lifting my feet off the footrest didn't help one little bit.

My double-barrelled dentist must have been brought up by Scottish Presbyterians or some other puritanical sect (he wore open sandals without socks in winter as well) because he ignored all my agonised 'oohs' and 'aahs' while he was drilling a hole into my gums. He even disapproved of my grimacing. 'What's the matter? Can't take a little bit of pain?' was his pet phrase. I was so relieved when I left that neighbourhood.

I have gone through scores of dentists in my life— from the austere Willoughby-Ouesely to the kindly Dr. Shah (full of *Lucknavi* graces but quite ineffectual) to the 'peaches and cream' Rosemary Meesham (who insisted I call her Rosemary) to the heavily moustached Dr. Parekh, whose breath reeked of stale radishes. These were but a few that I visited regularly. There were others who practiced their art on my teeth. Not one of them failed to strike terror in my heart except Amjad who decided to leave England for good. The squeal of the drill and the whiff of escaping gas strikes a fear in my soul. You must have gathered by now that I am an anxious patient. Even the smell of the antiseptic mouthwash sends a queasy shiver down my spine. If you think I am a sissy, what do you call all those beefy looking men who suffer panic attacks, heart palpitations, uncontrollable shaking and blackout at the thought of a dental appointment?

I have often wondered if my phobia is rooted in past experience of others. In all honesty, that is not the case. No one, that I know of, has told me harrowing tales of how their teeth were plucked out with a pair of pliers or a string tied to doorknobs. I carry no archetypal baggage. The adults in my family never transferred their own fears of dentistry to me for the simple reason that they never visited a dentist. Why then, do I shiver every time it becomes necessary to seek a dentist's help?

I think it is the needle. As a young boy, I went through a horrendous experience of having a big wound on my arm sewn up with a six inch needle without an anesthetic. Ever since then, the thought of a needle piercing my flesh churns my stomach. On more than one occasion I have turned down offers to visit certain countries because they required me to take four injections for yellow fever and at least two for cholera. Only those who have had cholera injections know how excruciatingly painful they are.

One of my dentists, the sweet-natured, Dr. Parekh, became so concerned about causing me pain that he referred me to a periodontal hospital where they only took patients referred to by dentists. The hospital was a training ground for the senior dentistry students. The specialists diagnosed the patient's problem and the prescribed treatment, supposedly under the supervision of a specialist, was carried out by trainee-dentists, who cut their teeth (pardon the poor pun) on the patient.

It was explained to me that my teeth had to be cut into but this could only be done by doing some undercuts (whatever that might mean). The treatment lasted several days. They had to give me not one but three pain-killing injections into my gums each time, but the process was still agonising. I mention it only to point out that, for all my squeamishness, I have been subjected to many kinds of dental surgeries barring orthodontics.

Children, I believe, now go happily to a dentist because right in front of their chair is a large-sized television screen which shows Tom and Jerry cartoons. They are so absorbed in the cartoon that they do not get distracted by the bobbing head of the dentist, dressed in a Mickey Mouse outfit, looking into their mouths. The surgery smells of strawberries because the gel that has been applied to their gums has a strong strawberry flavour.

Is this futuristic stuff? My placid dentist tells me it is not. And yet when I ask him why he has never given me a strawberry or a mint-coated gel to numb my gum instead of the dreaded injections, he says, he is not absolutely sure that it will work on me. 'You are extra sensitive,' he tells me.

My dentist and I now have a pact. He has given me a solemn assurance that if, at any time during the treatment, I feel uncomfortable, I should just raise my arm and he would instantly stop.

He thinks it makes me feel that I have the control and in this way I will not be fearful. The arm-raising happened frequently during the tediously long sessions when he was digging a canal out of my dental roots. Little did he realise that I had to draw on my last reserves of energy before I gave him the nod to continue.

My dear nephew, who reads medical journals for relaxation, informs me that dentistry has now been made trouble-free. There is a spray of an air-and-powder mix that cuts out tooth decay by a process akin to sand-blasting. Unlike the conventional drill, it is virtually silent, does not require an injection AND is pain-free. Since no smell or heat is generated, and because it is more precise, it does not affect the good tooth surrounding the decay, as the drill does. Also there is now a new gel which can dissolve tooth decay like paint remover. No injection. No pain.

My dentist nods, sagely, when I talk to him about these new discoveries, but says, after a while, that we mustn't believe everything we read.

FILM STAR IS ONE WORD

W.C. Fields incurred the wrath of many people when he said, 'Any man who hates little children and small dogs can't be all bad.' We love the remark because there are occasions when we all loathe small dogs and little children.

At some time in our lives we have all had cause to inveigh against some people or some things that get our hackles up for one reason or another. Unfortunately, our bluster, our vehemence, disappears harmlessly into the atmosphere. Invective is like steam.

What is one to do then? A well-aimed dig ought to do the trick, but it doesn't; it merely enlarges the circle of your enemies. It may be best to ignore everything that riles you, but it is not possible.

I pick up a women's magazine on a flight from Karachi to Lahore. It doesn't matter what the magazine is called — *The News of the Ladies* or *The News of the Universe* — they both are of the same size; they have the same format and, almost, the same tarty-looking, bejewelled lady on the cover.

The *piece de resistance* is the spread on the centre pages. The cover girl photographed in four different, equally tasteless outfits holds forth on love, life and ambition. It will be a tough test for anyone to find a shallower piece. And for vapidity it deserves a decanter of imitation Givenchy. I quote, verbatim:

> I have been successful at whatever I have done so far, whether it is the big or small screen. Some people don't think so but I believe that prayers have a great power, and the prayers of my mother and my family are always with me. People say to me, how come you always score when those who have been at it, far longer than you, don't? I don't know the answer. It is all because of His kindness and His Munificence. I say to fellow artists: be obedient to your elders. I respect all my seniors and I pray that I never give them any cause to be angry with me.

You can see from the photographs that in spite of her efforts to pull in her stomach; the folds in her frock betray an emerging paunch. Nobody minds that. Corpulence is a national characteristic and the stars of the big or small screen wear it with a touch of pride because it suggests good health and prosperity. I remember years ago, saying to a movie director that the leading lady opposite me was pretty stout and that she ought to do something about it. The director looked at me pityingly and said that in his views she was fine, just fine, but I needed to fill myself up a bit.

The cover girl, whose name is Farah Zuby, goes on to say that she has never once asked anyone for a role. Some girls, she is horrified to learn, go to the extent of giving favours, even money, to the directors, but she is not one of them. 'Pervaiz Sahib, the director, himself offered me a role.' She then lets us into a secret; 'There are heroines who sign a film on a single phone call from directors and producers. I never do.' Oh dear.

Does she mean to say that there ought to be at least half a dozen phone calls from directors and producers before a girl should sign a contract (signing in our show business parlance is a euphemism for accepting a portion of the money agreed to be given to you); or is it that she means that offers should not be accepted over the telephone?

The mystery is unfolded a couple of paragraphs later. She is against accepting any offer on the phone without first asking about her role. If and when she is assured that it is a 'good' one, she agrees. After all, standards have to be maintained.

The centre spread of the next magazine I go through features a cover girl known as Anju (sic). No less complacent than the previous lady, she has chosen to appear in a garish ensemble that only accentuates her ungainly figure. A simplified version of her outfit can be seen in places like the Dhoraji Colony of Karachi.

Anju says she prefers to work on TV because 'it is a very *knowledgeable* experience' (sic). TV directors always brief the artistes before hand. She thinks television is a medium that can get you popularity overnight while the situation in the films is totally different. 'There are many tensions in the film industry.'

Realising that she may have said something to offend the film wallahs, she is quick to recant and declares that working in films is her passion; it does not matter whether it is an Urdu, Pushto or a Punjabi film. Her performances are always 'satisfactory' for the producers. There was no substance in the rumours spread by some 'ill-wishers' that she did not cooperate with the producers. Only once did she fail to appear on the set because she had hurt her ankle. She had learnt to dance from the best choreographers of the country and was now a very good dancer. Indeed she could challenge all the top dancers. People ran down the film industry out of spite but she would always stand by it because she was a true Pakistani.

Where, oh where do they learn to mouth such platitudes? Perhaps they are not to blame. I get the feeling that the master mind behind these magazines has hired one man who writes the copy for all the ingénues and starlets, He probably chooses their dresses too; he certainly chooses the same photographer, who excels in making them all look like would-be Mesdames of a bordello.

The biggest disservice this Sevengali does to these strutting, over-sized ladies is to bestow the status of starhood upon them. Considering that there are 156 issues (a year) of these identical magazines, there are at least as many 'film stars' that emerge and disappear into obscurity every year. Burdened with the complex of starhood, how do they cope with oblivion? It didn't take me long to find the answer.

Going through a tabloid, I came across a whole page that carried nearly 75 passport sized snapshots of women with the word 'film star' (written boldly as one word) on top of most of the photographs. They were all members of the cast of various plays, currently being staged in Lahore. So that's where they all are.

It had not occurred to me until I looked carefully at the pages that our stage is graced with so many film stars. What on earth are they doing in the theatre? Are there no films being made? Or have they suddenly realised that the theatre is the real alma mater of thespians? Interestingly enough, the epithet 'filmstar' is not attached to the photograph of any actor. Obviously, the promoters of the plays feel that they can only attract customers to the box-office if they advertise that they have so many female film stars in their company.

I still cannot comprehend why anyone appearing in a leading part in a play should wish to be billed as a 'filmstar'. It just goes to show that, deep down, we consider the theatre to be a poor substitute of the cinema. May god have mercy upon us.

AN 'ISLAMIC' ROBBERY

The Americans are fascinated by violence. Go to any cinema in the United States and you would see that the film-goers have no inhibitions about expressing their enthusiasm during the screening of a 'Rambo'. At every unspeakably bloody act they leap to their feet cheering and applauding wildly.

The carnage is a fact of contemporary film. The vividness and the explicitness of violence in Hollywood film is overwhelming. You don't have to be a Marshal McLuhan to conclude that the films and audiences of the last ten years have been obsessed, that violence is the thing they most admire and wish to celebrate.

The format is familiar. As soon as you see the main title of the film appear on the blank screen, to the accompaniment of pounding percussion music, you know you are in for unending sequences of ear splitting explosions, crashing glass and screeching car brakes.

The makers of 'commercials' make sure that they are not predictable. They know that they have to whet your appetite in about 30 seconds so they give you a funky sequence followed by the logo of the advertising company that appears without comment on the screen. Companies who promote a perfume, for example, prefer a kind of siren who looks alluring, but aloof. The advertisers go after style and if the 'style' has a touch of sin, so much the better. They know that the youth market will not accept a message that is devoid of sinfulness. An ad these days is merely a miniaturised segment of a blockbuster.

Big movies in America open on thousands of screens across the country and if they survive the first week they are regarded as a success. This is a sudden-death way of testing a film for the market. The initial audience consists of 18 to 25 year old males, the sector of society most driven to violence. The movie-makers stimulate and exploit these men with graphic, sex-ridden violence.

The horrific evidence of the depravity of the film industry is found in cult movies like 'Natural Born Killers', which includes almost a hundred fictional murders. The movie has been blamed for nearly a dozen real murders. The fourteen year old boy who decapitated a thirteen year old girl in America told his friends that he wanted to be 'famous like the 'Natural born killers'.

Some sociologists and psychologists insist that there is no provable connection between screen violence and the street. Indeed, they say, screen violence may have a cathartic effect because it drains people of their impulse to shoot or stab people.

This may be so, but you have to be a cretin or intellectually corrupt not to feel and acknowledge the connection between the screen and the world. You may not become a different person the moment you leave the cinema, but the images stacked in your mind cannot be erased with a kleenex. I cannot help wondering about the states of mind of those who go to see carnage for fun. The gibbering hysteria of a bunch of people before the barrel of a gun that they know for certain is about to kill them, can be funny only for those who derive a special thrill in watching screaming people jumping to their death when the twin towers collapsed.

We may ignore ethical postures, but we cannot ignore the fact that the box office demands blood and mayhem and there is no way that the supply can be stopped. Cult movies may be described as a romantic truth about the edge of experience, but the romantic edge portrays a chilling reality about the psyche of a mass of people for whom entertainment has no meaning unless there are half a dozen murders.

There are dissenting voices (though some tend to focus purely on the film's cinematic flaws). Academics and social commentators are outraged, disconcerted and distressed about the cult of violence, but the hard facts of economics obliterate their pronouncements. An industry that engenders billions of dollars of cash flow is not going to allow squeamish academics to interfere with its business.

The bizarre scenario is that the American predilection for violence exports incredibly well. Blade, Terminator, Matrix, Killers — violence and its accessories — have been a commonplace of global culture. Bloodshed exhilarates in Karachi and Lahore as surely as it does in Chicago.

We may not have the laser guns, the remote control missiles and the sophisticated weaponry, but our movies are pretty heavy on gore; what we lack in technology is more than made up by the excessive emphasis on rhetoric. Fat-faced, porky men rant and scream and deliver long speeches before they are mown by our Rambos in unending gun battles.

This takes place in spite of the fact that we have a fairly heavy censorship. We condone screen violence because it is supposedly committed in the name of Islam or to uphold Islamic values and Islamic justice. Those who impose censorship are least concerned with how quickly we acquire the superficialities of western styles and graft them on to our layered culture.

The heart of the matter of screen violence is that it seeks myths and forms, outside society, which offer a kind of fulfilment that ordinary life does not.

Violence is therefore portrayed (in the West) as an elitist style. Witness the last three Bond films.

The exploration of 'style' necessarily demands that all kinds of extremities be indulged as the expression of the director's desire for a totality of experience. The seductive *femme fatales* seek gratification from lacerating their lovers; the hero who saves the world (the USA) from annihilation must be beaten into senselessness before he gets the Olympian strength to destroy the all powerful heathen.

In our part of the world we don't get to see films made by better directors (Scorsese, etc), films which are indeed a critique of American society. What is doled out to us is a 'bit of bloody fun'.

The impact of such fare on our youth has been tangible. Gun-brandishing has become a symbol of macho superiority. A musician friend of mine was accosted by four, unmasked, young men in one of the busiest streets of Karachi during mid-afternoon. They poked their guns in his ribs, took off his watch, and asked for his wallet. Infuriated, that he only had two hundred and forty rupees on him, they pushed him about. My friend said he found it unbelievable that none of the passers by noticed what was going on. In utter despair he asked if they planned to shoot him. 'Do you think we can't?' one of them said, raised his gun and fired a shot in the air; everyone around scurried for shelter, including a constable who stood a hundred meters away. They then took his car keys and asked him to lead them to where it was parked.

They took one look at the car, a discoloured jalopy, and handed him back his car keys with a warning that he had better be careful about walking on a busy commercial street with so little money in his pocket.

The four masked men armed with revolvers who raided my house did not display such wit. They terrorised my wife and our two retainers, ransacked the house, took her car keys, but, before leaving, produced a miniature Quran and made everyone swear, with their hands on the holy book, that they would make no attempt at following them. It was a genuine 'Islamic' robbery.

HUMOUR DOESN'T ALWAYS
CROSS BORDERS SAFELY

One of Christopher Isherwood's first literary engagements in New York was an invitation to a PEN (poets, essessayists and novelists) Club dinner, to which he went unaware that he was expected to speak. He was called on first. Off the cuff, he told a joke about a foreigner who arrives in New York for the first time and sees a woman fall out of a high office block window into a dust bin. 'America must be very wasteful,' the foreigner exclaims, 'that woman was good for another ten years at least.'

He was given icy stares, for the club dinner was a deadly serious women's lib affair.

Isherwoods' friend and contemporary, Auden, didn't much care for Isherwood's pursuit of Vedanta, which he referred to as a mumbo jumbo. Auden once wrote a scurrilous poem dedicated to Isherwood.

> *Dear Christopher*
> *Now reviewers are singing your praises*
> *And lovers are scratching your back*
> *But, Oh how unhappy your fact is so I wish you the*
> *peace that you lack.*

W.H Auden, who was regarded as a gigantic literary figure, if only because people started putting 'esque' after his name (Audenesque), is no longer a household name. A friend of mine once heard a woman on the radio say she had never read any Auden and had no intention of doing so, and he told this to his wife, who said, 'Auden, who?'

I can top this one or rather the late Harold Lang could. During a break in a rehearsal of 'Hamlet of Stepney Green', someone said that the British who went to America to get away from the war had their own group and it was called the Audenaires. Harold, ever so quick on the uptake, said, 'Do you mean Vin Audenaire?'

I write this not to denigrate Auden, but merely to suggest that none of these stories, even if adapted creatively, could mean anything to a Burmese.

The Vin Audenaire quip is a good example of a joke that doesn't travel, but then how many jokes do travel well? We are told that laughter crosses all borders and that humour is international, but it isn't. What makes people laugh in one country doesn't, necessarily, make them laugh in another.

A lot of Chinese conversation, I am told, is ribald and when a Chinaman laughs, it's quite probably because another Chinaman has told a risqué joke. But does this help an Italian to laugh at their jokes? Definitely not.

Miles Kington writes that when he went to Hyderabad, Deccan, to attend a World Congress of

Humour, there was an exhibition of cartoons there
with one from an Indian paper on the subject of goal
keepers. It had three frames: the first one showing a
goalie and a family on the goal line; the second one
showing the goalie going out to clear a ball; the third
one showing the family having moved into the goal
and set up home there. It didn't make any impression
on him. In fact he thought it was rather tasteless. But
then there was another cartoon from *Punch* (also on
the theme of goal keepers) showing a blind goal
keeper—with dark glasses and a white stick in the
corner of the goal—leaping one way to save the ball.
Unfortunately, the ball is going the other way.
Fortunately, his guide dog leaps up and saves it.

An Indian came up to Kington and said, 'Explain to
me this cartoon from *Punch*, please. Why is it funny?'

'Well,' said Kington, 'the goal keeper is blind'.

'How do you know he is blind?' asked the Indian.

Apparently the shorthand signs used for blindness—
dark glasses, white stick, guide dog—don't work in
India because they don't have guide dogs, etc. But
even after the Indian had understood the blindness,
he didn't think the cartoon was funny.

The story told by Christopher Isherwood about the
woman falling out of a window was not entirely
crude. It merely illustrated cross cultural
misunderstandings. Imagine the foreigner to be an
Irishman and we'd all chuckle heartily. The stories
about Sikhs that circulate throughout the
subcontinent and beyond (some generously

contributed by the Sikhs themselves) can be traced to the plethora of Irish jokes.

The only criterion in international humour is that every nation has its own version of the Polack joke. The French tell Belgian jokes, the English tell Irish jokes and we tell Sikh jokes.

I have been informed that Egypt is the country where the best Middle Eastern comedy comes from. If they are putting on a big show in Syria or Jordan, they send for an Egyptian comedian.

But an Egyptian stand-up comedian, Kington tells me, came to grief recently in Libya. He had been invited to compere a big concert in Tripoli and he decided to kick off his act with a joke about a roast chicken, a waiter and a difficult customer. Halfway through the story the audience started to shout and harangue him and make distinctly threatening noises. What he didn't realise was that the word used in Egyptian Arabic for chicken is the one used in Libya for a prostitute (this could be pure apocrypha) and as rather undignified things get done to the chicken, the comedian was digging a deeper and deeper hole for himself.

Humour doesn't always cross borders safely.

IGNORANCE OF CERTAINTY

A friend I had not seen for many years invited me, a few days ago, to lunch at his farm. My friend, who is anything but a farmer, is an urbane, slightly over-worked advertising executive, and he wanted to discuss his new publication on methods of disseminating information.

When I arrived, my friend was making a pretence at tending to his chrysanthemums. He took me on a walking tour. The farm was landscaped tastefully; the fruit orchards separated from the vegetable patches by rows of thick shrubberies. It was while I was admiring his roses that his brother-in-law's family descended upon us. I think it was an unexpected visit for my friend was over-cordial in receiving them. The balding husband wore glasses which must have been loose for he kept pushing them up to the bridge of his nose all the time. The plump wife, drenched in good fellowship, showed ample promise of early obesity. There was a daughter in tow, a pigtailed, solemn looking girl with her teeth bound in braces. The good woman, as soon as she was introduced to me, looked back at her daughter and said, 'You know who uncle is, na? Let uncle hear your speech.'

There are times when I regret having developed the reputation of a dramaturge. This was one of them. The wife then turned to me, 'She is so good in acting, so good. Last week she won a prize in her school.' My heart sank, not because the prize-winner was going to declaim, but because I knew there would be a long period during which the parents would coax and the daughter would decline. Parents have an enormous propensity for showing off their offspring to newly-acquired 'uncles'. I braced myself to wait. It came as a surprise when I found out that the earnest daughter needed no further prodding. She took up a stance, held an imaginary lantern in her left hand which she waved about frantically in an effort to search for her lover in the dark, but which looked more like she was warding off an evil—and burst forth into:

O Romeo Romeo wherefore art thou Romeo.......

This line—the ultimate in the amateur hour of schools the world over, is now the bane of my life for I have seen countless schoolgirls (and boys in outlandish wigs) inflecting the word 'wherefore' as though it was 'where'. In Shakespeare's time 'wherefore' did not mean 'where' and I don't think it does today. It simply means 'why'. The lines do not make any sense otherwise.

Romeo is a Montague and Juliet is a Capulet and even those who have not gone beyond the prologue are aware that this is the problem the lovers have. The Capulets and Montagues have had a bitter feud that has gone on for generations. Juliet cannot understand why it must be that Romeo has to be Romeo. She suggests that he stops calling himself Montague, but if he won't then she will 'no longer be a Capulet'. Juliet has no inkling that Romeo is lurking somewhere in the neighbourhood. If you recall the balcony scene, Romeo at this point is hiding in the shrubbery of the garden ('orchard'). Here is the complete passage, one of the most famous in romantic drama:

> *O Romeo, Romeo! Wherefore art thou Romeo.*
> *Deny the father, and refuse the name;*
> *Or if thou wilt not, be but sworn my love*
> *And I'll no longer be a Capulet.*

Similar misconceptions continue to exist about other famous Shakespearean lines. 'Get thee to a nunnery' is a prime example. Hamlet's famous injunction to Ophelia does not imply that she takes up holy orders. The word 'nunnery' was an Elizabethan slang for a whorehouse. Hamlet here assumes a cruelty which is not in his nature; he wants to spurn Ophelia's advances with cold brutality.

Gertrude's comments on the player queen in Hamlet: 'Methinks, the lady doth protest too much' (or 'the lady doth protest too much, methinks' as it appears in the Quartos) is another line usually misunderstood by those who forget that 'protest' here means 'proclaim'. The older meaning of the word 'protest' has now assumed a different connotation. We do not say, 'I protest my right to this land.'

Older meaning of words notwithstanding, our speech today still contains so many phrases based on misinformation. I do not know where the expression 'drink like a fish' comes from, but it is used quite often. Fish, as you know, don't drink. This is because their gullets are so tightly constricted that little, if any, water goes into their stomach. The water they take in passes through their gills. It was probably a sailor who saw bubbles gurgling out of a fish's mouth.

There are far too many misconceptions deeply ingrained in our system of thinking. I would not give them up for if I were to do so, I would have to acquire a new memory bank as well. I know that 'Chop Suey' is not a native Chinese dish, but I still expect to see it on the menu in a Chinese restaurant. It was Fredric March (a brilliant conversationalist apart from being a leading man on Broadway for years) who told me that Chop Suey originated in a California mining town, in the middle of the last century, when a Chinese cook simply threw together what he had left over and called it 'Tsa Sui' which in Chinese means a little bit of this and a little bit of that.

I also like the misconception about the expression 'humble pie' (if only because I have eaten it often enough). The 'humble' in 'umble pie' was, originally, 'umble', a term derived from umbilical. The 'umble pie' eaten by the poor, a few centuries ago, included the umbilical cords of animals. To eat a 'umble pie', in the bygone days, signified poverty. When and why the 'umble' turned into humble is not known to me, but I am certain that I'd never be able to bring myself to eat 'umble' — in a pie or any other form — so I'd go on pandering to the misconstruction.

Misconstruction and misbelief plays a significant part not only in the enrichment of a language but in the framing of our perceptions as well. Take the term Epicureanism. Who would have thought that the kindly and moderate Epicurus would have inspired the name for a way of life that has become the paradigm of self indulgence and hedonism? Epicurus, historians of ancient Greece, will tell you, neither believed in, nor practised, the immodest pursuit of pleasure at all costs. He did propound that happiness is the *sumum bonum* of life, but he was not a sensualist. Indeed, he is said to have called for prudence and moderation as well as temperance in sensual pleasure.

Well, what do you do if someone says, 'Eat drink and be merry?' Do you say it was not Epicurus but Appolodours or Adolphous or Aristophanes. Of course not. The notion of Epicureanism cannot be transferred to Aristotelianism. Similarly, the entire romance — and with it a certain archetypal pleasure — goes out of the window when I learn that Delilah did not cut Samson's hair.

There are scores of almanacs and encyclopaedias which give you information; there are other books about odd facts and little known truths. I do not recommend them. I think we need to cherish some commonly accepted fallacies if only for the sake of cultural continuity. People who hold on to concepts — and concepts are beliefs, at times — without regard for scientific evidence, should be allowed to do so. Ignorance of certainty is a nice, warm feeling.

LANGUAGE THAT CONCEALS LANGUAGE

The language of diplomacy has always been double-edged. Speech, as Talleyrand said, is given to man, to conceal his thoughts. Take the lead story in your morning newspaper which tells you that 'there has been a full and frank exchange of views' between the Indian and the Pakistani foreign ministers. What it means, actually, is that there is total disagreement between the two sides, but they dare not announce it.

English is perhaps the only language that can cope with diplomatic equivoque. Connor Cruise O'Brien, the redoubtable Irish writer and diplomat, once recounted in a television interview, that a U.N. French interpreter was quite out of his depth when he translated a British delegate's carefully phrased speech on self-determination for Cyprus as 'When Her Majesty's Government talks about "independence", it clearly means "independence" and ...ahem...not independence... '. I recall an equally priceless comment made by Anthony Eden, after Britain invaded Egypt in 1956: 'Far from being at war,' Eden said in the Commons, 'Britain and Egypt are only in a state of armed conflict.' Such gems are rare to come by.

Language is not necessarily a means of communication, not when it comes to parleys between nations because both sides, like Humpty Dumpty, use a word to mean exactly what they choose. Nothing illustrates the meaninglessness of language better than the Theatre of the Absurd. It deliberately attempts to renew the language of drama in order to expose the barrenness of conventional speech. Ionesco's *The Bald Soprano* is a classic example.

It has long been felt by dramatists who are popularly referred to as avant garde, that stereotyped language, which is made up of nothing but clichés and slogans has atrophied and has been degraded into a mere conventional token of human intercourse. Playwrights like Beckett and Ionesco, who are concerned with genuine meaning and emotion, have demonstrated again and again that conventional stage speech has ceased to be the expression of anything alive or vital. Lucky's famous speech in *Waiting for Godot* is soaked in the colour of the language of philosophical argument, but it is a flood of gibberish, thus making a mockery of bombastic, scholastic discourse.

The dialogue in Ionesco's *The Lesson* becomes divorced from the real action in the play. Both the professor and the pupil go through a repetition of school-book phrases, but behind this smoke-screen the action of the play takes an entirely different course, culminating in the final moment when the professor plunges his knife into the pupil's body. It is a dialectical contrast to the pointlessness of the meaning of the lines. In an essay, Ionesco says:

> As our language becomes increasingly divorced from real life, our culture no longer contains ourselves or only contains an insignificant part of ourselves — and forms a social context in which we are not integrated. The problem thus becomes that of again reconciling our culture with our life by making our culture a living culture once more. But to achieve this end we shall first have to kill the respect for that which is written.... it becomes necessary to break up our language so that it may become possible to put it together again and to re-establish contact with the absolute, or I should prefer to call it, multiple reality.

Reality to Ionesco is multiple, complex, many dimensional and exists on a number of different levels at one and the same time. In conventional drama every word is supposed to mean what it says, the situations are clear-cut, and at the end, all conflicts are tidily resolved. Ionesco, Becket, Adamov, Artaud et al..., the major contributors to the Theatre of the Absurd, make a defiant rejection of language as the main vehicle of the dramatic action so that they can carry out an onslaught on conventional logic and conventional thinking. They want to penetrate to deeper layers of meaning and to offer a more complex picture of reality. They avoid the simplification (of the realistic dramatists) which results from leaving out all the undertones and inherent contradictions of any human situation.

The dissolution of language has preoccupied most of the serious playwrights of the 20th century, simply because they wanted the world to know that most of the (logically arrived at) conclusions are mere rationalisations of emotive impulses. Reality, they feel, can never be explored through conventional language, which only obeys the arbitrary conventions of grammar. Not everything we say means what we intend it to mean. The real effort must be to penetrate to the content of thought, which is masked by grammatical rules and conventions. The sense of the absurd is what makes mankind survive.

Man has been, and is, unable to understand the world in all its hopelessness and absurdity. Communication between human beings is, often, impossible. Complex reality, as we are well aware, exists on a number of different levels at one and the same time. It can only be conveyed by being acted out in all its intricacy. The theatre, therefore, (and not literature) is the only instrument to express the bewildering nature of the human condition.

Waiting for Godot is one of the greatest masterpieces to emerge out of the movement known as 'Theatre of the Absurd'. It is a play which has posed the question that has been debated for half a century and will go on being debated: does Godot stand for God or is he the ever elusive tomorrow, man's hope that something will happen that will render his existence meaningful? It is the impossibility of ever reaching a conclusive answer that gives the play its poetic power.

In a wide number of social circumstances some things have changed considerably. Television and Radio presenters used to be paradigms of genteel politeness and probity; today they have to be cocky and brash, and be able to speak with a Cockney or Geordie accent (in our case the most ill-educated Urdu accent). There are other changes; the answer to something as straightforward as 'how are you?', used to be 'fine thanks, and you?' has fallen out of favour. It is now *de rigeueur* to say 'absolutely knackered, absolutely..' To say that you are 'fit as a fiddle' or 'couldn't be better', implies that you have nothing better to do than to play with your dumb bells. 'Absolutely knackered' might suggest you are obsessed with your tiredness, but it doesn't not commit you to further conversation and it effectively conceals your real feelings.

Curiously enough, it is all done through language, even though it is language that conceals language. The 20th century excelled in creating the awareness that language reveals as much as it conceals. The world, meanwhile, continues to be harsh and ludicrous, and as difficult to interpret as reality itself. Amidst the ideologies, which are pursued with equal fervour and equal futility, the human condition continues to remain, dare I say, 'absolutely knackered.'

LET'S PLAY CULTURE

Hypocrisy is a part of our cultural upbringing. Let me illustrate: a few years ago, when the Taliban wantonly destroyed the Bamiyan Buddha, we felt bad, but not bad enough to make any serious protest. What's more, many of us had a twinge of guilt about feeling bad.

We have been brought up to condone the smashing of idols. In all our primers, Mahmood Ghaznavi's forays into Somnath and the destruction he caused to the idols of its temples, have been written up as feats for the glorification of Islam. We become het up when we learn that, on the other side of the border, some historians describe Mahmood Ghaznavi as a marauder, whose sole aim was to plunder the wealth of Somnath.

Pray consider another scenario. We don't really mind if some of our 'misguided' young men become involved in the learning of music, but we take an exception if our young women do. Again, we don't make too much of a fuss if men decide to paint nudes, but we bristle and fume if young women do. The fact is that the condition of being a male or female determines the form of culture we are allowed to imbibe.

True, some middle and upper middle-class girls show an interest in the learning of music and their well-to-do parents, grudgingly, (sometimes willingly) employ male tutors to visit their homes, but they do that only to indulge their daughters' 'fondness' for music. Music is not something that a girl is allowed to pursue professionally.

The problem lies with the word 'professional'. It has been embedded into our psyche that the profession of music and dance belongs to a different breed of people, a breed with whom the 'decent folk' have no truck. Music and dance are, therefore, considered to be lewd, worthless pursuits.

Oddly enough, the taboo extends to the *Meerasees* as well. The *Meerasees* (preservers of heritage) who are hereditarily — and professionally — committed to singing, do not allow their women to perform in public. They have no compunction in instructing girls (commonly known as prostitutes) in the art of singing, but they forbid their own women to learn the craft.

The late Salamat Ali Khan, a colossus amongst the subcontinental musicians, once confided in me that one or two girls in his family could sing the most complicated phrases of the Raga *Maluha Kedara* with such command and ease that, as a learner, he was often put to shame. They had, naturally, acquired the facility while listening to the young Salamat Ali being put through his paces. Had they shown any desire to be present during his lessons, they would have been given a hiding. His father was a man of strict principles, he told me, not without a touch of pride.

In the days when I ran a Dance Academy, headlines often appeared in jingoistic Urdu papers accusing me of destroying the moral fibre of our society. Since I had sold my soul to the West, I was instigating a well thought-out plan to incite *sharif* young girls to take up dancing in public. It is not easy to translate this word. Suffice it to say that in our social context a *sharif* is a person who doesn't succumb to what is considered to be louche and ignoble, and he certainly does not take up a profession that is socially unacceptable.

The scenario has not altered that much. Within the boundaries of Islamic ideology which, officially, determines our cultural guidelines, it is clearly understood that whatever went on in the pre-Islamic period is to be rejected outright. All such activities (classical dance etc,) are regarded to be alien transgressions on our Islamic culture. This became the official state policy in the eighties. And yet even during the 'dark decade', classical dance was performed — and it still is — on the make-shift stages of five star hotels and the small theatres of Alliance Francais and the Goethe Institute. The most ludicrous phenomenon has been the unfettered growth of the lascivious 'film' dance.

The 'culture' game was first played in the columns of *Zamindar* soon after the Great Leader's death. The worthies, who contributed to the paper, proposed that henceforth anyone who wanted to write, paint or sculpt should 'Pakistanise' himself, that is to say, he should begin everything in the name of the Almighty, and end with a prayer for redemption.

Perhaps it was in the wake of this furore that the newly established Broadcasting Service of Pakistan decided that instrumentalists and singers should not perform ragas that had Hindi and Sanskritic names. *Shiv Ranjani, Hem Kalyan, Anand Bharion, Ram Kali,* etc, were chucked out of the window.This was a time when *Aiman* (considered, for some reasons, to be a properly circumcised raga) reigned supreme. *Ghazals, geets, taranas,* Iqbal's hortatory verse, were all set to the *Rag Aiman.* The initiators of this move probably thought that they were sowing the seeds of a new 'Pakistani' culture.

But it didn't work out; and slowly, but surely, the *Jai Jai Vantis* and the *Bageshwaris* crawled back into the musical repertoire of singers. You cannot erase 'centuries of memories' by imposing a new mode of artistic expressions. We enjoy and cherish music not just because the singer is skilled, but because he sings a raga that is present in our unconscious. Our appreciation of classical music is archetypal.

We are playing the 'culture' game again. I have been reading reports about the meetings, which are going on in the corridors of power to coordinate and formulate the ideological aspects of a new cultural policy. Apparently, UNESCO too, is involved. The UNESCO involvement, I presume, is only confined to the restoration of monuments. I shudder to think what the new edicts would be.

In our part of the world, no two people can ever come to terms on the definition of 'culture'. Culture is perhaps the most amorphous word. We either equate culture with high-falutin learning or look upon it in terms of speech, manners and eating habits.

We admire looking at the bust of a Moenjodaro priest because we feel an atavistic thrill. Are we ever going to accept that our culture has been culled out of the multi-civilisational ethos of South Asia? Even if we think it is, we dare not profess it; and this is what give rise to a hypocrisy which is now deeply ingrained in our make-up. It is just as well that we have turned this hypocrisy into a kind of resilience.

NEW YORK, NEW YORK...

Walking through the downtown streets of Manhattan, it occurred to me that every fourth shop now sells food. The glistening on spare ribs in Chinese take-aways outshines the sheen on a seargent-major's boots and is quite revolting. There are new restaurants everywhere, offering fake French or fake Italian food at astronomical prices and smart new food shops selling limited editions of olive oil guaranteed to be so virginal that no male is supposed to have set eyes on them. As for the price, you would probably pay less for the Dead Sea scrolls.

Manhattan seems to be thriving on the threshold of a new kind of expensiveness. Rent and property values have never been higher; cosmetics have never been more cosmetic. Everyone wants to do away with fashion (to be fashionable is considered *déclassé*) but in their attempt to be 'unfashionably' chic, they hope to create a fashion. It's not just the women; men too, strut about in their newly coiffed spiked hair, wearing $200 dollar designer ties over baggy safari trousers. A two day stubble seems to be a must with this outfit.

There has always been money in New York, but I have not seen it chasing goods so relentlessly. Is it the aftermath of 9/11? There are long waiting lists for specially created bidets and carved fireplaces, mahogany shoe trees, and Italian finials. You can order a swizzle stick for $350 — and wait.

The well-heeled Manhattanites, unless they go to see a fight at Madison Square Gardens, rarely venture to go downtown beyond 42nd Street. They would rather not be seen shopping at Macy's (which happens to be on the 34th Street) even though it claims to be the world's largest department store. But Macy's 'White Sale' is an event that the well-groomed women of the Dakotas and Park Avenue find difficult to resist. They put on dark glasses and wipe off their lipstick and thus, disguised, mingle with the plebeians in the all-in fun of snatching counterpanes and fleecy towels from each other's hands.

From the 34th Street downwards, there are thrift shops and discounts emporiums with mounds of cast-off clothing, soft furnishings, reject china and counterfeit, designer-label bargains. Women with peroxided hair, black women with false nails glued to their stubby fingers, fish out a pair of trousers or a cardigan, examine it minutely before spreading it across their chests in front of a mirror. Not pleased, they go back to the mound and start digging all over again.

Elsewhere, there are street markets. On the corner of every block, goods are piled high on cut price barrows: millions of watches and sunglasses, rings and bracelets — and talismans. The black men, who stand behind the barrows, have a hurried manner because they know that they can be chivvied off any moment for crowding the pavement.

The outcasts of society, dubbed locally as bums, are no longer confined to the Bowery. They are everywhere, outside swank Madison Avenue galleries, Fifth Avenue hotels; on the steps of the grand library and even outside the entrance of Radio City Music Hall. They don't beg; they walk slowly with a vacant look in their eyes. They have no destination. Occasionally they rummage into a trash bin.

The newspaper kiosks on Lower East Side that also sell phone cards and peanut packets, chewing gum and chocolate slabs, soda and coke, and now, *paan masala* and *paans* are, more often than not, manned by that enterprising fraternity known as the Patels. They are the left-overs. Their predecessors, who began life similarly, moved on to own hotel chains in North Carolina and Texas. Times were different then, one of the Patels told me. Today he and his rotund wife are on their feet for ten hours or more. The husband and wife have a permanently tired look on their faces.

The affluent New Yorkers spend vast sums on sable capes and ivory bird-cages; the rest of the Americans watch gamblers making or losing vast sums on television. The latest craze is a tele game called 'Texas Hold 'Em', in which any player at any time can put all his money in the pot. It's also called 'All In'. The game has stormed across television and computer screens and given poker a boost that it has never known before. Where else, but in America, can you win 2 ½ million dollars in a poker game?

A revolutionary new camera technique enables you to see the player's cards through a window on the table. A player who is dealt what is called a 'nothing hand', looks at his cards and silently works out the mathematical possibilities measured in thousands. Is he going to bluff? How successful will his bluff be? The viewer is hooked. He watches goggle-eyed as the player bets a million dollars on the flip of a single card.

Middle-brow New Yorkers are concerned that the world doesn't like America. An increasing number of people are beginning to feel that they don't need the god-damned world. Others, innocently, wonder why. It's this lot that attends lectures and seminars in which tweed-jacketed, bow-tied experts tell them why people do what they do. And when they learn that those who use a four-wheel drive just to go to the supermarket do so in order to hide their impotence, they feel they have learnt a thing or two. America has always been in awe of psychology.

My friend Ann Farber, a teacher-turned literary agent, tells me that most of the Upper East Side New Yorkers now feel the urge to acquire some kind of a guru, a cultural anthropologist, if you like. They think they need to learn about themselves because sometimes their behaviour doesn't make sense to them. They want someone to tell them why they get lured by certain words.

There are gurus galore in New York and I am not counting the psychoanalysts, or the Maharishis. Of the Eastern pundits only the Dalai Lama disciples have a good trade, but marketing advisers, college professors, Rabbis and Monsignors don't do badly either.

The highest paid Guru is the Frenchman, Clotaire Rapaille, once a former French embassy cultural attaché, but now a naturalised American. Since taking up residence in America, he has become the darling of big American companies like Ford and AT&T. He advises them on the importance of sub-text in their ads. Even presidential candidates have sought his counsel on how to appeal to the American public. Rapaille does not mince his words. Sometime ago, he said in an interview that America was an adolescent culture, 'Right now the world needs parents and the world's parent is the US and it is an adolescent.'

Ann Farber agrees.

OH FOR A SWIZZLE STICK

The most tedious aspect of air travel in America is the waiting period between connecting flights. You have time, oodles of time, to kill. The airport designers, aware of this plight, have been astute enough to install scores of inviting stores and stalls, thereby creating an itch in you to buy a gift or to treat yourself. I have taken countless turns among the boutiques and nifty little shops that now inhabit every airport from Saginaw to Sacramento.

It speaks well for my persistence that knowing the trite selection on display, I first head for the bookshop. Going past the circular tables with stacks of John Grishams and Stephen Kings, you come across revolving stands adorned with glittering paperbacks, either with a naked couple entwined on the front cover, or a nubile sprawled on satin sheets. The shelves, when you circumvent these stands, have similar books except for their covers, which haven't quite got the same lamination.

Airport bookstalls have two kinds of books: pulpfiction and what school masters refer to as

'improving books'. Apart from buying a *New Yorker*
—hard to locate amidst such periodicals as *Handy
Man* and *Hard Porn*—I do not remember having
actually bought a book there. Wearily, I leave the
bookstore to go past The 'Tie Rack', the 'Juice Bar',
the sheepskin stores to find myself in front of the
'Gadget Corner'.

The whole idea of a Do-It-Yourself outfit is to induce
in you the feeling that you are going to spend your
money on something really useful. I fall into the trap
again and again. There are impenetrable packs of
plastic objects welded to a cardboard back, like an
all purpose glue or a bottle opener that doubles up
as a toe-nail clipper, I always feel a tinge of
excitement before taking a close look at corkscrews
and swizzle sticks. I am the world's most committed
non Do-It-Yourself man: I have never been able to
put a nail into a wall without bending the nail,
ruining the wall and damaging my thumb. Yet, my
pulse begins to race when I look at the sleek, rubber-
handled hammers; and I begin to dream of a patio in
which the trelliswork has been created entirely by
myself.

There are innumerable sets of drills and screwdrivers
and apple corers, indeed all the things which you
never knew you needed but now that you have seen
them you wonder how you ever managed without:
the mug with a concealed cache for depositing the
tea bag, the striped criss-cross belt that stops your
suitcase from ripping apart on the conveyor belt, the
lovely, egg-shell white electric plug adapter
guaranteed to fit into any socket from Ulan Bator to

Ulster. (In actual fact, my little plastic bag in which I keep my toiletries has three different adapters, none of which worked in Dade County so, I remained unshaven until I bought a new electric shaver). I move on to the alarm clock section.

Other than collar stays, which I forget to take out of the shirt before it goes for a wash, I have bought more alarm clocks than most people buy packets of crisps. This is after the advent of the Quartz era. Before that, there was the old-fashioned 'time piece' which clicked noisily and sounded like death knell and never went wrong. Quartz clocks and I don't have an understanding: they stop at will, and the sound of their alarm, out of deference to musicality, is so faint that I am up most of the night for fear I won't hear it. The last gadget-clock I bought was in Cleveland, Ohio. It used to produce a distorted female voice, which announced the time on the East as well as the West Coast. After a while I got so fed up with the voice that I gave it to my cook who was mightily pleased because he thought it would help him learn English. He left one day to attend a funeral, and never returned. I have no way of finding out how he is getting on with his English.

I wonder if there is anyone anywhere who hasn't succumbed, at one time or another, to the lure of the gadget. A gadget is a toy we all want to play with. Gadgets vouch shortcuts, ease, and magic. They appeal to the most vulnerable side of our lives and they hold the promise of a more fruitful life until we begin to use them. My own experience is that they lead to frustration and disillusionment. I tried a runner bean shredder and it turned the beans into a shapeless mess. I tried a potato chopper and it reduced the objects it was supposed to be chopping into a grey pulp. All the shredders and peelers and egg separators that I ever bought ended up gathering rust in a drawer.

I put all my gadgets in kitchen drawers. Here, in our part of the world, our kitchens may not be equipped with honey twirlers or dough cutters or a variety of whisks, but there is one gadget that has found its way in — the microwave. We use it to heat the leftovers in the fridge. In the west, the microwave is an icon; the entire family depends on it to support its gastronomic existence. I must admit I have never had a tasty meal cooked in the microwave.

It would be futile to calculate the number of hours I have had to kill (in Lahore and Islamabad) before my flight is called. Our airport concourses do not have distractions; there are no arcades, no popcorn kiosks and no shoeshine stands. The only thing to do is to sit in one of the unbroken chairs and stare. I used to read a book but it did not help. Someone would approach, apologize for disturbing my study, if I didn't mind, and begin a banal conversation. I minded very much, but I have been too well brought up to have been dismissive. On one occasion, the book was taken out of my hand, its title examined, a few pages flicked through before it was returned to me with the moronic witticism. '*Aap itne dublay patlay hain aur itni bhari kitaaben parhtay hain*' (You are so light of weight and yet you read such heavy books).

Oh, for a swizzle stick.

PUNCTUAL OR INTELLECTUAL?

I have often wondered why we are so committed to being unpunctual. Is it laziness? Or is it because we believe that time is a philosophical concept and that it has no relationship to the hour of appointment? People say they are sorry if they are late and think no more of it. The three most used expressions in Urdu (or Pushto and Punjabi) are 'Sorry, Jee', 'Sorry, yaar' and 'Sorry, Sir'.

The word 'Sir' crept into our speech some decades ago, as a result of a hangover from the military rule, that we have never quite shaken off. It may carry overtones of deference and servility, but more often than not, it is used in a derisory manner. It does not have to be attached to the male gender either. Many ladies in a position of authority are addressed as 'Sir'. The only Madam in the country was a singer of considerable repute who refused to take the slightest notice of the fact that a Madam in the late 20th century was not a high class dame, but one whose connections were more with the boudoir than with breeding.

I digress. Our speech these days is not just a mixture of two or three languages; it is a mingle mangle, reflecting our thinking which is hybrid. We speak like half-breeds. I offer two examples; the first a conversation overhead in a plane, travelling from Karachi to Lahore:

> *Main vaisay bohat* careful *hoon magar kya hota hai* sometimes, you know *kutch aisa* I feel the pressure *ke jaisey aap ki* request, if it is rejected *to phir insan* aakhir, *you know* kutch ghabrah sa....yaani we are all suckers yaar.......

And this one from a television programme:

> *Yahan jitney larkay – girls bhi, hain in sub ko hum voh opportunities......*I mean *in ke liyay* we want to open their eyes *mutlab in ki* technical awareness *ho jai ke jub yey kisi* different environment *main pohnchen to in ki* approach...

Was this the language that this worthy (talking of an international academy in Islamabad) learnt at his mother's knee? I cannot imagine it. But he grew up, as so many others have, choosing to express himself in a bastardised admixture of English and whatever tongue he prefers to call his mother's.

The loss of intellectual curiosity is one of the most damaging aspects of our existence today. 'Intellect' and 'intellectual' have become disparaging words. We seem to regard intellectuals as impractical people, far removed from reality, existing in a universal space and not bound by national identity.

An intellectual does not live in a void; he has a nationality and a native language and a tradition. Even so, he needs to be questioning and at times – skeptical.

An intellectual needs not oppose for opposition's sake. But he needs to ask questions, making distinctions, restoring to memory all those things that tend to be overlooked in the rush to collective judgment and action.

Ours is not the only country where the nationalist parties have degenerated into coteries and cliques. Look at India which has long been ruled since independence by a secular nationalist party. Today there are strong Hindu groups who assert that they have a holy duty to bring back the glorious *Ram Rajya*. In Egypt and Tunisia, there are so many Islamic groups and they claim to have a mandate granted them by the urban poor and peasants of the countryside, to restore and reconstruct the Islamic past. They are willing to fight to the death for their ideas. Their chants are dogmatic and populist.

The task for the intellectual is not to deny these groups their right to pursue their cause, but to point out that simply to say 'Islam is the way' is not the answer. Islam is a religion and it is the faith and identity of a vast majority of people. But there are widely divergent interpretations of Islam. As Edward Said points out: 'Islam of the rulers is one thing, but Islam of a dissenting poet and sects is another credo. And who but the intellectual will stand up to the charismatic demagogues to face the challenges of

women's rights, of modernity itself, and the
challenges of non-Islamic minorities?'

This is a major question for the intellectual today.
Does the fact of nationality commit the individual
intellectual to the slogans of a political meeting for
reasons of national patriotism? Or, can he dissent?
And what is his fate if he does?

But where does punctuality come into all this? Well,
quite a few intellectuals I have known are notoriously
unpunctual. The trouble with being punctual is that
there is no one there to appreciate, and, as Bob
Monkhouse says, if you are punctual people think
you have nothing better to do. I have found this out
to my cost.

PUNCTUATION — A MATTER OF TASTE?

There are times when I wonder if the battle for good English hasn't been lost for all times — at least in the subcontinent. The howlers that I come across are becoming almost unbearable. Not so long ago, I received a letter which was full of 'complements' (sic). The second para read: 'I feel rightly convinced that your artful personage shall perpetually endure to actuate your fanciers for the times to come. Please accept my passionate complements.' He then went on to say, 'May Almighty grant you the cogency to accomplish the aggrandised obligations.'

For a moment I was nonplussed, then I realised that my well-wisher felt — perhaps quite rightly — that I did not have the logical capacity to achieve whatever artificially enhanced obligations I had been entrusted with. Or did he mean something else?

The letter-writer has picked a few words and pieced them together without giving any thought to what they purport. Stringing words together is the first step towards articulation. Most of us do it haphazardly without any regard to grammar.

Words move; music moves
Only in time...

says Mr.Eliot, but he also warns that:

Words strain, crack and sometimes
break under the burden, under the
tension... Slip slide perish
Decay with imprecision... Shrieking
voices... scolding or merely chattering
always assail them...

Everytime I look at our newspapers I am appalled at the gross disregard of logic in the coverage of 'stories' (as the journalists call their pieces). Grammar is logic. Logic helps make clear the grammatical relations between parts of a sentence or a paragraph. Logical and grammatical principles are the same. Years ago I wrote a piece on this subject. I reproduce it here, unabashedly.

My father, who taught English most of his life, once told me that the finest grammarian he had come across was his schoolmaster, Sardar Kharak Singh. Way back in 1897, Kharak Singh told his class that there were only six stops: comma, semicolon, colon, full stop, question mark, and exclamation mark. The work of three of them - full stop, question mark, exclamation - is so clear that mistakes about their use can hardly occur without gross carelessness. The three stops (,) (;) (:) are tones rather than stops, each directing us to pause for so many units of time before proceeding.

The work of punctuation is mainly to show or hint at the grammatical relation between words, phrases, clauses and sentences, but it is not always so. Fowler rightly points out that in two sentences of nearly similar pattern, one of which has its parts separated by commas, the other by semicolons, there can be a difference accounted for by the intrusion of rhetoric. Logical writing, he suggests, is vastly different from rhetorical writing. If logical sentences help to make clear the grammatical relations between parts of a paragraph, the rhetorical sentences contribute to emphasis and heightening effect. When logic becomes rhetorical the language becomes heightened.

I begin to moan the absence of teachers like Kharak Singh. Here is a passage I spotted in an English daily which claims to have all the hi-tech resources at its command:

> he said that what he is doing is nothing and why police is not doing their work properly. He went on to assert that when things come to pretty pass noisy pillars of society start making speeches about how they will change face of the earth...

I showed this incredible piece of literature to a few friends and, curiously enough, no one was surprised. Indeed, one of them produced his own collection of 'colourful' writing and, I must admit, some of it was far more hilarious. One expert in social sciences staunchly defended this kind of journalese. 'Who cares about past and participles?' he said, 'this is our style, this is the Pakistani way of using the language.' Long live anacoluthon—is all I can say.

Sardar Kharak Singh may or may not have heard of H.W.Fowler, but he made sure that his pupils soaked up adverbial and adjectival clauses, participles, prepositions — and punctuation. A classic example he drummed into his students was this sentence:

> The master beat the pupil with a strap.
> The master beat the pupil, with a strap.

The comma has turned a matter of fact statement into an indignant statement. The strap, we understand from the comma, becomes a lethal instrument.

The value of the comma is well-known - or is it? In today's prose it is omitted as often as it is inserted. Too many commas are like too many cooks. And what of the full stops? We would all do well to heed Fowler's advice:

> It is a sound principle that as few stops should be used as will do the trick.... stops are not to alter meaning but to show it up.... Full stopping that is incorrect is also unpardonable. The objection to full stopping that is correct is the discomfort inflicted upon readers, who are perpetually being checked like a horse with a fidgety driver.

Dickens and Trollope certainly do not believe in using the full stop as a device; they sometimes exasperate you by offering a sentence that keeps on prolonging itself by additional phrases, each joint of which gives the readers hopes of a full stop. We are happy with them because the power of their narrative matches the magic of their storytelling. But what about the following sentence? The author is an American.

> Here may still be seen by the watchful eye the Louisiana heron and smaller egret, all that rapacious plume-hunters have left of their race, tripping like timid fairies in and out the leafy screen that hides the rank jungles of sawgrass and the grisly swamp where dwells the alligator, which lies basking, its nostrils just level with the dirty water of its bath, or burrows swiftly in the upper earth to evade the pursuit of those who seek to dislodge it rope and axe that they may still its hide to make souvenirs for the tourist who, at the approach of summer, hie them north or east with grateful memories of that fruitful land.

Phew! Punctuation is also a matter of taste.

I can understand the contempt our reporters feel for such things as a comma or a colon; they are probably in a hurry to file their stories. What I find inexcusable are the solecisms to be found in the political and literary columns. The slipshod writing in our newspapers has obscured the language into something trite and meaningless. When we mutilate a language we debase ourselves.

CULTURE, COLONIZATION AND FORSTER

It is now an accepted axiom that literature should not be studied in isolation from its social and political contexts. The approach to set a literary work in the ideas, conventions and attitudes of the period in which it was written is, I believe, called historicism. (there is now New Historicism, which focuses on the intertexuality of literary and non-literary texts, but that is another issue)

Those who are against historicism feel that critics are not really capable of gauging the conventions and attitudes of a certain period because they appraise cultural values of that period with today's sensibilities. Critical practices that explore the functioning of culture are often amorphous.

In the last fifty years there has been a great deal of argumentation about culture. Is culture the outcome of a whole way of life? Or is it simply the selected highlights of a society's most intellectually, or artistically enlightened citizens? Is it the best of a civilization, or is it a conglomeration of disparate and antagonistic forces which reflect the vibrancy and the vitality of a society at a given moment?

If you were to look upon the areas of mass culture and take as its texts newspapers, magazines, pulpfiction, film, television, racy songs, it would not take you long to come to the conclusion that most people are influenced by what is known as popular culture. It may not be your cup of tea but you cannot ignore the fact that the majority of people tend to gravitate to those forms of expression known as *awami*.

But if I were to say that culture is a body of values, transmitted from the past to the future through imaginative works, I would be dubbed as a recluse and a snob who is unable to see that culture is the totality of human habits, customs, traditions, monuments artefacts etc. — and that culture is the throbbing force that governs a community or a nation's behaviour.

Does culture generate sensibility and taste? I doubt it. It is true that when culture becomes a mode of perception concepts like sensibility and taste evolve, but in countries like ours — dominated by ideological concerns rather than cultural — individuals alone worry about matters like taste. In our society the taste that we profess publicly is more often than not, in conflict with what we cherish in our privacy.

Films, television, internet and a whole range of technological devices for the distribution of images and information call into question traditional standards and accepted forms. In the face of its threats our younger audiences—who like to reject traditional modes—develop a sense of guilt because they dare not openly reject traditional pronouncements. What they learn then is not a new sensibility but hypocrisy.

I grew up under an education system devised by the Empire builders. Its main aim was to establish superiority of the British in every field. I remember being awestruck when one of my primary school teachers told us that the streets of Britannia were made of glass. *(Bartanya mein sheeshay kee sarkin hotee hain).*

The colonizers did not hesitate to use literature to legitimize their power. The role of Shakespeare in schools (and universities) was to promote Englishness and to justify the principle of hierarchy. Shakespeare's Henry V asserted the value of English monarchy. As far back as 1878, Bulwer-Lytton, a Viceroy of India, had expressed the view that Great Britain must never ignore the essential and insurmountable distinctions of race qualities which were fundamental to its position in India. 'The conceit and the vanity of the half-educated natives must never be pampered.'

The imperialists justified the legitimacy of their rule in India by impressing upon the people the independence and integrity of their own culture—and by constantly downgrading the 'native' cultures which, they insisted, led to nothing but indolence and irregularities.

There was, of course, résistance to the colonial rule. The British rule did not affect life in the villages much, but in the cities there were people opposed to the cultural — and political — dominination of the British Sahib. There were murmurings everywhere. There were many committees, nationalist in tendency, that often met and gave vent to their anti-British feelings.

The question that intrigued E.M. Forster was how did the 'half-educated natives' interact with their rulers? It led him to write 'A Passage to India', a book dear to my heart, not because my name has been associated with it for nearly half a century, but because I consider it to be a monumental novel of the 20th century.

When I got to know him a bit better, I asked Forster how his novel was received when it first appeared way back in the 20's. The great man, the most self-effacing individual I have ever come across, smiled. 'Well,' he said, as though recalling a painful memory, 'A lots of letters appeared in the Morning Post saying, 'How dare he paint our women like this.' 'You mean the Memsahibs', I asked. 'Exactly,' he said. The Morning Post was the mouthpiece of the Conservative party; later on it acquired the title of 'Daily Telegraph'.

As a cultural study, Forster's novel is an excellent example of how the 'natives' and the liberal Englishmen understood each other (or didn't understand each other). Fielding, the sensitive, sympathetic school master, is deeply perturbed when Aziz — whom he has befriended — is imprisoned for making advances toward Miss Quested. After the trial, during which it becomes clear that the accusations are false, Aziz is released; he leaves the court house as an embittered man.

Fielding is pleased for his friend, but realizes that the chasm which has developed between the two, cannot be bridged. They ride together and remain apart. Fielding puts it down to India and its complexities, resigns his job and returns to England. Aziz, for the time being, has become a hardened critic of the Raj.

Forster, whose views were liberal and humane, depicts the muddled atmosphere that existed in India at the turn of the 20th century, with absolute brilliance. His India is a country unapprehendable and vast where nothing is identifiable, not even the birds. The English were in India to govern the Indians whom most of the pucca sahibs considered to be barbaric, lazy, uncivilized. 'I have never known anything but disaster result when English people and Indians attempt to be intimate socially. Courtesy by all means. Intimacy—never, never' says the young Assistant Commissioner of the district of Chandrapore, where the action takes place. The crux of the novel is, to me, not the sustained encounter between the English colonials whom he described as 'well-developed bodies, fairly developed minds, and underdeveloped hearts'—and the Indians, as one critic puts it, but the search for that 'quite something' which makes human beings connect with each other.

'SOUNDS OF THE HEART'

I am sure it's known to many of you that the word 'admiral' has nothing to do with 'admire' or 'admiration'—as one of my students surmised—but that it comes from the Arabic word '*amir-al-bahr*', meaning commander (*amir*) of the (*al*) sea (*bahr*), which was the title the Arabs created for the leader of their navy after he had conquered Spain and Sicily.

The phrase was adopted by the English (and the French as well) who apparently misunderstood the individual parts of the phrase and thought that the definite article '*al*' meant 'sea'. They dropped the final word *bahr* because they didn't know it meant the sea and ended up with a rather eccentric official title, '*amiir-al*,' which literally meant 'commander of the'.

Lexicographers tell us that '*amiiral*' was introduced to the English language around 1500 AD. The letter 'a' often stood for the Latin preposition 'ad' (for example, admirable) so the 'a' changed to 'ad' and soon the title of the ruler of the Queen's Navy became 'admiral'.

Words have intrigued me for a long time. I am whole-heartedly in agreement with the old Chinese proverb that 'words are the sounds of the heart'. But, if, I were to be honest, I would say that I am interested in words largely for phonological reasons.

Wordsmiths, that is, people who live in a universe of words and are seriously obsessed by them, have often published lists of their most favoured words. The author, Williams Espy's list contained: 'gonorrhea', 'lullaby', 'meandering', 'mellifluous', 'murmuring', 'onomatopoeia', 'wisteria'... For me it was cornucopia. Roll these words round your tongue, they are sharp and silvery against the teeth; whisper them, speak them full-throatedly; these words delight your senses like a sip from a vintage Beaujolais.

In the last few decades there have been many competitions held in newspapers and Radio inviting people to send in their favourite English words. The results in the *Sunday Times* competition showed that 'parakeet', 'chrysalis', 'sycamore', 'antimacassar', 'chinchilla', and 'doppelganger' were among the top ten words. These words were obviously chosen for their sounds and not for their meaning.

It would seem that a word perceived to be beautiful has to have two or three syllables. In our language too, words of two or more syllables are, phonetically speaking, much more attractive: *'sansanahat'*, *'muzmahil'*. There are, of course, other criteria: the vowel sounds varying from syllable to syllable, but this is the territory of my friend, Khalid Ahmed, and I do not wish to step into it.

Khalid Ahmed is a wordbuff, a wordaholic and a wordsmith; he is a polymath. He is a linguist and an etymologist and he can tell you, with great ease, how words can be pressed, squeezed and manipulated into all kinds of shapes when they travel from one country to another and from one culture to another. For years he has been showing us how an *Amharic* word finds its way through Slavic languages into Persian and how a Sanskirit word sneaks into Greek or vice versa. I wonder if he is as amused as I am that given the prominence of alcohol in British society, the word alcohol is not originally English, but another import from Arabia.

I must confess I don't know half as much as I would like to about the meaning of many words — leave alone their origins. And it depressed me no end when I took the vocabulary test devised by that distinguished professor of linguistics, David Crystal.

Professor Crystal's method is simple. In order to estimate the size of your vocabulary, take a medium-sized dictionary, one between 1500 and 2000 pages. (*Collins, Chambers* or *Oxford* would do). Aim for a sample of pages. If the dictionary is 1500 pages pick only 30 pages, that is, two per cent of the number of pages (forty if it has 2,000 pages).

You then break the sample down into a series of selections from different parts of the dictionary. For a thirty page sample you have six choices of five pages each, or ten choices of three pages. A representative sample, he recommends, is to pick your pages beginning with CA, EX JA, OB, PL, SC, TO and UN.

You begin with the first full page, and go through all the words on each page of your sample. If you think you know a word or any of its meanings, put a tick against it. (It doesn't matter if you do not know the alternative meanings). For your active vocabulary, you only need to be certain that you can use the word often, occasionally or not all. Do not ignore words which are clustered together just showing their endings as in nation—al—ize. You can also tick idioms and phrases such as *call up* and *call the tune*. Add up the ticks and jot the total down on a piece of paper. Then add up all the page totals and multiply by 50—and you will get (more or less) the size of your vocabulary.

I sat down with my *Concise Oxford* which has 1562 pages. I selected three sections of ten pages, and chose PL SC and UN. My vanity took a severe knocking as I totted up the figures. Of the 395 words spread over ten pages I only knew 165, not even fifty per cent. Gamely, I went on to the next section and my result was slightly worse, but I perked up when I got to the section beginning with the prefix 'UN'. Here I scored heavily (who wouldn't?); the only words (in these ten pages) I did not know were: 'unaneled', 'uncial', 'unciform', 'uncinariasis', 'uncinate', unguiculate', 'unaxial'.

My vocabulary, judging by the Crystal test, would be a little over 34,000 words. Pretty dismal, I thought, considering that most writers insert into their sentences the best part of a hundred thousand words. Never mind, I told myself. There are scrabble players who are familiar with thousands of words without knowing their meaning. But it was no consolation.

The *Oxford English Dictionary* had over 500,000 words in the edition which came out in the nineties. Scholars and lexicographers are busy preparing a newer edition which will probably have two million entries. Even if I were to disregard a large number of entries from earlier periods in the history of the language, as well as names, places and acronyms, I will still be left with hundreds of thousands of words which I shall never know. Dictionaries are expanding by the hour. It is estimated that about 900 new words enter the language every year.

I am reminded of the Emily Dickinson poem:

> *A word is dead*
> *It is said,*
> *Some say.*
> *I say it just*
> *Begins to live*
> *That day.*

STIRRINGS

Good prose depends on clear meaning, but not good poetry: that goes beyond meaning. Poetry depends for its magic on the associations and sounds of words. Never once have I been able to comprehend fully, a poem by Cavafy or Rilke and yet I am always moved when I read either of these two poets. It is something to do with what I call 'stirrings'. When reading a passage there are so many emotions that rise and billow before they subside, leaving me buoyant, cleansed, and yes, I would go as far as to say, purified. Take these lines from D.H. Lawrence:

> And yet out of eternity, a thread
> separated itself on the blackness,
> a horizontal thread that fumes a little with pallor upon
> the dark.

The lines are from the 'The Ship of Death', a poem in which Lawrence talks of apples falling like great drops of dew so they can make an 'exit from themselves'. I know that he wants me to build a ship (of death) for the voyage of oblivion that awaits me, but in writing the above lines, does he mean what I think he means? The image of a thread fuming with pallor haunts me. It matters not whether the pallor can fume; the lines send a tingling sensation down my spine.

Poetry is one of the divinest pleasures created by man. It is beautiful when it is inspirational: 'and jocund day stands tiptoe on the misty mountain tops'. It is no less beautiful when it is structured:

> *The room was suddenly rich and the great*
> *bay window was*
> *spawning snow and pink roses against it Soundlessly*
> *collateral and incompatible:*
> *World is suddener than we fancy it.*

The last line takes you into a different layer of comprehension. Louis MacNeice is an undervalued poet. A contemporary of Auden, Isherwood and Spender, he was a self-effacing man who worked as a producer for BBC Radio. I have already written about how he would stand with a quiet and dignified manner while Dylan Thomas, sitting on a bar stool, held forth. He has the outstanding ability of beginning a theme—or making a point—and then bringing in the counter-point sharply within a line or two. Here is an example, a short poem called 'Sunday Morning':

> *Down the road someone is practising scales,*
> *The notes like little fishes vanish with a wink of tails,*
> *Man's heart expands to tinker with his car.*
> *For this is Sunday morning. Fate's great bazaar:*

'A wink of tails' is a metaphor not easy to translate into prose. The idyllic Sunday morning scene — the sound of piano music — is quickly dissolved into the activity dearest to an Englishman's heart on a Sunday, which is, tinkering with his motor car.

Auden had great affection for MacNeice. He was the same age and when MacNeice died in 1963, Auden wrote a moving poem called 'The Cave of Making' in which he wrote'...... Here silence/is turned into objects/I wish Louis, I could have shown it you/ while you were still in public/and from your perspective you'd notice/sights I overlook, and in turn take a scholar's interest'. The poem is sub-titled ('In memoriam Louis MacNeice,') and ends with:

> .....*for your elegy*
> *I should have been able to manage*
> *something more like   you than   the egocentric monologue,*
> *but accept it for friendship's sake....*

When I listen to poetry it is primarily the reader's voice which shapes my feelings. Words assume the colour that he assigns them. Sometimes a reader does not embrace the emotive word and that gives a tingling pleasure to me like the anticipation of a cold shower while wallowing in a hot bath. The word not emphasised hovers round the corner and when it is uttered it assumes a hidden, recondite importance.

The late Alan Badel spoke Shakespeare beautifully. He was an excellent Romeo for while he made you aware of the finest love poetry ever written, he avoided the hackneyed method of giving weight to words other actors caressed and milked. His voice was rich and silken smooth and had that delicious graininess which made me want to shut my eyes and listen to him even though he was a very personable actor to watch. In the balcony scene, after he had already created a shimmering aura of 'rich jewels in an Ethiop's ear', he languidly leaned against a pillar and said, softly, 'I am no pilot; yet wert thou as far as that vast shore washed with the farthest sea, I should adventure for such merchandise'. The humdrum word (merchandise) acquired a unique and imaginative particularity which sent goose-pimples all over me.

Those who enjoy reading poetry know that not every poem can be labelled major or great. Sometimes you find a poem to be endearing or enchanting for reasons best known to you. English poetry is so rich and so vast—and there have been so many great poets—that the temptation is to read only the prescribed masters. Every year brings forth anthologies which include more than a hundred entries from the celebrated poets to the all but unknown. The Web Site Poetry Daily publishes a new poem every day. In New York the subway posters greet travellers with stanzas from Blake to Langston Hughes.

When you come across a poem like Yeats' 'The Spur', that offers an attitude or an opinion that you empathise with, you take it to heart. But the joy of joys is to find a poetic work of great quality in an airline brochure. Thus it was that I came across Rick

Moody, a poet unknown to me. His 'Verse Collage'
is a poem redolent with nostalgia of early love, with
relationships that flounced out in a huff or a tiff, and
with lost memories. The verse is shot through with a
tender ironic melancholy. The poem takes its impetus
from Romeo and Juliet. For your pleasure I quote
two disjointed stanzas:

In immature birds the neck is reddish brown.
Too soon marr'd are those so early made.
*A lot of hugging, holding hands sometimes. He always
used to push the hair out of my face.*
Both briskly preen their feathers....
With love's light wings did I o'er perch these walls.
*We were always aware of the volume and sometimes
I bit my hand — so that I wouldn't make any noise
The constant use of the beak inevitably causes wear and
tear
please be my friend
The girl floats around in her nightgown, C'mon it's me
I intend to reclaim my family life for my family
She had complained that he was making no effort to get
to know her.
She wanted to have sexual intercourse with him at least
once*
Call me but love and I'll be new baptized.
She told me I looked fat in the dress.......

Have no qualms if it does not stir you. There's
always Mathew Arnold.

TEN MEN AND A HORSE

The cricket that I cherish most is played on a field full of daisies and buttercups and dandelion with a rectangular patch in the centre, freshly mown and rolled and known as the wicket. All around the field small parties of villagers squat on the ground and wait patiently for the game to begin. Invariably, there is a row of elderly men dozing in deck chairs; others wearing floppy felt hats loll about outside the pub, which is close to the ground. They have clean-shaven chins and long whiskers and they hold pint-sized tankards in their hands.

The match never begins on time because one or two of the visiting players have failed to turn up or have sneaked into the pub to fortify themselves against the demon bowler the home team prizes. No one is impatient; the world stands still.

There are, often, long parleys about whether the visiting team, which is one man short, should be provided with a local player or whether the match should be held ten-a-side. One of the two friends whom the captain of the home team has brought to stand as umpire is then coaxed to play for the visitors. He protests that he hasn't got the right gear but everyone makes allowances for that. The problem of finding a second umpire is solved by the Vicar, who agrees to stand in, not before cracking a joke about the lbw rules.

It doesn't always work out smoothly. In a match I played at Chorley Wood, our captain had tricky negotiations — we were two men short — with the Chorley Wood captain and it was agreed that two substitutes would be lent to us so that we could field eleven men and that nine men on each side would bat.

The two young men, who had been detailed for the unpleasant task of fielding for both sides and batting for neither, went off in high dudgeon. The match was about to be called off when our two defaulters turned up in a smart sports car with a third man, none other than Gerald Harper, the matinee idol himself. Gerald had ferried the defaulters and he declared stoutly that he was jolly well going to play. Whoever stood down it wasn't going to be him. He was not a star for nothing. Fresh talks ensued and the match was played on a twelve-a-side basis.

The game itself was played with exemplary exactitude. Everyone except for the odd substitute was dressed in perfectly creased flannels; everyone took guard meticulously (through most of them didn't quite know what to do with it); everyone looked imperiously at every fielder in turn as if he knew precisely where to score. No one wore a helmet.

There is nothing quite like *Ye Olde Englyshe* Village cricket. A match against the TV travellers from London is an event in a village. Tea ladies quiver with excitement at the thought of seeing their favourite TV celebrities in the flesh. The inn-keepers open their backdoors to let them have their pre-match half of mild-and-bitter, sometimes on the house. Their freshly coiffured wives flirt with them. The beaming Vicar keeps reminding the celebrities that the apse, being in need of repair, they must not sign an autograph without ensuring that the autograph hunter has put in his sixpence in the collection box, which he has placed on the signing table.

The debonair Tim Aspell, was our captain when we played at Epsom. He used to bat number four. (Great captains bat one or two down). Everyone, except Tim, knew that he was not the Traveller's answer to Peter May. Our start was disastrous: three runs for two wickets down. Just as Tim, dressed immaculately in a silk shirt, went in, the telephone rang. Leslie Glazier, our twelfth man, reserve, scorer and a mordant wit, picked up the phone. It was Tim's wife and she wanted to speak to him. Leslie never mentioned that Tim had gone in to bat. 'Would you hold, love?' he said over the phone, 'Tim won't be long.' And he wasn't.

The late Trevor Howard was a cricket enthusiast and a great raconteur. We once played together in a seven-a-side match against an erstwhile Maharajah's team in Simla. The Maharaja had converted his palace into a hotel. Trevor and I were staying in his hotel. Listening to Trevor's cricket tales, he organised a match in the compound of the hotel. The ground behind the wicket was level for a few yards and then sloped away rather dangerously so that the bowler seemed to appear from nowhere. It was only in the last few yards of his run that he was visible to the batsman, or indeed any of the fielders.

When Trevor Howard went out to bat—left leg padded up (the other pad was used by the batsman at the opposite end)—the Maharajah took up the bowling. He was a spinner and as he only had a short start, he was visible throughout. Trevor scored most of his runs in byes. He would charge and miss, but the wicket keeper, the fat head-cook of the hotel, could never grab the ball cleanly to stump him. The Maharajah glared at the wicket-keeper everytime he missed an easy chance, but the fat cook folded his hands in obeisance and intoned, 'Galti hogya Maharaj.' (I made an error, my lord). The Maharajah couldn't sack him because he was a wizard of a cook and the entire hotel clientele swooned over the better than cordon bleu cuisine he created. His roulades and his crepe suzettes were the best I have ever had.

I am grateful to Trevor Howard for telling me one of the finest cricket yarns: in a match in Bucks County, the visiting team arrived, ten men and a horse. The visitors lost the toss and were put in to bat. They lost one player after another until they were twenty nine for eight. The horse was sent in next and he began to thrash the bowlers; he hooked and he cut and he drove and he pulled, a four and a six and a six and a four, until the score reached 219 with the horse not out at 179. It was now the home team's turn to bat. The captain of the home team turned to the visiting captain, 'I suppose, you are now going to ask your horse to bowl?' he asked in utter weariness. 'Don't be silly,' said the visitor's captain. 'Whoever has heard of a horse that can bowl?'

Doug Blackwell took over the captaincy of TV Travellers from Tim Aspell. Lady luck had deserted Doug as an actor and he had become resigned to playing bit parts. His soul passion was talking about cricket statistics and his own swinging off-breaks and leg-cutters. Unfortunately, his direction was somewhat askew; one of his deliveries was always aimed at first slip. On one occasion, his first ball was not a good one, due mainly to the fact that it slipped out of his hand. It went up and came down about six feet wide of the off stump. The batsman had plenty of time to make up his mind; he could leave it alone, contemptuously, and let it be counted as a wide or he could spring forward and hit a terrific six. He chose to leap forward, whirled his bat and missed the ball by about two feet. The wicket keeper, never a quick mover, somehow reached the ball and kicked it towards the wicket. By an incredible fluke, the ball hit the wicket. Leslie Glazier, never one to miss an opportunity, said, 'I suppose you bowled for that Dougie.'

'YOU DON'T MIND, IS IT?'

My dear nephew, who keeps me amused by sending me odd bits of humour, has emailed me a letter written by a Mr. S.R.H to his doctor:

> 'With respectfully stated that the letter is writing to your goodself in respect of the confirmation about the fee for checkup and time as well, I am directed by the Newzealand (sic) embassy to be checked and got some medical paper from you to produced in Embassy. You are therefore requested to kindly let me know that what kind of the checkup will be processed and how much fee come over it and how many time will be borne in issuing report.'

Some years ago, I would have moaned pleasurably after reading this galimatias. I don't, any more. English in the subcontinent has not only developed its own pronunciation but its own vocabulary and — judging from the letter quoted above — its own distinctive grammar.

The young man sitting next to me on a plane to Delhi last year, raised himself from his seat to address someone in the row behind, 'I say old chap, what do you say shall we order some bloody Marys?' His friend mumbled something which I couldn't hear. My fellow passenger sat down with a big smile on his face. I thought I ought to save him the embarrassment and so I leaned towards him to inform him that the airline did not serve any alcohol. 'I know, I know,' he chuckled, 'I was only pulling his legs.'

This is not the only saying which we, in the subcontinent, have altered to satisfy our sense of syntax, 'Thanks God' is another most commonly used expression. We have a propensity not only for variations in noun numbers but for progressive verbs. 'He is not knowing the answer' or 'I am believing that he can't be telling the truth.'

Other words are English terms that have taken on a whole new meaning such as bearer, which (in Pakistan) means a waiter; and eartops, which (in India) means earrings. In both countries boots (or boot) means shoes, tennis shoes, shoes with laces or moccasins.

In the sub-continental jargon some standard phrases are often rearranged or abbreviated. ('Give me the scissor' instead of a pair of scissors; 'a key bunch' instead of a bunch of keys). Duplication is often used for emphasis. 'I like hot hot coffee.' 'Oh she has been crying crying all night.'

English is spoken by millions of people in India. It is still the language of India's judicial system. English is also the preferred language of Indian universities. In Pakistan too, most of the high profile lawyers use English when they appear in the law courts. Needless to say that English in the subcontinent has developed a distinctive vocabulary. The number of regional words that have crept into the Oxford English Dictionary is now over two thousand. I do not mean words like *Bhaji, Chappati* or *Vindaloo,* (which entered the jargon of most Midlanders as a result of the influx of Pakistani and Indian eateries), but hybrid words like *policewalla* and his weapon, the *lathi.*

Indian English was, in the fifties and sixties, a source of endless delight for stand-up comics. The late Peter Sellers became an icon because of his renditions of what he considered to be 'the Indian accent' in the BBC's popular programme *Take it From Here.* Indians were often belittled by being addressed with a 'Goodness gracious me' (spoken in the manner of Peter Sellers) to make them aware that their speech was highly risible.

That era, which lasted nearly thirty years, is over. Indians and Pakistanis may not be welcome in England, but they are, no longer, derided for their manner of speech. The new forms of English emerging in Asia have now come to be accepted as an innovative branch of a language that already has a multitude of dialects with their own distinctive pronunciation.

On a visit to Singapore I was intrigued to note that the Singaporeans mostly speak Singlish to each other. I was informed that the strange Singapore pidgin was once banned from television, but Singlish, refused to be stamped out. This was not surprising, considering that the people who spoke it were influenced by Malay and Chinese dialects. They found it more colourful to call someone a *kambing* instead of a fool. (Kambing in Malay means goat). Malay words entered the flow of English and some English words took on eccentric uses. If someone offers to 'follow you home' in Singapore, it does not mean that he is going to stalk you but rather offering to accompany you to your house.

Singaporeans also like to say *no* in almost every sentence: 'You are joining *no*, next week?'; 'You are coming, *no* to my party?' This is very similar to the *na* that we use in our everyday English. 'I was going there, *na*, but I couldn't'; 'I can't refuse a chocolate *na*'. We also use *na* as a suffix just as the Singaporeans use *lah*. We say, 'I should have finished it *na*' with almost exactly the same inflection as a Singaporean says, 'Give him a buzz, *lah*.' The most typical example common to both Singapore and the subcontinent is the usage of the question tag: *is it*? without any reference to the verb that has gone before, resulting in: 'You don't mind *is it*?'

It has always been known that Asian English is famously different from Queen's English. I am not here talking about the strong rhythmic pronunciation which differs from region to region, but the language as it is spoken. The other day, a movie star who has now decided to converse only in English showed off her newly acquired skill by telling me, 'It is very pleasure meeting you.'

Three hundred million people use English as their native tongue, but nearly 400 million across the world, speak it as a foreign tongue. The movie star's expression may not be typical of their speech, but it is just to show how a language, when it is a living thing, changes and acquires attributes such as its own local slang. Some observers feel that the striking individuality of the new English dialects ought to be appreciated as a celebration of linguistic diversity. I may not be one of those, but I admire their generosity.

My nephew's remarks about Mr. Shah's letter to his doctor (that I quoted at the beginning of this piece), are rather revealing. He writes: 'I showed this to an Australian friend and he thought the language of the letter was similar to the kind of writing he comes across in New Zealand.' I would like to know what the New Zealanders think of the Australian English.

THE RATTLING OF BONES

Our delight in nonsense poetry has its roots in childhood when we string words together without having to bother about their meanings or implications. *Akkar Bakkar Bumbay Bau/Ikee Nabbay Pooray Sau*: I remember chanting this verse while running aimlessly when I was four. My father once told me the story of a man who was so lazy that when he was asked to *uchro* (utter) something. He replied '*uchro muchro duchro*'(*muchro* and *duchro* are just rhyming words like *Bifzi-Bafzi*). It delighted me no end. It was a perfect release from all constraints and rules. Why hadn't I washed my hands? Why was I wrestling with the branch of a tree and not doing my homework? The answer, of course, was '*Uchro muchro duchro.*' It didn't always prevent me from getting a smack on my bottom, but it was a temporary deliverance from the serious, adult life.

Our own Sufi Ghulam Mustafa Tabassum produced delightful nonsense verse though it was confined to what is known as 'nursery rhymes'. He created a world in which dolls and animals and human beings are all friends who share each other's pains. It's a world in which snakes dance on trees and cats eat berries; mice sing classical ragas, tigers jump over the moon and lions and lambs go out boating. Sufi Tabassum's poem about a boy known as *Tot Batot,* is one of the most enchanting parables of our cultural lore, simply because it challenges the arbitrariness of the world determined by the propriety of logic.

In this climate of fear and hatred I turn to Edward Lear. I do not know whether you are fond of this 19th century poet or not, I certainly am. He was a naturalist. His *Nonsense Botany* has flowers like 'Tickia Orologica' (with blossoms in the form of pocket watches), or 'Shoebootia Utilis' (which grows boots and shoes). He also invented unheard of creatures who receive their existence from their names. 'His Younghy Bonghy-Bo', an adorable poem that I once knew by heart—who inhabits the coast of Coromandel, 'where the early pumpkins blow', who proposes to Lady Jingly because 'he is tired of living singly' is a magnificent creation of fantasy. Lady Jingly turns down his proposal because she is already committed to Handel Jones Esquire & Co. Heartbroken, Younghy Bonghy-Bo bids her farewell and goes away to his death through the silent ocean, but Lady Jingly stays on the coast of Coromandel and 'on that heap of stones she mourns' for the Younghy Bonghy-Bo.

Poetry and cruelty, tenderness and destructiveness are closely linked in the nonsense verse of Edward Lear, as in this limerick:

> *There was an old Person of Buda,*
> *Whose conduct grew ruder and ruder;*
> *Till at last, with a hammer,*
> *they silenced his clamour,*
> *By smashing that Person of Buda.*

Literature — and the theatre in particular — has, in an increasing manner, given room to that liberation through nonsense which the grim, bourgeois world would not admit in any guise. Nonsense verse gives a powerful release from the strictures of prudery and sanctimoniousness. It is not just children who sing it, adults, too, have been enchanted by it for many centuries. When you find the rhetorical jargon incomprehensible, (or when you are landed with a dummy with no aces or kings) what better way to react than to rattle off:

> *Bifzi Bafzi, hulalemi,*
> *quasti basti bo,*
> *Lalu Lalu Lalu Lalu la.*

The literature of verbal nonsense brings into focus the human condition itself. This is what gives it a dimension larger than mere playfulness.

The real world is cruel; its inhabitants are crushed by accidents of birth or environment and they are unable to break the pattern which has been ordained for them. In the simplest language Lear says:

> *There was an old man of Cape Horn*
> *Who wished he had never been born*
> *So he sat on a chair, till he died of despair*
> *That dolorous man of Cape Horn.*

It is not surprising that Lewis Carroll, one of the greatest exponents of nonsense verse and the author of those immortal 'Alice' books, was a logician. He was a man steeped in the world of syllogisms and equations, in which determinism of meaning could not be shaken off. So, he resorts to the absurd:

> *'When I use a word' Humpty Dumpty said, in rather a scornful tone, it means just what I choose it to mean–neither more nor less'.*
> *'The question is, said Alice, Whether you can make words mean so many different things'.*
> *'The question is', said, Humpty Dumpty, 'which is master – that's all'.*

In 'Through the Looking Glass', there is a wood where things have no names and in this very wood, Alice, having forgotten her own name, meets a fawn who has also forgotten her identity. They walk on together, Alice's arms clasped round the soft neck of the fawn, but when they come out to an open field, the fawn suddenly shakes itself free from Alice's arm, leaps into the air — and darts away. There is a suggestion here that when you have an identity defined by language, having a name, you have restrictions imposed upon you, but when you lose your name you gain freedom in some way.

The field of nonsense poetry — and prose — is as large as it is fluid. Most of the works explore the mysteries of being and the self to the limits of anguish as well as absurdity. It portrays a sense of the senselessness of life, of the devaluation of ideals, purity and purpose and it strives to express the inadequacy of rational approach. In many ways nonsense poetry and prose is the direct antecedent of the 'Theatre of the Absurd', which doesn't argue about the absurdity of the human condition; it merely presents it in concrete theatre images.

In our part of the world, there is an unending tirade of misused and overused words which are churned out day after day in the name of honour, valour and glory. Any one with the slightest sense of discernment knows that they have a trite, hollow ring to them. I am reminded of that marvellous passage from the 'Hunting of the Snack' (by Lewis Carroll) and I quote a few lines, not for those that they are aimed at (they never take any notice), but for those who think the printed word matters:

> 'To the horror of all those who were
> present that day
> He uprose in full evening dress
> And with senseless grimaces endeavoured
> to say
> What his tongue could no longer express
>
> Down he sank in his chair — ran his
> hands through his hair —
> And chanted in mimsiest tones
> Words whose utter inanity, proved his insanity,
> while he rattled a couple of bones'.

THE UNPRINTABLE POETRY

It was the late Shaukat Thanvi, who pointed out to me, way back in 1950, that nearly every renowned classical Urdu poet had, at one time or another, created poetry which was—and still is—unprintable. Shaukat Thanvi was a wit par excellence and the august literary figures of his times went out of their way not to cross swords with him for fear that he would ridicule them with his repartee. He was not a regular poet but he did write some hilarious erotic poetry.

I remember a gathering when Shaukat Thanvi regaled the company with snatches of the unprintable poetry, not of his own creation, but that of the *asatiza* (the masters). He had a sharp memory and he came out with droll pieces attributed to the venerable Mir Taqi Mir and that highly complex, whimsical poet, Inshah Allah Khan Insha.

We were sitting in a circle in the courtyard of Mehmood Nizami's house adjacent to the Lahore Broadcasting House. The grim looking Ansari (whose job was to provide sound effects during live productions of features and plays; (he was a wizard at drumming his fingers on a cardboard box to simulate the sound of horse's hooves) was also present. He grimaced and kept touching his earlobes, a gesture calculated to invoke the Almighty's forgiveness for listening to such racy stuff. Thanvi who loved to ruffle those with a holier-than-thou attitude, leaned towards him and, with mock seriousness, said, 'Tell me Ansari, do you beg for His forgiveness in a similar fashion *before* or *after* copulation?'

In our poetic literature some 'daring' verse can be found in '*masnavis*', but the bulk of the ribald verse, written by the classicists, has been handed down from one generation to the other. Some years ago, Amjad Hussain, my friend from Toledo, Ohio, a surgeon by profession and a man of wide literary tastes, told me that he was putting together an anthology of risqué poetry. His intention was to have the book printed for private circulation. I suggested that he should seek the help of Shan-ul-Haq Haqqi, probably the only living authority on bawdy verse. Haqqi's memory is prodigious and his research impeccable. For some inexplicable reason, Haqqi was disinclined to cooperate, and the project fizzled out.

It is not difficult to understand why some of our most illustrious poets wrote pornographic poetry. It was, partly, to get away from the tedium of having to compose 'creative' ghazals day in and day out; but, largely, to find some kind of a release from the stranglehold of the ever-elusive, cruel, even sadistic, *mashooq*, (the loved one). The theme most often used in our poetry is that the beloved remains perversely indifferent to the entreaties of the poet. Pick up any collection of Mir or Sauda, Jur'at or Mushafi, Nasikh or Dard, and you would see that the 'I' character constantly groans under the tyranny of the idolised beloved. In the unprintable poetry, the poet subjugates the beloved (albeit a comely boy) and relishes a union in which the *mashooq* helplessly pleads for mercy against his ever increasing libidinous advances.

The complexion of bawdy poetry changed in the 20th century. The man responsible for the change was Rafi Ahmed Khan, a professor of English at Lucknow University. He gave it an altogether different dimension. His poetry, unlike that of some of his predecessors, is not pornographic doggerel, it is shot through with lively, scintillating humour and it is remarkably devoid of scatology. Often the first line of his couplet depicts man's helplessness in a hostile world and then, with a remarkable twist of a phrase or a word, which, to quote the Duke of Buckingham, 'cannot be used in the presence of ladies', turns the entire content into a wildly funny situation. Rafi Ahmed Khan parodied rather than celebrated amorous conquests.

Those who came in the wake of Rafi Ahmed Khan found it distasteful to write in the mould of Jan Sahib and Charkeen. Erotic poetry now shunned smuttiness. Hafeez Hoshiarpuri, a ghazalist of considerable stature, composed eloquent salacious poems and Shan-ul-Haq Haqqi has written pungent and witty erotic verse, which is Ghalibesque in style.

Pornographic poetry in English is mostly confined to the form known as the limerick. Limericks are usually full of jokes about genitalia and scatological puns. Could you ever suspect the Nobel Prize winner, T.S. Eliot, to indulge in this form? He did. In his early days, Eliot frequently wrote pornographic doggerel in his notebook. He used to rip the pages off and send them to his great friend Ezra Pound, who was an avowed admirer of the ribald verse. Later he sold some of these poems to a New York lawyer (for a little over a $100) with a plea, 'I am sure you will agree that these verses never ought to be printed,' he wrote, 'and in putting them in your hands I beg you fervently to keep them to yourself and see that they are never printed.'

But they were printed. And by Faber and Faber, Eliot's own firm. When the book—*Inventions of a March Hare*—came out, many critics and scholars winced at the violent obscenity of some of the lines. The author of *Eliot's Early Years*, Lyndall Gordon, said that the pornographic verses underlined the misogyny behind much of Eliot's writing. Another Eliot scholar, Anthony Julius, who has written extensively on anti-semitism in Eliot's work, characterised the coarse verse as drawing on puerile racist ideas about sexual superiority.

King Bolo's swarthy bodyguard
Were called the Jersey lilies
A wild and hardy set of blacks

Undaunted by syphilis
They wore the national uniform
Of a garland of verbenas
And a pair of great big hairy balls
And a big black knotty penis

This is an extract from the poem that Eliot called 'King Bolo Verses'. It probably bears out Anthony Julius's contention, but Eliot claimed that these verses were merely an attempt to make fun of the pompous tone struck by early anthropologists.

The appearance of *Inventions of a March Hare* has once again brought up the controversy surrounding Eliot's dislike for women. He was supposed to have been instrumental in committing his first wife to be confined to a mental asylum. It has been argued by many, including Bertrand Russel, that his wife didn't deserve such treatment. Faber, who brought out the collection, defended it vehemently, saying it was a wonderful book. The director of Faber and Faber declared that some of the poems in the book were extremely beautiful and that it was certainly not possible to establish Eliot's misogyny from the bawdy lines because Eliot was equally critical of all human beings. Ah well!

I am not entirely convinced that the poems in the new Eliot collection are beautiful. Some of them are excellent bits of scholarly ribaldry; others are the sort of limericks that schoolboys make up to entertain each other. Indeed, all scabrous poetry reflects, to some extent, a schoolboyish fascination with genitalia. Some critics in the West accused Eliot of a

rather sad kind of depravity. But is he the only one
to show this depravity? If you were to draw a list,
then, to quote Taseer: *'is men kutch parda nasheeno kay
bhi nam aatay hein'*.

The climate in the West can allow for the publication
of *Inventions*, but if a collection of Rafi Ahmed Khan
or Haqqi's erotic verse were to be published, our
prudery would create a havoc. The bookshop that
included such a work would be burnt down and the
publisher lynched publicly. The gulf between what
we enjoy privately and what we condemn publicly
has never been greater.

VAIN FAITH AND COURAGE VAIN

The genius of Oscar Wilde turned art into philosophy and philosophy into art. The paramount quality of literature is that it alters the minds of men. It widens the range of perception. Wilde was not being vainglorious when he said, 'Drama, novel, poem in prose, poem in rhythm, subtle and fantastic dialogue, whatever I touched, I made beautiful in a new mode of beauty.'

Wilde gave a new dimension to paradox. He summed up all systems in a phrase and then gave the phrase a paradoxical twist.

> *I don't mind hard work where there is no object of any kind.*

> *There is nothing romantic about a proposal. Why, one may be accepted.*

Oscar Wilde is certainly not a supremely important writer, but he wrote *The Importance of Being Ernest,* one of the lightest, gayest, most scintillating plays in English, an exquisite, carefree comedy. Oscar Wilde's tutor at Oxford was Walter Pater. Pater was a dry old stick, devoted to handsome athletes. Wilde had a life long respect for him. It was Pater who encouraged Wilde in his first literary efforts. After seeing Wilde's first essay, he wrote to him:

> You possess some beautiful, and for your age, quite exceptionally cultivated tastes and a considerable knowledge too of many beautiful things. I hope you will write a great deal in time to come.
> Very truly yours....

It was this note of encouragement more than anything else that aroused my interest in Pater (Fellow and Tutor of Brasenose College). It's a long time since I picked up his *Marius the Epicurean*. I did the other day. His prose is cold and coiled:

> 'By them the religion of Numa', so staid ideal and comely, the object of so much jealous conversation though of direct services as leading sanction to a sort of high scrupulosity especially in the chief points of domestic conduct, was mainly prized as being, through its hereditary character, something like a personal distinction as contributing among the other accessories of an ancient house, to the production of that aristocratic atmosphere which separated them from newly-made people'.

Pater's *History of Renaissance* is soaked in scholarship, but his reserve is chilling and the only viewpoint it promotes, as far as I am concerned, is ennui.

Pater I can do without. I admire him for what he saw in Oscar Wilde. Upon receiving a copy of *The Happy Prince* he wrote: 'Your genuine little poems in prose... and the whole, too brief, book abounds with delicate touché and pure English.'

Wilde, who cared so deeply for the purpose and nuance of his prose became downright prosy and didactic when he went to prison. In *De Profundis*, he writes with the fervor of a religious mystic. The tone is pontifical, if anything. Perhaps something of Pater rubbed off on him after all.

> Yet the whole of Christ, so entirely may sorrow and beauty be made one in their meaning and manifestation, is really an idyll, though it ends with the veil of the temple being rent, and the darkness coming over the face of the earth, and the stone rolled to the door of the sepulchre.

I don't know why I have picked on Walter Pater. There are others with huge reputations who are equally, if not more, ponderous. Take Thomas Mann, whom I find to be legendarily boring though many of my literary friends swear by the profundities he reveals to them. Then there is Herman Melville: (forget that you have seen the movie of *Mobie Dick*). I place Melville and Nathaniel Hawthorne in the same category as Thomas Mann.

The number of romantic poets who have produced dramatic works is awe-inspiring. Dryden, Byron, Coleridge, Keats, Tennyson, Southey, Wordsworth and others, have all written pseudo-classic drama. It is the epitome of tedium. One of Dryden's heroic tragedies, *The Conquest of Granada*, runs into ten acts, and some of his rhetoric makes the long winded speeches of Ulysses (*Troilus and Cressida*) sound like crisp, Noel Coward passages.

I used to think that it is only drama (such as I have mentioned above) which came under the label of soporific stuff. I was wrong. There are scores of authors, placed vertically on shelves in sections known as 'classics', who produce the same result. Let me give a thought to Carlyle, of whom Samuel Butler said in a letter, 'It was very good of God to let Carlyle and Mrs. Carlyle marry one another, and so make only two people miserable instead of four.' I was once presented three volumes of his *Miscellaneous Essays* by a Cypriot plumber who used to do all kinds of odd jobs for me. His wife, he told me rather sheepishly, had forgotten to take them with her when she left him.

Talking of essays, what about the complete works of Addison including his poems and a play? Addison and Steele are always mentioned together, (like Sutcliffe and Hobbs) because they both contributed to the *Spectator*. We were always exhorted to read their essays. I never did—not until a wet afternoon when I picked up two old numbers of the Spectator for sixpence at Ipswich. I decided afterwards to leave well alone.

Of poets I can say with hand on heart that there are so many who are tedious beyond belief. Longfellow heads the list.

As for George Gordon: (he was nearly forgotten even by his own contemporaries) all his exhortations would have gone astray if he had not been known as Byron, a member of the aristocracy. Byron is forever singing about the glories of Greece:

> *When a man hath no freedom to fight for at home. Let him combat for that of his neighbours.*
> *Let him think of the glories of Greece and Rome.*
> *And get knocked on his head for his labours.*

I grant you that George Gordon, Lord Byron's 'Don Juan' has some wonderful passages, but if you were to remove the rest of Byron from my collection it wouldn't pain me at all.

There are many other books you have seen—bound in leather—behind glass doors, Ovid, Cicero, Menander. The list is unending.

You can also keep that other aristocrat, Lord Macaulay:

> *To my true king I offer free from stain*
> *Courage and faith, vain faith and courage vain...*

Then there is the third Lord, Alfred, whose eyes remained brimmed with tears from the depth of some divine despair. His musings have dulled the minds of many a schoolboy. Tennyson too, (and not because he is a member of the aristocracy) is on my list of unwanted classics.

I am not talking about a shift in taste. (Trollope, in, after a long period; Lamb, out, after having been immensely well-known once). I merely want to suggest that there are some volumes of enormous historical importance which nobody reads unless they have to, like the plays of Bjonstjerne Bjornson.

There are many promising, famous but unreadable authors, but I have no time to mention them now, Time was when I used to collect them in the hope that I might, one day, muster enough courage to read them. I realised some years ago that I wasn't going to be able to do it, so I took out of my shelves, Edward Bulwer Lytton and Charlotte Bronte and Maeterlinck and a volume called *The Sayings of Plutarch* and put them in a kitchen cupboard, that also contained disused gadgets, school photographs and numerous books on the 'purpose of life' that people had presented to me. My apartment was ransacked some months ago. The burglars took nearly everything, but left me, my unwanted classics.

WATTLE AND WOOZLE

Newspapers in America are laden with leaflets, flyers and an innumerable number of mini catalogues. I find them fascinating, not because they display, attractively, goods that I may want to acquire, but because of the language used to entice me. No, I am not talking about the heady description of a holiday resort (the Loire Valley's Chateau de la Guillonnier, which I can hire for a mere $10,000 a week), but the text written to advertise ordinary garden compost, hammocks, outdoor shirts, camping and farming gear.

Most people toss away the neatly stapled sheets and pick up the 'Business' section of their newspaper before looking at the main headlines. I find that these catalogues give me hours of reading pleasure; they reveal a world of possibility I scarcely knew existed. The descriptions are written so artfully that you would be a fool not to be taken in by them.

P J Adams, in their glossy booklet, show a tanned, rugged, Robert Redford look-alike, eyeing a stack of flannel shirts. The copy says, 'Our outdoor shirt features, among other things, gauntlet buttons, long sleeved plackets, and two ply 40 S yarn construction for a superior nap. It has boxed pleat, double stitching at stress points, handy locker loop and non-fused collar...'

What 'other things' they have they left out, I wonder. I have never worn a shirt with a non-fused collar. I haven't the faintest idea about a non fused collar, and the two ply 40 S yarn construction, but I am tempted, if only to be able to have a superior nap. I must confess that I do not, and indeed, cannot sleep if I am wearing a shirt. Maybe this is why I have never had a 'superior nap' in my life.

The other day I flew from Philadelphia to Chicago. The in-flight magazine in the seat pocket in front of me was an absolute delight. In the stationery section was a thing called 'The Briefcase Valet'. Here is the copy: 'Available in dark or natural cherry at a modest price of $199, it is designed to alleviate one of the most intractable storage problems of what to do with our briefcase when we put it down at home. That's why we designed the "Briefcase Valet". It holds your briefcase up off the floor, making it easier to insert and retrieve things'.

Now my briefcase never fails to mystify me. I do not think I can retrieve anything out of it, unless I dump everything on the floor and rummage through the mess. What do I have on the floor? Assorted papers, rulers, old address books, erasers, tiny plastic boxes full of cardamom seeds, sleeping pills, paper clips, markers, a dozen pens with different nibs, countless newspaper clippings from the Urdu dailies, (which I found amusing at the time), ball points, cheque books, visiting cards, used envelopes with my jottings on the back (I keep them for the definitive novel that I am about to begin) and at least two passports which are well past their expiry date.

More often than not, I am unable to retrieve what I am looking for. A month ago, my wife asked me to check the date when I paid our daughter's astronomically heavy school fee. My daughter hasn't seriously begun school yet; she only attends a Montessori. I shudder to think what her school fee would be when she is ready for it.

I knew that I had paid it because my banker friend's assistant was good enough to carry the cash (the school refuses to accept cheques) to the school accountant's office. He gave me the receipt in an envelope which I, naturally, shoved into my briefcase. When after a thorough search, I failed to trace the envelope; I suggested to my wife that she should check with the school, since they keep a record of such matters. My wife wasn't too happy about it. I discovered the envelope last week in Hartford, Connecticut. It was wedged in between a doctor's report on my cardiovascular graph. I have not yet mentioned it to my wife, in case she asks me about the '20% discount on all toiletries at Heathrow' voucher, that she asked me to keep and which, my briefcase had mysteriously swallowed.

The copywriters who write the blurbs for swank restaurants use a language that I can only describe as expensive hyperbole. American food, no matter which state you are in, is not known for the subtlety of its cuisine. This is why the well-heeled nobs prefer to eat in dimly lit French or Italian restaurants which boast of their roulades and ratatouilles in anthropomorphic terms. The restaurants, apart from the exaggerated accents of their maitre d's (which thrills their patrons) are neither French nor Italian, but posh and pricy. The satirist, Bryson, once wrote a magnificent piece spoofing the haughty manner of a head waiter: 'Our crepe galette of a sea chortle kept in rich mal de mer sauce is seasoned in dishevelled herbs layered with steamed wattle and woozle leaves.'

The description is seductive enough for anyone to believe that wattle—slender leaves of interlaced twine—may, when steamed, taste a bit like fettuccine, but what about woozle? Anyway, wattle and woozle sounds nice. Next time somebody asks me who my bootmakers are, I shall have no hesitation in answering, 'Wattle and Woozle, of course'.

It is my experience that in swank eateries, one must disregard the advice of the head waiter. Some years ago I was lured into trying a soup with steamed bay leaves. It tasted like Optrex eye drops, and that is a taste I know well. You may be cleverer than I am, but when I bathe my eyes with the eye glass pressed close to my eye sockets, I cannot prevent a drop or two trickling down to my lips. It's not a taste I cherish.

The taste of American bread, white or brown, never rises beyond a chewy, limp, listlessness. Toasting or frying it doesn't help. Everyday American food is squishy. As for the real American burger, it is so tall I can never accommodate it in my mouth without taking off a couple of layers from the top. I defy anyone to bite into a proper American hamburger — that mound of onions, lettuce, tomatoes and the yellowest cheese imaginable — without squirting some bits on his shirt.

There is a giddying abundance of absolutely everything in America. Who is going to pick which item and why? This is where the marketing gurus come in. It is under their tutelage that the would-be Updikes dare to suggest that herbs should be described as dishevelled and not smooth. Oddly enough, the concept catches on. There are, of course, special schools that train writers to produce copy for the concoctions offered by the superior restaurants.

The secret of clever promotion of marketable goods lies in decoding the unconscious thoughts hidden behind words and expressions. Gauntlet buttons evokes the image of a Hollywood cowboy on a ranch and the one thing that appeals to American sensibilities, more that anything else, is a ranch.

'WHAT ELSE IS ON'

The full meaning of the slogan 'Workers of the world, unite', dawned on me when I visited the offices of Geo television. Hundreds of people were huddled together in a makeshift hall; each one having no more than about thirty six inches of space around him. Nearly every one of them seemed fairly absorbed in whatever task they had been assigned. Amazingly enough, none of them looked morose or down-trodden.

I was led thorough the narrowest of corridors to the office of the supremo, a glassed booth, at one end of the hall, that could just about hold a desk and three chairs. 'Wouldn't the fire department consider the presence of so many bodies under one roof a serious hazard?' I asked him. The supremo, a lean, handsome man with a sprinkling of gray hair that gave him an intellectual countenance, nodded, 'We are trying to find another office, but until then...' he spread his hands to convey '*ce la vie*'.

Before I could say that I felt hemmed in, he was gracious enough to escort me to a spacious reception room in the inner sanctum of the network several floors below. I learnt that those bright looking, earnest young men and women that I saw upstairs, were graphic designers, mostly.

Since my visit, I have begun to take an interest in the Geo network. The first time I tuned in, the screen displayed a frozen image of a devastated street, with the same inconsequential music in the background that blares at you when you enter the Grand Central Station in New York. From time to time an adenoidal announcer said that full details of the horrific accident would be revealed to me shortly. I waited, but the image stayed frozen.

The gismo known as the remote control is a lethal weapon. Once you hold it in your hand you are goaded by unknown forces to press your thumb on the channel button. The very next channel was showing New Zealand v India in a One Day International in which New Zealand needed only 21 runs to win off 29 balls with 3 wickets in hand. Who, I ask you, wouldn't wish to see the finish of that match?

Strange things happen when I begin to flick channels. On my screen, channels 12 and 13 have a permanent blank screen, as indeed, channel 39, 51 and 53. Channel 52 is the same as channel 7; from 54 onwards, every channel is a repetition of earlier channels. I take great comfort in the knowledge that, technically, I have access to 69 channels.

Do you remember the movie 'Bad Day At Black Rock'? It was made in the late 50's and it starred Spencer Tracy, supported by such luminous and powerful actors as Robert Ryan, Lee Marvin, Richard Widmark, etc. In the movie, Spencer Tracy arrives in a ghost town to unravel a murder committed a long time ago. He meets nothing but resistance. The common guilt that the town folk share compels them to make several attempts on Tracy's life. In keeping with the Hollywood tradition, our hero, though defenseless—he has lost the use of his right arm in the war—packs a few hefty punches with his left arm, which make the 'baddies' curl up. I do not have all the details right because I did not watch this movie except in glimpses and that was because, last year, one of my cable channels showed it at least 23 times.

The cable people who come to collect the rent tell me that, in actual fact, they are giving me access to 28 channels, and that if I was to raise my rent I would receive as many as a 120 channels. You would think that I would be spoilt for choice, but I have come to the conclusion that the idea of TV these days is simply to fill the air with commercials; for fillers, they screen cheaply available, old programmes.

In America, the fare under the category of 'Drama' means offerings of 'Dallas', 'Gumsmoke' and 'Little House on the Prairie'. And, of course, whichever channel you turn to, at whatever hour, you are bound to see Angela Lansbury rolling her eyes in 'Murder, She Wrote'.

What bewilders me is that the same programmes are shown over and over at the same time each night. If you turn on Discovery channel to find a programme on Hollywood stunts, you can be certain that the next time you switch to the Discovery channel at the same hour, it will be Hollywood stunts again. In all likelihood it will be the same episode. I have fond memories of many old programmes — 'Bilko', 'Rawhide', 'Wagon Train' — but I don't want to watch any of them night after night. In any case the best of the old programmes like '77 Sunset Strip' and 'Burns and Allen' are never seen.

I moan about this because our cable system is governed by the machinations of American television networks. With so many channels to choose from and nearly all of them interrupted every few minutes with advertisements, I am reminded of Bill Bryson's priceless comment; 'You don't watch television to see what's on, you watch to see what else is on.'

The various Indian channels, which keep dishing out an endless fare of so-called 'family entertainment', have come to an amicable agreement with each other. Their soaps and serials may have different titles, but the same simpering, bejewelled, over made-up actresses appear in every one of them. Also, they make sure that the ten-year-old girls in their sit-coms are played by pigtailed, revoltingly precocious children that you ache to push out of a high window.

But back to Geo: I am glad that they have established themselves as a channel that gives us news as and when it happens, but I wish they had a better lot of 'news-givers'. The crop of newsreaders that they have been hand picked, are ill-clad (one of them often wears a pseudo-Norfolk jacket) and lack the one quality a newsreader has to have; communicable integrity.

I am not suggesting that Geo should have Tom Beurk look-alikes, but they should work on finding men (and women) whose diction is clear, who can simulate a demeanour of trust-worthiness and who make you feel that they are giving you the news and not reading a bulletin written, devised and doctored by the powers that be.

SANTA

The word 'egghead' never fitted any one more than the late Adlai Stevenson, an American intellectual turned politician who neither talked nor behaved like a politician. He cared a great deal about the world, particularly the Third World. The yellow Press referred to him as 'Madlai Adlai'. The right wing newspapers often chided him for not being American enough. Why he allowed himself to be pushed into contesting the Presidential election—which he lost obviously—was a puzzle for most of his admirers.

I was once made to sit next to him at a dinner party hosted in his honour by Lawrence Langner, the head of Theatre Guild of America. Until then, most thinking Americans that I had met thought that the best way to engage some one from the sub-continent into a conversation was to talk about Nehru or Tagore. I was quite prepared to discuss Tagore's effete dramatic works, but he surprised me by talking most amusingly about his visit to Peru and an ingenious method the Peruvians had devised for irrigating some of their barren lands.

I was introduced to Adlai Stevenson by Santha Rama Rau, who knew everyone worth knowing in New York. Santa — as the Americans pronounced her name — short story writer, novelist, dramatist, had adapted Forster's famous novel, 'A Passage to India' into a play that was about to open on Broadway. I soon found out after my arrival in America that, socially, she was one of the most sought-after authors in New York.

Santa's dramatization of the Forster novel had already been much praised during the play's run in the West-End. The audiences in London could relate to the British presence in India during the days of the Raj. But Santa was not entirely sure how an American audience would react to a play which was not a part of American history. Her friends, experienced theatre-goers, assured her that Broadway theatre-goers were used to seeing plays which had no American presence, but Santa was a little apprehensive. She knew that a West-End triumph did not necessarily mean a Broadway success.

Once the play was on — and it did not turn out to be a flop — she was, invariably, complimented on its success. 'Oh, it was mostly Forster', she would say without the slightest trace of false humility, 'I only did a cut and paste job'. This was far from true. She had transformed a major novel into a terse and moving two hour play — and it wasn't as though she had just lifted much of the dialogue from the novel and bunged it together into three acts. Her treatment of Mrs Moore (Forster's most enigmatic character) in the context of the play was subtle and astute.

Mrs Moore, an elderly woman, who instinctively feels attuned to Eastern mysticism is a fascinating character. She goes on walks, unaccompanied, in Chandrapore, a provincial town in India , an act that the colonial rulers consider to be nothing short of madness. She befriends Aziz, an Indian doctor, which also annoys the English authorities. Mrs. Moore remains unconcerned and, in spite of warnings, accepts Aziz's invitation to join in a picnic to explore the Marabar caves, Chandrapore's historical monument.

It is here, in the caves, that Mrs Moore feels an odd sense of nothingness. The echo in the caves affects her intensely. When questioned about it, she says, 'Boum is as near as I can get it. Bou-oun, ou-boum – utterly dull. It undermined one's hold on life. It said, piety, pathos, courage—they exist but they are identical and so is filth. Everything exists, nothing has value. If one had spoken vileness in that place or recited poetry the comment would have been the same—Ou boum.'

Characters like Mrs. Moore are all right in a novel where the author can describe her thoughts and subject her to analysis, but how do you put over Mrs Moore on the stage? If you assign too many lines to her, she becomes a chatter box and the essence of her thought is diffused. If you try to set her up by having other characters describe the drift of her thinking, the scene loses its tautness.

I remember a late afternoon in Cambridge when Forster treated me to tea and crumpets roasted over the log fire in his sitting room. The Cambridge Don, George Rylands a.k.a Dadie, (one of the most outstanding Shakespearian scholars of his era) was also present. For some reason, perhaps because of my presence, the conversation turned to 'A Passage' and Mrs. Moore. 'Tell me, Morgan,' Rylands said', What did the old bat mean by that boom-boom speech?' A flicker of a smile appeared on Forster's face'. I don't know Dadie, I'm not entirely sure she knew what she was saying.' Then he sighed and said, 'She was such a tiresome woman'.

This conversation took place well after the run of the play had come to an end, but I know that Santa held many sessions with Forster over Mrs. Moore. He couldn't help her much. The job of creating Mrs. Moore on the stage, he told me, was left to Santa. And she did a splendid job. Picking on threads she managed to create a role that leaned heavily on the inner resources of the actress (what role doesn't?) but at the same time aided with deftly conceived dialogue that managed to be significant without getting out of character.

Santa was a handsome, silver-haired woman, unusually tall for an Indian. She had an irrepressible good humour running into gestures and laughter.

Her pearl-white teeth glistened as she smiled. During the day she wore western clothes, but in the evening she was dressed in beautiful *Kanjivaram* saris. There was hardly an evening when she wasn't invited out and she somehow persuaded me to accompany her. When I protested that I would be an imposition she assured me that the hosts knew about me and would be delighted with my presence. If I still demurred she insisted that she had to show me off and that she was taking me around for her sake and would I mind obliging her? With Santa as my chaperone, Manhattan was an unending glitter.

But for Santa I would not have met Truman Capote, a weasel of a man whose resentment against the world was so deeply ingrained that he wore a permanent sneer as a guard against a hostile universe: Norman Mailer, who held court every evening, demolishing anyone who interrupted him with a choice invective. He had a huge collection of invectives. There were a host of others; Algonquin left-overs, jazz musicians, architects; I wish I had kept a diary.

In my professional career I can think of many people who sheltered me, protected me and rooted for me. I cannot think of anyone other than Vsanthi Rama Ran Bowers, who went so out of her way to lionise me — and with such grace.

A CARROT IS A CARROT

What are the roots that clutch? asks Elliot—and I have been trying to grapple with mine. Is it the past that never disappears?

The past clings to us as sticky as glue. Traditions. Customs. Why do you go to a shrine and touch the ground with your forehead? Why does a woman fast on certain days? Why do hand-maidens carry oil lamps or prepare henna paste a night or two before a wedding? It is the custom, the tradition. No further explanation is required. It has always been so. It must continue to be so.

What will happen if there is a break in that tradition? Things too terrible to be named. The downfall of the family, the society, of religion—of the fabric of the country itself.

So a woman will paint 'kohl' on her child's eye, a marriage needs to be approved by the elders of the family and so life is lived according to its rules, rules prescribed by time, centuries of time.

Those who do not live by the rules, those who flaunt them—or some of those who now live in far off shores and have subjected themselves to the rules of other lands—feel a twinge of guilt and will go on feeling it.

Of course, time moves in other directions as well. Television invades homes and imposes its own ethos even upon the devout viewers; the shalwar is given up for jeans, the old soothsayer is laughed at, the transvestite wandering minstrels shunned: the past scorned. But it remains: like the colour of one's skin and eyes, it remains. It does not leave.

The past, however, does not maintain its dignity and repose. It has not remained unaffected by the upheavals of the present. Would that it were so. The walls and boundaries of monuments are plastered with cinema posters and loud pronouncements of quacks who would restore your lost youth; grotesquely large portraits of politicians hang from balconies of old houses. Ruins of old buildings litter the streets.

Nightmarish scenes confront me in every city. Women scooping up torn plastic bags from dung heaps; men with twisted arms and tortured limbs lurch towards you at traffic lights, drooling and invoking luke-warm benedictions; children with wrinkled knees and runny noses asking for money, disinterestedly, whimpering and cajoling as soon as they realise they are being eyed by the surrogate father or uncle; filthy lanes with huge, muddy gashes in the middle; sidewalks taken over by hawkers, juice-makers, spice-sellers, plastic wares, sweetmeats and bicycle wheels. Wherever you go there is a smell of skewered meat tinged with urine.

Every available tree and lamp post is abloom with hideous banners (and flyers) proclaiming extraordinary spiritual powers of faith-healers along with brazen declarations that the true followers of the Prophet will not hesitate to shed their blood in the cause of Kashmir.

Almost every commercial street has pools of putrid water. Around them people sit, talk, make deals, sigh, belch, pick their noses and gleefully rub the skin off their big toes. Eliot again:

The lot of man is ceaseless labour
Or ceaseless idleness...

The crudely amplified voice of the muezzin, mechanical as it is non-musical, does not invoke a sense of piety (upon hearing some merely check the time of the day). It is no longer an invitation to share the simple prayer. Only the truly devout stop whatever they are doing and supplicate.

The past for most of us is a sacredness that can only be coveted—a wistful feeling that the world THEN was devoid of sin. Time past is not necessarily contained in time present. In most pronouncements from the pulpit the past is presented as high Moral Purpose. The men of the past—forever shunning worldly pleasure—are all upright, their turbaned heads bowed in supplication; the women, sedentary,

swathed in cloaks, forever serving them silently in a
state of perpetual obeisance. The past is remembered
with awe, hardly ever with affection. Is it any wonder
that the young of today want to run away from it as
far as they possibly can?

Here is another dilemma: if we take pleasure in 'Once
upon a time....stories' (oh what a rich feast) we are
accused of pandering to escapism. We are chided for
not preparing ourselves for life's grim battles. On the
intellectual plane, Iqbal denounced Hafiz and other
Sufi poets because their verse was tainted with lyrical
romanticism, (Later on he withdrew the ban, but more
of that anon.)

In the work — not my bread and butter work — which I
undertake to transcend my own inadequacies: reading,
interpreting, projecting other people's thoughts, I keep
making forays into the past. It is, indeed, a monument
to the past. A monument suggests a gravestone, cold
and immutable. I like to think that it reflects the play
of sunlight and rain. I hope that some people feel
that it enables them to stray into a past that was not
mute but vibrant.

I do not mean to imply that I want my effort to be
regarded as an unreserved paean of praise for the
past and that I regard 'modernism' to be destructive
of the old traditional culture. The old traditional
culture was full of cruelties and injustices, but it was
a pattern of life known and understood and,
therefore, more acceptable and more fitting than an
alien culture that has neither been fully understood,

nor assimilated. I have an inherited, instinctive love for the past.

For me the past is concrete, physical and palpable. It is not all repression and internecine struggles and the subdued social status of women. The past is beautiful gardens laid out with symmetry and order; the past is musical soirees of extreme refinement; the past is nimble-witted symposiums on logic and scintillating conversations on aesthetics. In our past you talked with your friend late into the night and then walked him home. He, your friend, returned your courtesy and walked all the way back to your home (the distances were perhaps not too large) and you once again accompanied him all the way—and so the night wore on until the early morning was heralded by the *muezzin*, whereupon you parted. A laughable ritual, you might say, but it symbolised graciousness of which we are devoid today. What we have today is life shorn of the past and unheedful of the future. Life today is a carrot.

'You ask me what life is?' Chekhov wrote to his wife just before his death, 'It's like asking what a carrot is. A carrot is a carrot and nothing more is known...'

INDEX

A

A history of moral philosophy 58
A Passage to India 250, 301,303
A Streetcar Named Desire 86, 87
Abdali, Ahmed Shah 10
Abdul Aziz Khan Beenkar 16
Abul Fazl 132
Abul-Asar see Hafiz Jallundhri
Actor (s) 19, 193, 105, 23, 167, 262
Adamov, Arthur 221
Adams, P. J. 290
Addison, Joseph 287
Agha Hashr 32
Ahmad Bashir 110
Ahmed Nadeem Qasmi 168
Ahsan 101
Akhtari Bai Faizabadi 147-149
Akram Kazmi 65, 66, 74
Alfred, Lord 284
Ali Akbar Khan, Ustad 158,163
Alice 275-276
All India Radio 50, 173
Allen, Steve 112
Alliance Francais 222
America 71-75, 86, 87, 96, 100, 102, 105, 112, 114, 117, 120, 144, 176-177, 180, 188, 204,-205, 208, 232-234, 290, 294, 297, 300-301
American (s) 100, 105, 117, 176, 204, 207, 208, 233, 246, 293-294, 300-301
Amir Elahi 34
Amir Khan 163
Amir Minai 147
Amjad, Dr 195
Amjad Hussain 275
Amman 99, 103
Amritsar 167
Amy Minwalla 128
An Equal Music 144-145, 165
Anti-Catholic policy 66
Anti-Catholicism 59, 63
Anwar, Dr 85, 87
Anwar Jalal Shamza 167
Anwar Kamal Pasha 31, 32,33
Arabic 116, 122, 213, 252
Arlott, John 71
Armada 61
Arnold, Mathew 125, 261
Arts Council 55
As you like it 81
Ashby 41, 42, 43

Aslam Khan 101
Aspell, Tim 117, 264
Asquith, Clare 59, 60, 61, 64, 66
Auden, W. H. 68, 210-211,258

B
Bad Day at Black Rock 297
Badayun 35
Badell, Alan 259
Bahadur Yar Jung 105
Bahadur Shah Zafar 147
Baldev, Raj 37, 39
Bamiyan Buddha 224
Barabanki 35
Bare Ghulam Ali Khan 54, 148, 156
Barkat Ali Khan 148
Barnes and Noble 176-178
Barrymore, John 85
Basil Street Hotel 93, 99, 100, 102
BBC Radio 72, 258,
BBC 69, 71, 137, 269
Beckett, Samuel 220-221
Bengal 127
Bermans, Pandro 103
Bhai Lal Mohmmad 57
Bhajans 48
Big Daddy 87
Birmingham 118, 135, 137
Bjornson, Bjornstjerne 289
Blackwell, Doug 266
Blade 207
Bombay 93, 101, 129, 172-174
Book of Verse 71
Booker Prize 142
Brabham, Nobby 90, 91, 94
Brasenose College 285
Bridge 151-155
Britain 219-220, 249

British Columbia 87
British Raj 131, 251, 301
British 23, 48, 118, 211, 219, 249-250
Broadcasting Service of Pakistan 227
Bronte, Charlotte 289
Bryson, Bill 289, 294
Buddha 220
Burton, Richard 72
Butler, Samuel 287
Buxton 69, 70
Byron, Lord 286, 288

C
Calcutta 51
Calligraphy 127
Cambridge 95, 303
Capote, Truman 304
Carlyle, Thomas 287
Carroll, Lewis 275-276
Carson, Johnny 114
Cat on a Hot Tin Roof 87
Catholic Church 63
Catholic(s) 59, 61, 62, 64
Catholicism 60, 61, 64
Cavafy, C. P. 257
Cecil, William 63
Chamberlain, Lord 87
Chambers 254
Charkeen 280
Chekhov, Anton 308
Chicago 207, 291
China 153
Chinaman 211
Chinese 211,217, 229, 253, 270
Chinese restaurant 213
Chorley Wood 259
Chu Chin Chow 22
Chughtai 157

Cine-View 58
Clotaire, Rapaille 229
Cockney 41-43, 219
Coleridge 286
Collected Poems 76
Collins 254
Concise Oxford 255
Contemporary fiction 138, 142
Corpus Christi 59
Cricket 30, 37, 38, 71, 75, 76, 85, 258, 262, 264, 265-266
Cricketer (s) 29, 75, 76
Crisp, Quentin 111
Crystal, David 254-255
Cukor, George 106
Culture 26, 130, 136, 204,207, 212, 217, 227-228, 233, 248

D
Dagh Dehalvi 147
Daily Telegraph 250
Dalai Lama 233
Dallas 297
Dance 225
Dance, classical 134, 226
  Bharatanatym 126, 133
  Ghungroos (ankle-balls) 130
  Kathak 126,131-133, 135
  Khuchipudi 133
  Nritta (pure dance) 134-135
  Orissi 133
  Tatkar 135
  Toras (short dance pieces) 131
Dance Academy 226
Dance troupe 128
Dante 243
De Profundis 282
Dead Sea 229
Death of a Salesman 87
Dehlavi, Nawab Shakir 35

Dehlavi, Shahid Ahmed 56
Delhi 35, 267
Delilah 214
Derby Rep 44
Daruwalla, Jal 37, 38
Desai, Leela 51
Dain (witch) 02, 03, 04
Dickens, Charles 80, 245
Dickinson, Emily 256
Dictionary 250, 252
Dilip Kumar 94, 101
Don Juan 284
Doubleday, Kay 70
Drama 19, 138, 280, 284, 286-287, 297, 300
Drama Academy 69
Dryden 287
Dubai 146, 150

E
Eden, Anthony 219
Edgbaston 85
Egypt 213, 219-220, 240, 281
Eliot, T. S. 68, 243, 277- 278, 281, 282, 305, 307
Elizabeth 60, 61, 63, 66
Encyclopedia Britannica 176
England 19, 20, 21-23, 41, 59, 61-63, 65, 69, 77, 86, 93, 112, 118, 142, 170, 195, 251
English 23, 41, 61, 76, 80, 81, 103, 123-125, 129, 138, 146, 166, 171, 182, 183, 213, 219, 236, 242, 244, 252, 253, 267, 268, 269-271, 280, 281,285-286
English Reformation 65
Epsom 260
Ervin, St. John 61
Espy, Williams 253
Esther 90, 91, 94

Europe 96, 112, 156
Evernew Studios 60, 62

F
Faber and Faber 281-282
Face to Face 112
Faiz Ahmad Faiz 36, 136, 137
Fani Badayuni 35
Faqir Hussain Saga 128
Faqir of Ippi 118
Farah Zuby 201
Farber, Ann 232
Fareeddoon 58, 59, 60, 63
Fareedoon-e-Garakani 58
Faridah 101
Faryn, Michael 118
Fass, Ekbart 179
Fateh Ali Khan, Ustad 57
Fayyaz Khan 163
Feroze Nizami 55
Ferozepur 23
Ferrer, Jose 105
Fields, W. C 199
Film (s) 102, 110, 113, 115, 118, 173-174, 204-206, 208
Fine arts 127
Firaq Gorukhpuri 36
Forster, E. M. 95-96, 250, 297-299, 301-302
Fowler, H. W. 245
Fraser, Antonia 60
Freeman, John 112
Fromm, Eric 58
Frost, David 117

G
Ganesh 133
Ganesh Vardana 135
Gatting, Mike 34
Gauhar Jan 144

GCDC (Government College Dramatic Club) 19
Geets 48, 223
Geo Television 295-296, 298-299
Ghalib, Asadullah Khan 104, 148, 166
Ghanshyam School of Dancing 128
Ghazal (s) 133, 146-150, 227
Ghazal gayaki 148
Ghungroos (ankle-balls) 130
Gidwani Pictures 173
Gielgud, John 69, 77, 78, 79
Glazier, Leslie 264, 266
Gods & Goddesses 130
Goethe Institute 226
Golden Gate 144
Gordon, George 288
Gordon, Lyndall 277
Grand Central Station 296
Gray, John 69, 70
Greece 218, 288
Grisham, John 143, 234
Grosvenor House Hotel 105
Group Theatre 58
Gunsmoke 297

H
Hafeez Hoshiarpuri 276
Hafiz Jallundhri 110, 111, 113
Hafiz Shirazi 308
Hakims 108
Hameed Naseem 53
Hamilton 102
Hamlet 60, 61, 62, 63, 64,81, 216
Hamlet of Stepney Green 211
Hangal, Gangubai 104
Harborne 194

Harding, Gilbert 112
Harper, Gerald 263
Harty, Russel 117
Hawthorne, Nathaniel 286
Heathrow 185, 292
Henley-on-Arden 77
Henrietta 90-91
Henry IV 81
Henry V 249
Henry VIII 59, 81
Hindi 94, 160, 227
Hindu (s) 18, 26, 48, 132, 240
History of Renaissance 285
Hobbs, Jack 287
Holden, William 102
Hollywood 95, 96, 102, 115,
142, 204, 294, 297-298
Howard, Trevor 264-265
Howard-Stepney, Marged 73
Howe, G. D. 23
Hudson, Rock 102
Hyderabad, Deccan 94, 96-97,
102, 105, 211

I
Ibne Insha 110
Inayat Ali Khan 164
Inayat Bai Dheruwali 156
Ince Henrietta 88-89
India 10, 36, 48, 54, 56, 58, 92-
94, 102, 127, 131-133,150,166,
170, 249, 251, 268, 296, 298,
Indian universities 269
Insha, Insha Allah Khan 123,278
Inventions of March Hare 281-283
Ionesco, Eugene 220-221
IPTA (Indian People's Theatre
Association) 59
Iqbal, Allama Muhammad 35,
36, 53, 146, 227, 308

Ireland 61
Isherwood, Christopher 210,
212, 258
Ishiguru, Kazuo 142
Islam 18, 52, 129,130, 204,207,
226, 240
Islamabad 237, 239
Islamia College 18
Ismat Chughtai 173
Israel 117
Italian restaurants 289

J
Jalaluddin Akbar 47
Jalota, Anup 148
Jamshoro 27
Japanese 116
Jhande Khan, Ustad 47
Jhang 23
Jigr Moradabadi 36
John, Sir 78
Johnson, Samuel 270
Josh Maleehabadi 36
Juliet 215-216, 261
Julius Caesar 78, 140
Julius, Anthony 281, 282
Jur'at 280

K
Kajjan Begum 144
Kalidasa Raza Gupta 126, 166
Karachi 82, 127, 129, 194,199,
201, 207-208, 239
Karachi, University of 183
Kashmir 138, 140, 307
Kasur 46
Kathaks (story tellers) 132
Kathas (stories) 129
Kazan, Elia 88
Keats 124, 286

Khajuraho temples 92
Khalid Ahmed 254
Khilafat Movement 17
Khurshid 129
Killers 207
King Bolo Verses 281-282
Kings, Stephen 234
Kington, Miles 78, 211-213
Kot Fateh Din Khan 10
Kot Hakim Khan 11
Kot Lukamdeen 11
Kot Murad Khan 11
Kot Rukunuddin 10, 11
Krishen Chander 167
Krishna of Kathak 133
Kucha Vakilan 167
Kyd 64

L
Lahore 10, 13, 18, 32, 50, 52,
55, 84, 153, 156,158, 171, 172,
199, 200, 204, 207, 237, 239
  Coffee House 67
  Kashmir Road 59, 60
  Lawrence Garden 69
  Mcleod Road 51
  Museum 67
  Muslim Town 62
  Nedous Hotel 63
  Parsi Temple 29
  Regent Cinema 51
  Rattigan Road 29
Lahore Broadcasting House
278
Lahore Radio 61, 170
Lahore Veterinary College 29
Lala Musa 54
Lancaster Gate 88
Lang, Harold 211

Language (s) 66, 112-113, 149,
180, 184, 213, 235-236, 240,
242, 249, 250, 252, 264,272
Lansbury, Angela 297
Latafat Hussain, Ustad 57
Laugharne 71, 72
Lawrence of Arabia 05, 97, 98,
102
Lawrence, D. H. 257
Laxmi Mansions 164
Lean, David 93-96-99, 102-
104, 107
Lear 64
Lear, Edward 273-275
Lexicographers 252
Library 176, 178, 180, 231
Literary fiction 139
Literature 138, 144, 154, 240,
268
Little House on the Prairie 293
London 20, 40, 44, 60, 69, 87,
93, 108, 157, 162, 177, 187, 264
Long Island 102
Lord's 77
Los Angeles 106, 117
Lucifer 60
Lucknow, University of 280
Lyallpur 45, 46, 50
Lytton, Edward Bulwer 249,
289

M
Macaulay, Lord 284
Macbeth 79, 80, 81
Macintyre, Alasdair 58
MacNeice, Louis 70, 72, 258-
259
Macy's 226
Madam Azurie 128-129
Madison Avenue 226

Madison Square Garden 230
Maeterlinck 285
Maharashtra 17, 47
Maharishi (s) 99, 229
Mahavidyallah (music learning institutes) 48
Mahmood Ghaznavi 224
Mailer, Norman 304
Majrooh Sultanpuri 36
Malang, Khan ,Ustad 45, 46, 49
Man for himself 58
Manhattan 100-101, 229
Mann, Thomas 286
Manto Nama 166
Manto, Saadat Hasan 166-175
Marius the Epicuream 285
Marquez 143
Marshall and Snelgrove 20, 21
Maeterlinck, Maurice 289
Marvin, Lee 297
Matisse 157
Matrix 207
Mattoo, Jeevan Lal 50, 51
Mayur 126-127
MCC 77, 78
McCarthy 88
M. D. Taseer 279
Meeraji 36, 170
Meerasees 225
Mehdi Hassan 149
Mehmood Nizami 274
Melville, Herman 286
Meredith, Burgess 85
Merry Wives of Windsor 79, 81
Mianjee 5-6, 11
Miller, Arthur 87
Milton 243
Mir Dard 280
Mir Taqi Mir 146, 278, 280
Mirasi jokes 110

Miscellaneous Essays 283
Moeen Najmi 167
Moenjodaro 228
Mohammad Bin Qasim 130
Moniza Alvi 245
Moody, Rick 260
Morning Post 250
Morgenstern 270
Mortimer, John 179
Mozart 49, 178
Mughal miniatures 132
Mughals 132-133
Muharram 125
Muir 68
Mummy 83, 84
Muneer, Justice 166
Murder She Wrote 297
Mushafi 280
Music 16, 18-19, 27-28, 49-50, 53, 55, 147,148, 161, 178, 225, 259
Music composers 17, 47, 67
Music, classical18, 47-48, 55-57, 148-149, 153, 156, 160, 163
Alap 162
Bandish 17, 164-165
Dadra 146
Gharana 48, 54, 56, 57, 164
Guru 17, 47, 99
Kajri 146
Mantras 105
Raga Aiman 53, 54, 227
Raga Asawari 104, 109
Raga Bageshwaris 227
Raga Bhatiar 149
Raga Bhopali 46
Raga Charukeshi 149
Raga Devgiri Bilawal 190
Raga Hameer 165
Raga JaiJjai Vantis 227
Raga Malkaus 46, 69

Raga Maluha Kedara 225
Raga Poorya Kalian 28, 164
Raga Sarswati 52
Raga Shiv Raranjini 52
Raga Shudh Kalyan 55
Raga Yaman 54
Raga sikhsh a (learning of
rags) 50
Ragas 17-18, 47, 53, 55, 144,
146, 160
Taranas 227
Taals (Metric cycle) 50, 131
Thumri 126, 146
Music, Pop 138
Musical instrument 117
Dilruba 16
Drut 156
Ghara 47
Harmonium 16, 47, 147
Pakhawaj 130
Sarangi 57, 150, 156
Sarood 57
Sitar 16, 57, 159, 162
Tabla 16, 45-46, 49, 57, 130
Tanpura 57, 97, 102, 104, 150
Vichitar Veena 16
Musicologists 157
Musicology 160
Muslim Rulers 133
Muslim (s) 18, 48, 53, 132, 144,
172
Muzzaffar Ghaffar 158
Mystery Cycles 59

N
Nahid Siddiqui 134-135
Nairang Galleries 157-159
Narvekar, Shrimati Bai 28
Nasikh 280

National Health Service 40,
194
Nationalist parties 236
Natural born 205
Nawab Chhattari, 97, 105
Nawabs 47
Nayyar Dada 156-157, 160
Nayyara Noor 136
Nazir Ahmad 52
Nehru 300
New York 74, 85, 93, 100, 101,
104,106, 206, 210, 260, 281,
296, 301
New Yorker (s) 231, 235
New Zealand 267, 267, 271,
296
Newspapers 146, 181, 183,
248, 290, 300
Nobel Prize 281
Non-Islamic minorities 237
Noon Meem Rashed 35, 36,
52, 67
North Carolina 231
North West Frontier Province
118

O
O'Brien, Connor Cruise 219
Ohio 236, 279
Okri, Ben 142
Olivier, Lawrence 75
Omar Hayat Malik 52
Ophelia 64, 216
Oscar 93, 103
Othello 64
Oudh 124
Ouesely, Willoughby 194-195
Oxford English Dictionary 254,
256, 269

Oxford University Press 245
Oxford 90, 285

P

Painting (s) 154-155
Pakistan 51, 54, 56, 129-130,
135, 176, 219,244, 268
Pakistan Broadcasting Service
223
Panna 128
Papacy 60
Parekh, Dr 195, 196
Parkinson, Michael 113, 117
Pater, Walter 285-286
Patiala 16
Patrick, Johnny 48
PEN (poets, essayists and
novelists) Club 210
Performing arts 125, 127
Perry Barr 85
Persian 06, 47, 52, 53, 54, 122,
133, 157, 184, 254
Petit, Pascale 247
Philip of Spain 61
Picasso 157
Poetry Centre 74
Poetry 9, 89, 110, 121-125,
133, 148, 149, 179, 257-259,
274, 276, 278, 280, 282
Plomer, William 74
Poets of Persia 36
Polonius 64
Poona 17, 47
Pope 60
Post-Reformation 65
Pound, Ezra 68, 281
Pre-Reformation days 60
Prince of Wales 45
Professor Sahib 18

Progressive Writers
Association 174
Protestantism 60-61
PTV 137
Pullman, Philip 142
Punch 208
Punjab
36, 127
Punjab, Government of 52
Punjab, University of 18, 50,
52, 65
Punjabi 06, 52, 160, 167, 202,
238
Punjabi-Urdu 138
Pushto 202, 238

Q

Quacks 111
Queen of England 61
Queen's Navy 252
Quinn, Anthony 105
Qusoor 01 see *also Kasur*

R

Radio Pakistan 52, 53, 54,
173
Radio 71, 112, 211, 223, 253
Radio City Music Hall 231
RAF 72
Rafi Ahmed Khan 280, 283,
Rafi Anwar 127-128
Ram Gopal 127
Rambo 204, 207
Rasoolan Bai 144
Ratan, Jai 166
Rau, Santha Rama 301
Riaz Khairabad 36
Richard III 80,
Rilke 257

River Kwai 93
Roman Catholic 60
Rome 21, 211-212, 255, 260
Romeo 215-216, 261
Roshan Ara Begum 54
Royal Albert Hall 162, 165
Rudauli 35, 36
Ruqaiya, Aunt 1, 4-7, 9, 12-13
Russell, Bertrand 140, 282
Ryan, Robert 297
Rylands, George 303

S
Sacramento 234
Saginaw 234
Sahir Ludhayanvi 36, 39
Said, Edward 240
Salamat Ali Khan, Ustad 56, 225, 226
Saleemullah 29, 30, 33
Salinger 170
Samson 218
San Francisco 75
Sanskritic 227, 254
Sarafian, Richard 115
Sauda, Mirza Rafi 280
Schonberg 178
Sellars, Peter 269
Shafi, Khwaja Mohammad 35
Shaggan, GhulamHussain 57
Shah, Dr 195, 271
Shakeb 35
Shakeel Badayuni 35
Shakespeare 59, 60, 61-66, 78, 79, 80, 215-216, 249,259, 303
Shakir Ali Museum 158-159
Shan-ul-Haq Haqqi 279, 281, 283
Shanks, Edward 71
Shaukat Hussian 57

Shaukat Thanvi 278
Shaw, Bernard 144
Sheikhupura 23
Shuja, Hakim Ahmed 32
Siddique 38, 39
Sidney, Sir Philip 61-63
Sikhs 23, 26, 39, 212-213
Simla 265
Sindh 130
Singh, Jagjit 146
Singapore 192, 269-270
Singlish 269-270
Singh, Sardar Jaswant 46
Singh, Sardar Kharak 243-245
Sirajuddin, Professor 25, 26
Slater, Geoffrey 70
Somnath 224
Southey 286
Spanish tragedy 65
Spectator 287
Spectre, Maud 96
Speight, Robert 125
Spender, Stephen 76, 258
Spiegel, Sam 102-103
Staccato rhythm 17
Stage 19, 20, 28, 160
Stanley 87
Steele, Richard 287
Stevenson, Adlai 300-301
Sufi Ghulam Mustafa Tabassam 52, 273
Sunday Morning 258-259
Sunday Times 253
Sutcliffe, Herbert 287

T
Tagore 300
Taijee 78
Take it From Here 269
Taliban 220

Talleyrand 215
Taming of Shrew 81
Tani 129
Tansen 47, 129
Tari, Ustad 57
Tele game 226
Television 82, 111, 112, 113,
114, 118,136-137, 139, 201, 223,
231, 239, 264, 266, 297, 306
Tennyson 288
Terminator 207
Texas Hold Em (tele game) 226
Texas 226
Thanda Gosht 168-169
The Cave of Making 254
The Conquest of Granada 287
The Duchess of Malfi 32
The Flying Bum 74
The Glass Menagerie 86, 87
The Happy Prince 286
The Importance of Being Ernest
284
The Lesson 220
The Merchant of Venice 32, 80
The Sayings of Plutarch 289
The Ship of Death 257
The Spur 256
*The story of life of Caleb Smith
— told by himself* 178
The Tempest 60
The Thespians 77
Theatre (s) 6, 20, 51, 88-89,
149, 151, 203, 222, 226
Theatre Guild of America 300
Third World 119, 300
Thomas, Dylan 124, 170, 258
Time magazine 86
Toba Tek Singh 171-172
Tom and Jerry cartoons 197
Tonight Show 111

Toynbee, Philip 76
Tracys, Spencer 103, 297
Trollope 245, 289
TV Travelers 77, 259, 264
Tynan, Ken 89

U
Ulysses 287
UNESCO 228
UNICEF 120
United States see America
Updike 170
Urdu literature 166, 171
Urdu Mousiki 159-160
Urdu papers 222
Urdu 06, 16, 19, 94, 97, 100, 122,
130, 148, 159-160, 166, 171, 183,
202, 223, 226, 238, 278, 292
Ustinov, Peter 115-118, 120

V
Vallee, Rudy 20
Vedanta 210
Verma, Pawan Kumar 166
Vicar 259-260
Vidal, Gore 144, 176
Vikram Seth 144-145, 165
Vilayat Khan 162-165
Vishnu 133
Vivaldi 178

W
Wadhawan, Jagdish Chander
166-168, 175
Waiting for Godot 220, 222
Warne, Shane 29, 34
Web Site Poetry Daily 256
Wes-End 90, 102
West-End actors 88
West-End actress 88

West-End musical 22
Whitehead 68
Wickham-Flint, Lofty 91, 93,
94, 97, 118
Widmark, Richard 297
Wilde, Oscar 284-286
Wintertton 118
Woman in Repose 154
Wordsworth 286
World Congress of Humour
211
Writers Revealed 179

Y
Yahoodi ki larki (The Jew's
daughter) 32
Yeats 243, 256
Younghy Bonghy-Bo 273-274

Z
Zamindar 227
Zarif 111
Zia Mahmood 155
Zinneman, Fred 106
Zulfikar Ali Bokhari 53, 54,
173
Zutshi, Shyam Lal 51